IMAGES
of America

MALTA

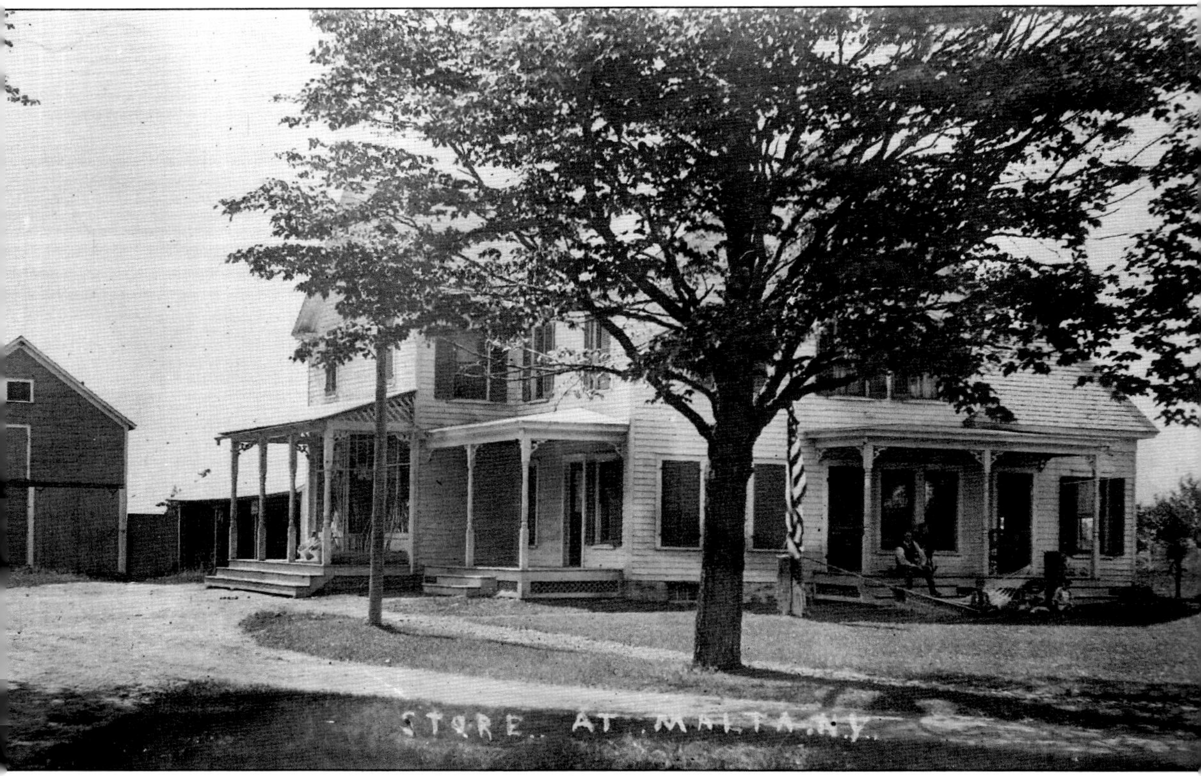

Rogers Store. The one-hundred-fifty-year-old Rogers Store was located on Dunning Street. On this site also stood the eighteenth-century tavern operated by Michael Dunning, a pioneer settler. It was at this place that the first Malta Town Board meeting was held on April 6, 1802. The Rogers Store building dates from about 1830 and became the first post office on Dunning Street. This historic landmark was razed on January 16, 1995. Today this location is the site of the Shops of Malta, the Gazebo, and the town clock.

IMAGES of America

MALTA

Ruth Weed Roerig

ARCADIA PUBLISHING

ISBN 978-0-7385-5698-7

Published by Arcadia Publishing
Charleston SC, Chicago IL, Portsmouth NH, San Francisco CA

Printed in the United States of America

Library of Congress Catalog Card Number: 2008922469

For all general information contact Arcadia Publishing at:
Telephone 843-853-2070
Fax 843-853-0044
E-mail sales@arcadiapublishing.com
For customer service and orders:
Toll-Free 1-888-313-2665

Visit us on the Internet at www.arcadiapublishing.com

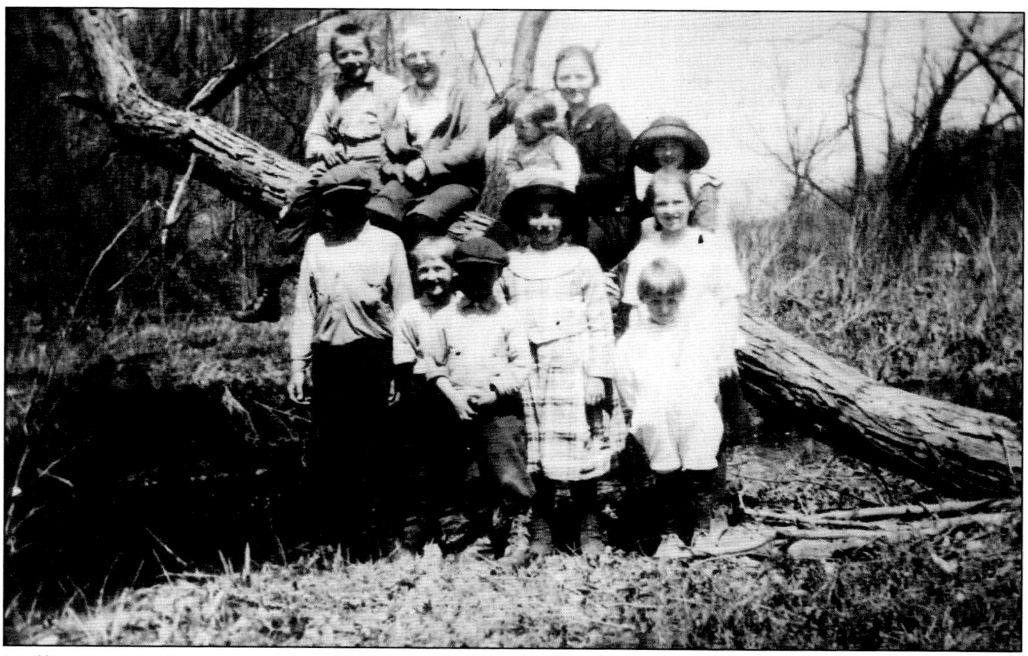

Hall's Corners Common School No. 6, *c.* 1922. The students of Hall's Corners Common School No. 6 are "mayflowering." It is a warm spring day, but the trees have yet to bud and the grass to turn green. We do not know the names or ages of these students, but some of them appear to be very young. The creek in the background could be the Mourningkill Creek, which is not too far from the site of the schoolhouse, or possibly the small stream at the foot of the hill called Brick Yard Hill.

Contents

Introduction		7
Acknowledgments		8
1.	Dunning Street	9
2.	East Line	27
3.	Malta Ridge	45
4.	Maltaville	65
5.	Round Lake	75
6.	Saratoga Lake	95
7.	Around the Town	109

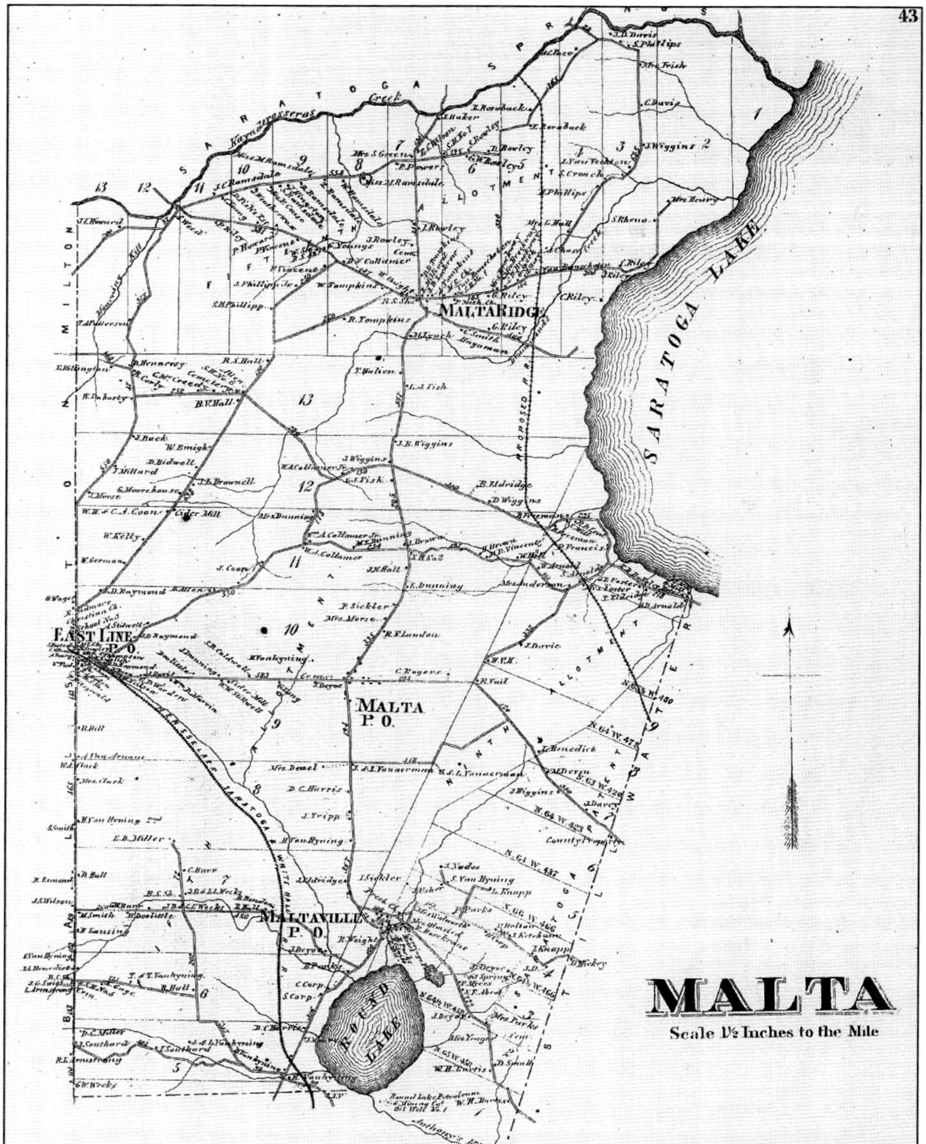

The town of Malta as it appeared on the 1866 map published by S.N. & D.G. Beers and Associates, entitled *The New Topographical Atlas of Saratoga County, N.Y.* Malta is located in the southeastern section of Saratoga County, and consists of approximately 17,000 acres of land. The Kayaderosseras Creek forms the northern boundary with Saratoga Springs to the north. The eastern boundary consists of Saratoga Lake on the upper portion of the line, and the town of Stillwater on the remainder. Malta is bounded on the south by the Anthony Kill Creek and the town of Clifton Park. The western boundary, formed by the towns of Ballston and Milton, is a straight line northward to the Kayaderosseras Creek, the place of beginning. This straight, man-made line is the eastern side of the famous "Five-Mile Square" that was set aside to defray the expenses of the survey and partition of the Kayaderosseras Patent. As an agricultural community, Malta developed no cities or towns. Today it is a largely residential community with limited light industry.

Introduction

The collection of photographs in this book generally covers the period of time from as early as 1860 to the present date; a few very early images have been inserted to portray Malta's beginnings. Many photographs were offered by the citizens of our town as well as by people of the neighboring towns and villages of Ballston, Milton, Clifton Park, Charlton, Saratoga Springs, and Round Lake. These kind people read the articles in the local newspapers requesting pictures, and were willing to provide a historic glimpse of their own families or the livelihoods of their ancestors. One call came from as far away as Washington, D.C., from a gentlemen who had been to the Saratoga Race Track in Saratoga Springs and phoned because of his early family ties to the area. While he had no pictures to share, he did have vital historic information to contribute.

At the beginning of this process of creating a pictorial history of the town of Malta, there was a genuine concern about the amount of information that would be available. This problem never materialized: there was never a shortage of information or pictures. Actually, it became necessary to be selective because there is more history available than we could possibly include in one book. Each interview scheduled to gather information took longer than anticipated due to the abundance of material gathered.

One benefit to the town of Malta generated by the gathering of this historical information is that important pictures, family histories, records of businesses (both past and present), and information about many early farms has been preserved for all time. This wealth of historical information has already been added to the town's historical records; the knowledge will enhance the historical research of future generations of Malta citizens.

The book is divided into seven chapters: Dunning Street, East Line, Malta Ridge, Maltaville, Round Lake, Saratoga Lake, and Around the Town. The final chapter includes images of people and communities in areas whose precise locations within the town cannot be specified. Examples of the types of areas featured in this chapter include Armstrong's Corners, Hall's Corners, Riley's Cove, and Silver Beach. These communities, while not large enough to require their own chapter, are vitally important to our township and must be acknowledged.

The town of Malta was created on March 3, 1802, when it was removed from the town of Stillwater. Three years later, on March 28, 1805, a portion of Saratoga was added to the northern part of Malta.

The first town meeting in Malta was held on April 6, 1802, at Dunning Street. Prior to February 7, 1791, when Saratoga County was set off from Albany County, the area today comprising Malta was a part of Albany County.

Always an agricultural community, the township contained no cities or towns; it does not even have such areas today. While communities all around the town of Malta have acquired a more metropolitan countenance, Malta has remained agricultural. Today it is still almost entirely residential, with a few remaining well-established farms. Our township is blessed with two lakes—Round Lake and Saratoga Lake—and several small streams. We have no mountains, just gently rolling beautiful countryside.

The creation of Route 9 (c. 1910) and the Adirondack Northway Interstate 87 (in the 1950s) did much to open up the town to commerce and tourism. There has also been a moderate amount of light industry coming into town in recent years. It is interesting to note how diversified the various communities of Malta became over time. Saratoga Lake developed as a lovely place both for its residents and for tourists who came to use its recreational facilities. Round Lake became very important as a religious center of the Methodist church. Both Maltaville and East Line were early settlements and seats of business and commerce; they contained two hotels, two blacksmith shops, a carriage shop, schools, churches, two post offices, and the railroad. As these two older communities declined, Malta Ridge and Dunning Street grew in importance. Today, Dunning Street in Malta is known as "Downtown Malta," as it contains controlled commercial enterprises and the seat of our local government.

This book is a history book intended for your enjoyment, and I am delighted to have taken part in its publication.

Ruth Weed Roerig
Ballston Lake, New York
September 1997

Acknowledgments

The majority of the photographs in this book came from the private collections of individuals either living within the town of Malta or in nearby towns. Another major source of images was the archive of the historian's office in the town of Malta.

My thanks go to Mrs. Jane D. Coffman, whose farsightedness in collecting pictures over the years made my job much easier. My gratitude is also expressed to Mrs. Mary Hesson, historian of the village of Round Lake, and to Mrs. Karen Campola, Saratoga County historian. Thanks also to Roy Arnold and Rachel Arnold Clothier, who together provided me with almost all the pictures of Malta Ridge. A very special thank you to Cynthia Young; Flo E. Sickels, town clerk; and Kathy Eitzmann, deputy town clerk, who assisted me in putting the final text onto the computer.

To all the other wonderful individuals who assisted me, I give thanks. There are so many of you that I cannot possibly name you all, but you know who you are, and I thank you.

May I also extend my appreciation to the personnel of the Malta Town Complex, who put up with me and my questions for weeks and weeks on end.

Thank you to the town board of the town of Malta for supporting me in this worthwhile and fulfilling endeavor.

—R.W.R.

One

Dunning Street

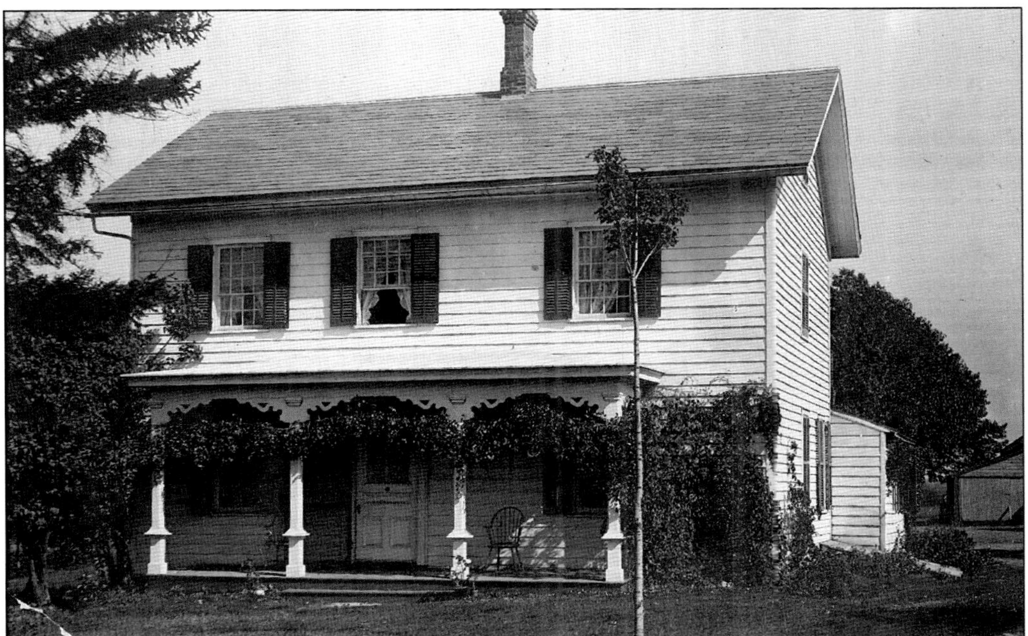

Hemphill Farmhouse. This is a photograph of the original Hemphill Farmhouse at Dunning Street, Malta. The beautiful old home stood on the southeast corner of the Parade Ground. It was destroyed by fire around 1939.

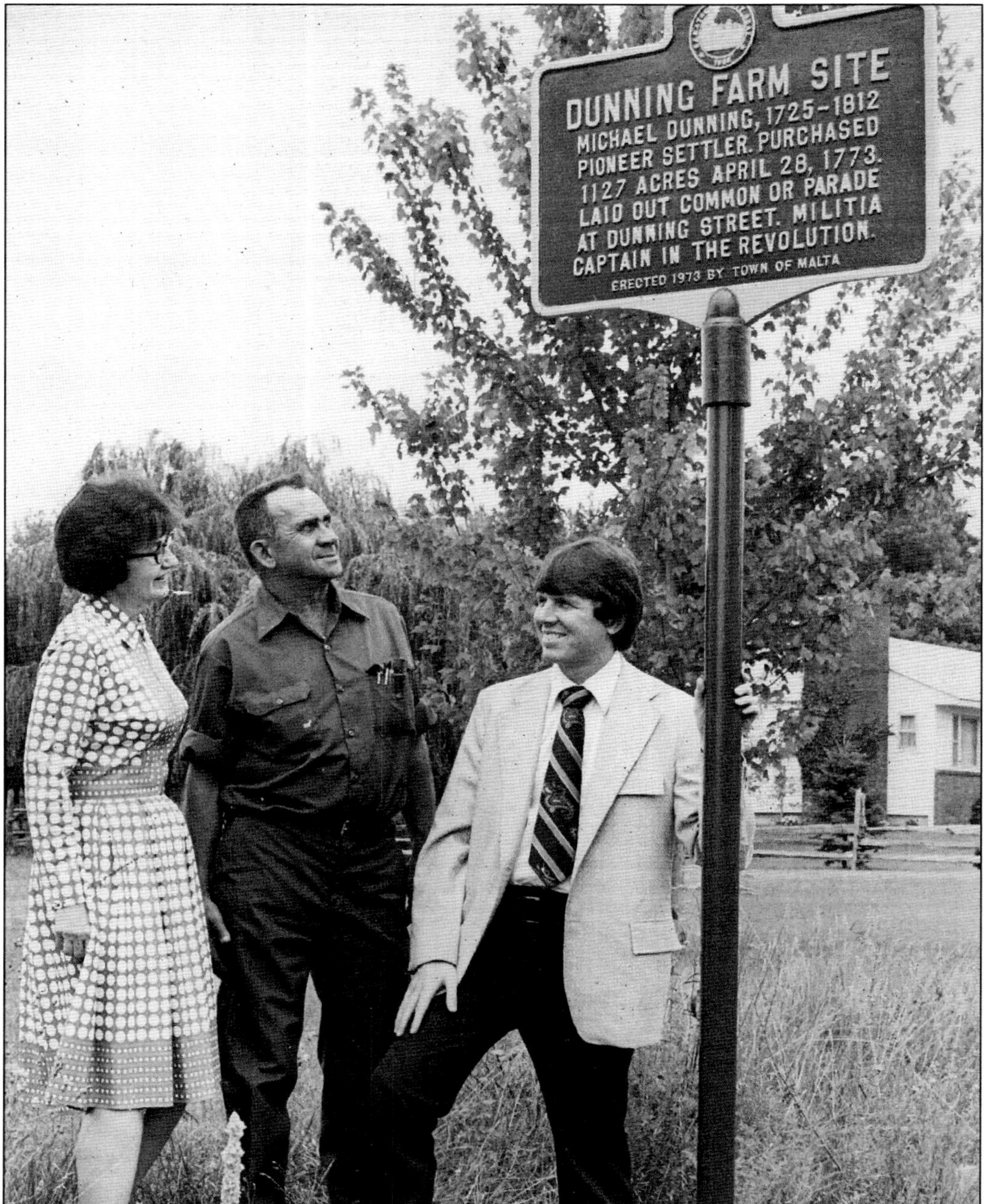

Dunning Farm Site. Michael Dunning (1725–1812), a pioneer settler of Malta, lived on this farm on Route 67, a 1/4 mile west of the intersection of Dunning Street and Route 9. On April 28, 1773, Dunning purchased 1,127 acres of land. It was Michael Dunning who gave the land for the Parade Ground, or Common, at Dunning Street. He also served as a captain in the militia during the American Revolution. The farm was designated as a historic landmark by the Town of Malta in 1973, and as such has a historical marker identifying it as the "Dunning Farm Site." Identified in the picture from left to right are Jane D. Coffman (historian of Malta), Royal Arnold (superintendent of highways), and David R. Meager (supervisor).

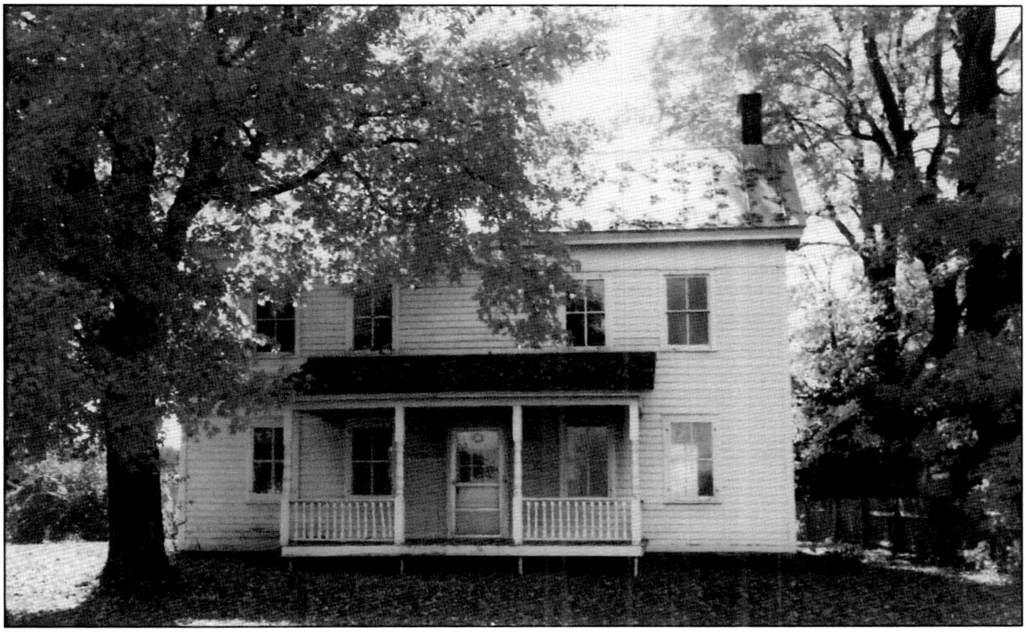

Betts Homestead. The Beer's Atlas of 1866 shows this stately old homestead as being the home of Mrs. S. Betts. Originally there were two Betts homes side by side. The other house was moved slightly to the south many years ago and was recently dismantled. The Trustco Bank is now located on the site of the demolished building.

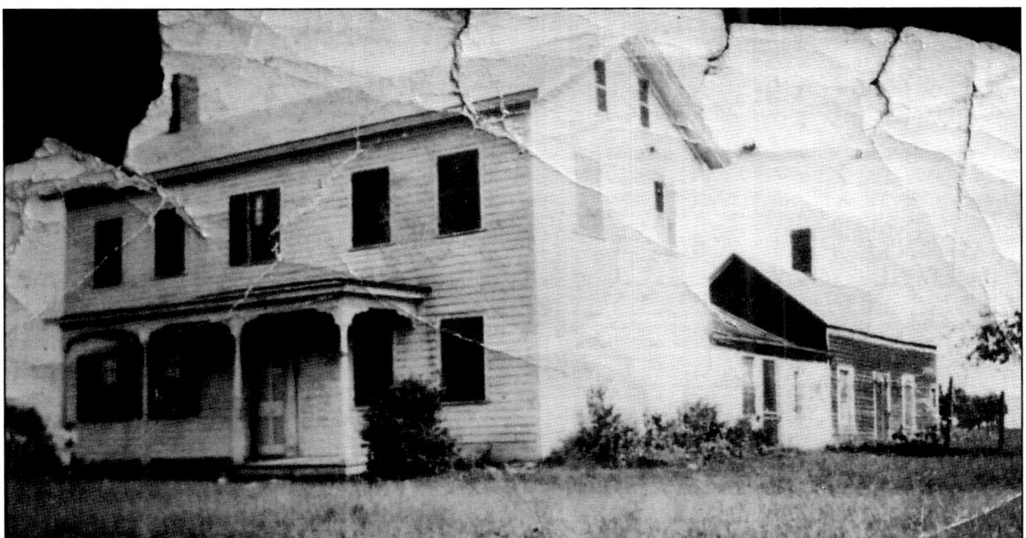

Deyoe/Bormann Homestead. The Samuel Deyoe/Edward G. Bormann Homestead was located on Route 67 (Dunning Street). Samuel Deyoe was a well-known and active participant in early town activities. In 1922–23, Edward G. and Emily Bormann purchased the property from George and May Deyoe, descendants of Samuel Deyoe. The home stayed in the Bormann family from 1922 until the property was sold by Edward R. and Jean Bormann in the 1980s. The house was demolished in order to make way for the Saratoga Village Mall, presently known as Malta Commons.

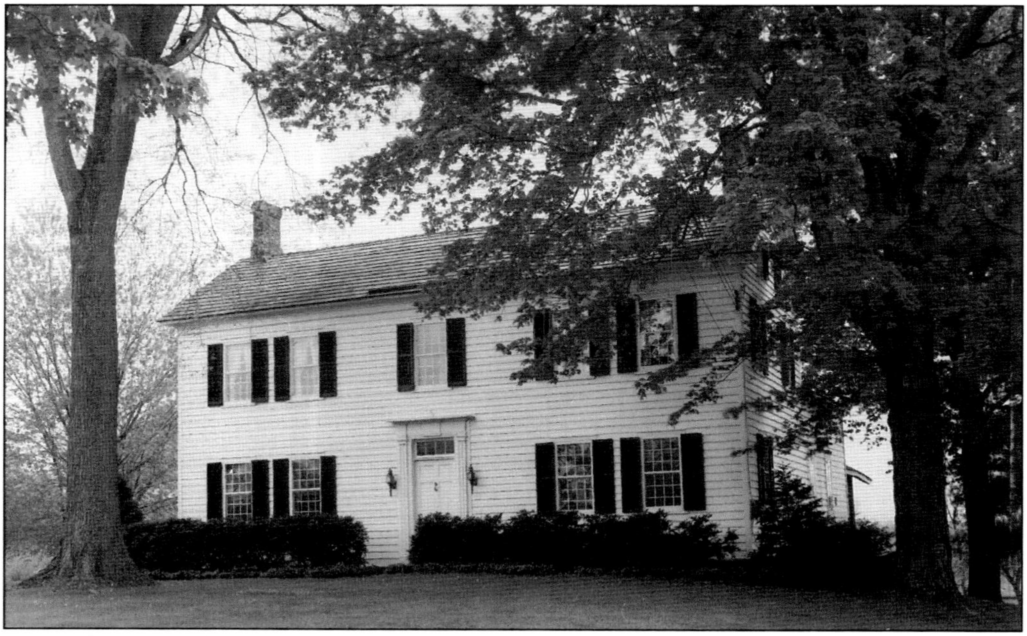

Marvin/Carpenter/Coffman Homestead. This home of pioneer settlers William and Susanna Wright Marvin was built about 1790 on land purchased in 1772. Today it is the home of John and Jane Coffman. Mrs. Coffman is the former historian of the town of Malta.

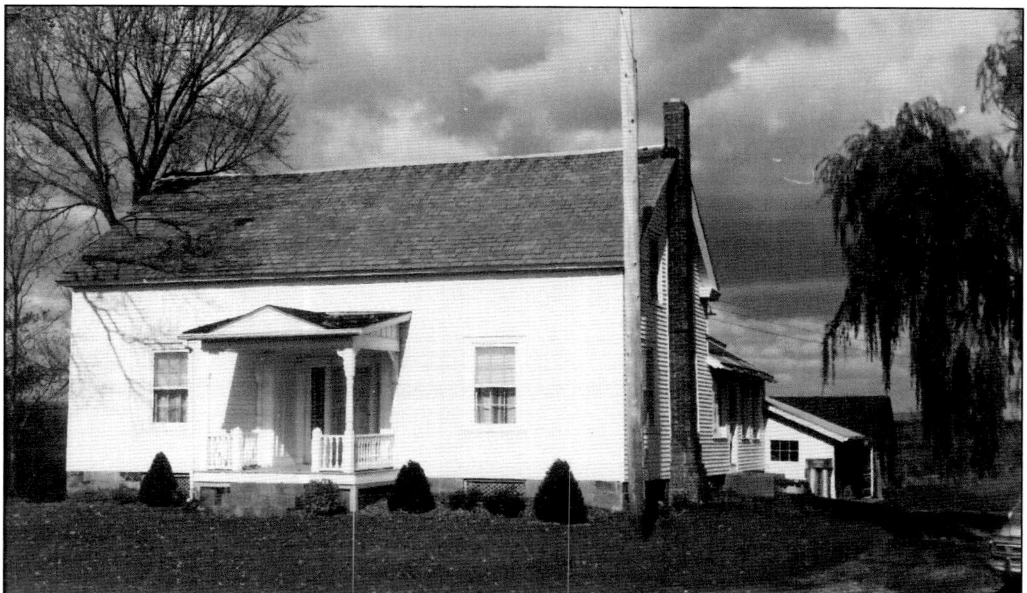

Caldwell/Van Aernem Homestead, situated on Route 67. In recent years, the Caldwell/Van Aernem residence became part of Saratoga Standardbred Farms, Inc. This home is thought to have been part of the Underground Railroad during the Civil War. The house has a double cellar, one section of which comes out in the kitchen and the other of which leads to a woodshed attached to the house. One bedroom upstairs has a passageway leading to the attic. Stairs from the attic also lead to the woodshed through a hallway.

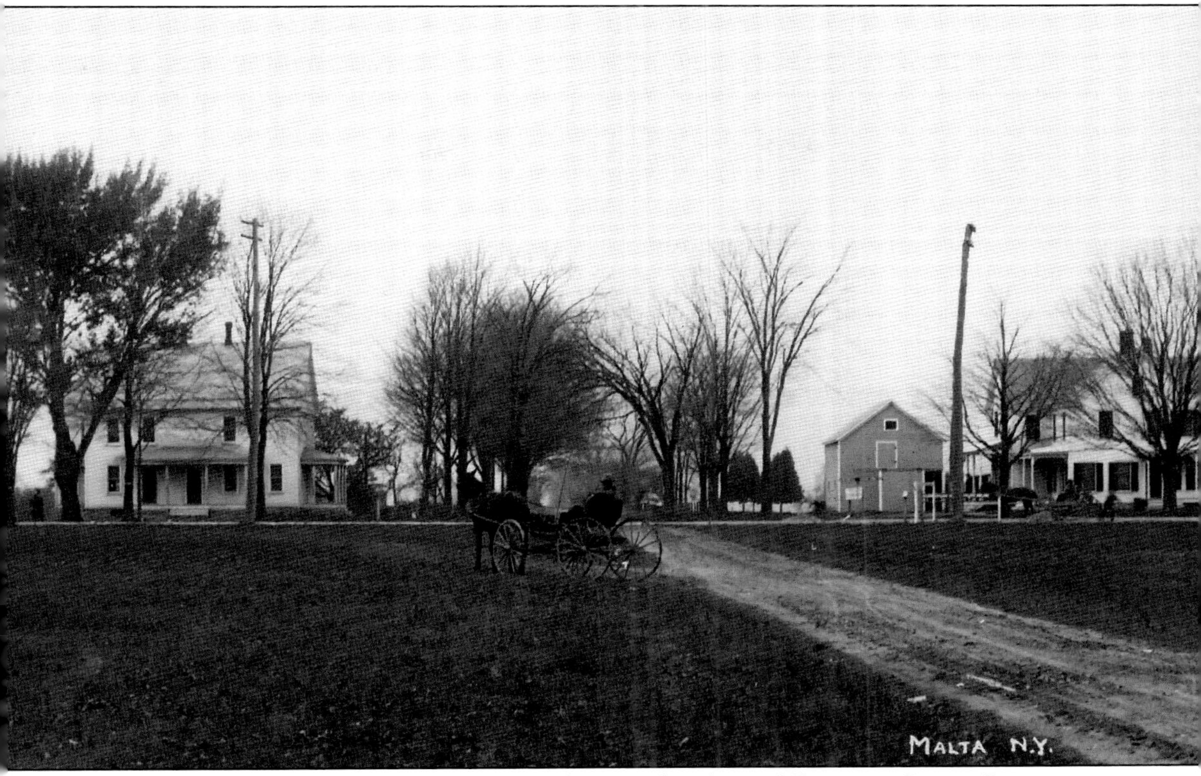

Dunning Street Corners, c. 1912. This photograph taken of Dunning Street Corners was obtained from a postcard with a 1912 postmark. The intersection was also known as Malta Corners. Looking west from the Parade Ground, on the right is the old Rogers Store and the post office, and the Rogers Hotel is on the left. This is the present site of the Malta Diner.

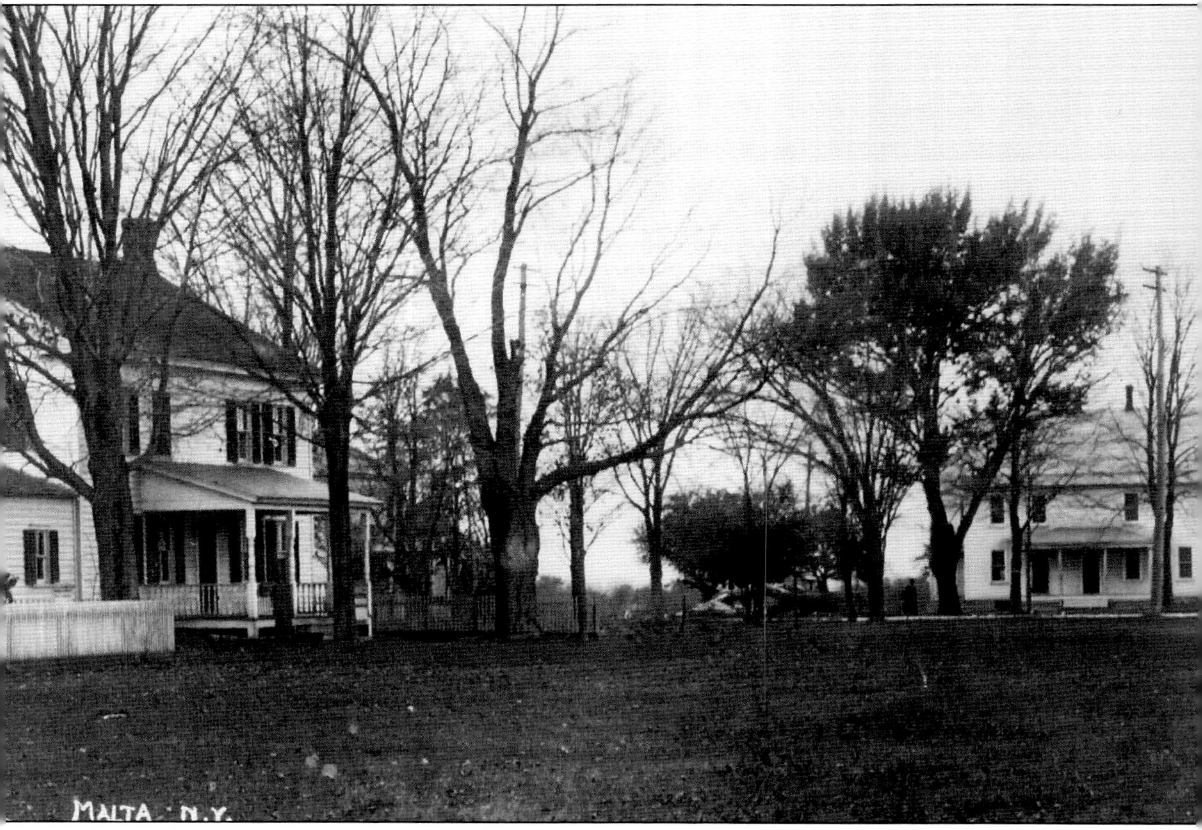

Dunning Street Corners, *c.* 1912. This photograph taken of the southeast and southwest sides of Dunning Street (or Malta) Corners was obtained from an old postcard with a 1912 postmark. The homestead of Mrs. Betts is on the left and the road, now U.S. Route 9, can be seen in front of the Rogers Hotel building site on the right. The Parade Ground is in the foreground. Presently Trustco Bank is located on this site.

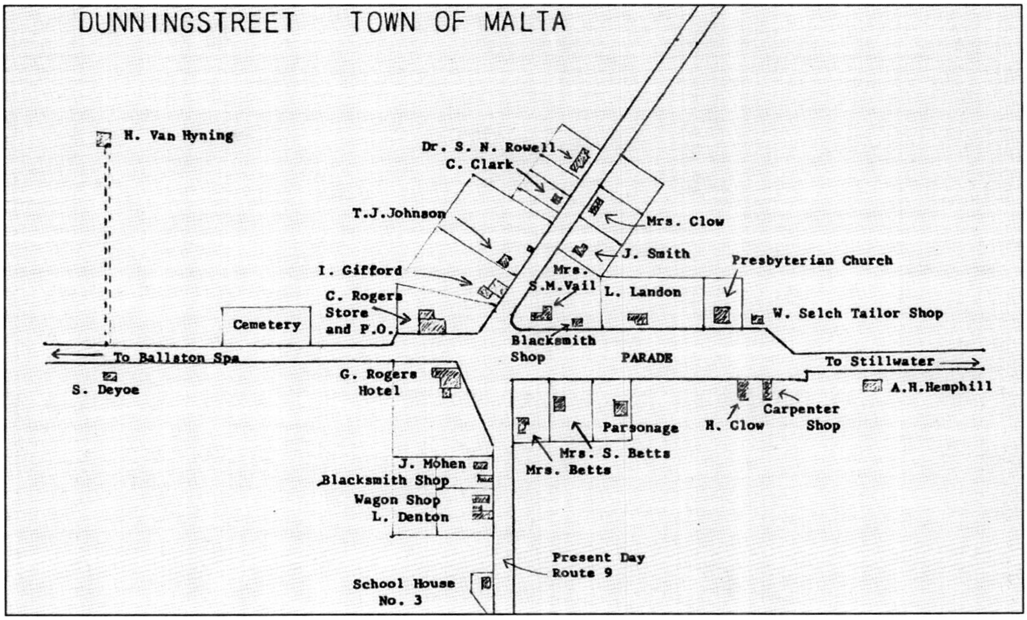

Dunning Street from the Beers 1866 atlas of Saratoga County. Identified here are the locations of local businesses and the names of the businesspeople as well as the surrounding residents.

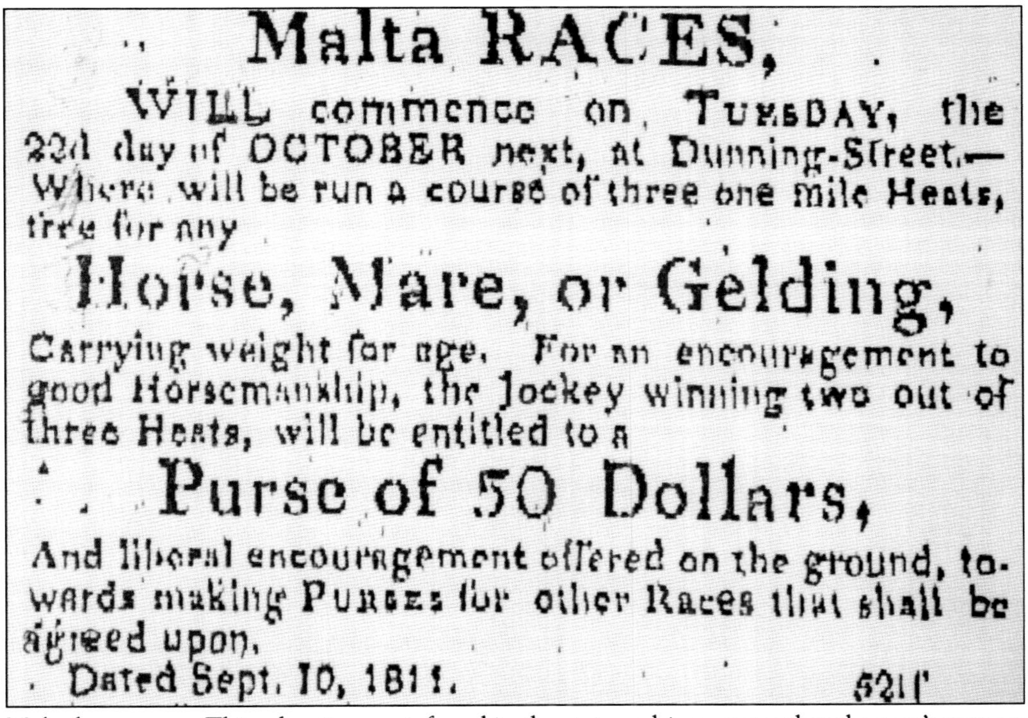

Malta RACES,

WILL commence on TUESDAY, the 22d day of OCTOBER next, at Dunning-Street.— Where will be run a course of three one mile Heats, free for any

Horse, Mare, or Gelding,

Carrying weight for age. For an encouragement to good Horsemanship, the Jockey winning two out of three Heats, will be entitled to a

Purse of 50 Dollars,

And liberal encouragement offered on the ground, towards making Purses for other Races that shall be agreed upon.

Dated Sept. 10, 1811. 521f

Malta horse races. This advertisement, found in the state archives, states that the race's purpose was to encourage good horsemanship. There were two 2-mile courses: one ran from Dunning Street to the top of Round Lake Hill, while the second ran from Dunning Street west on Route 67 to the farm of Orlando Woodruff.

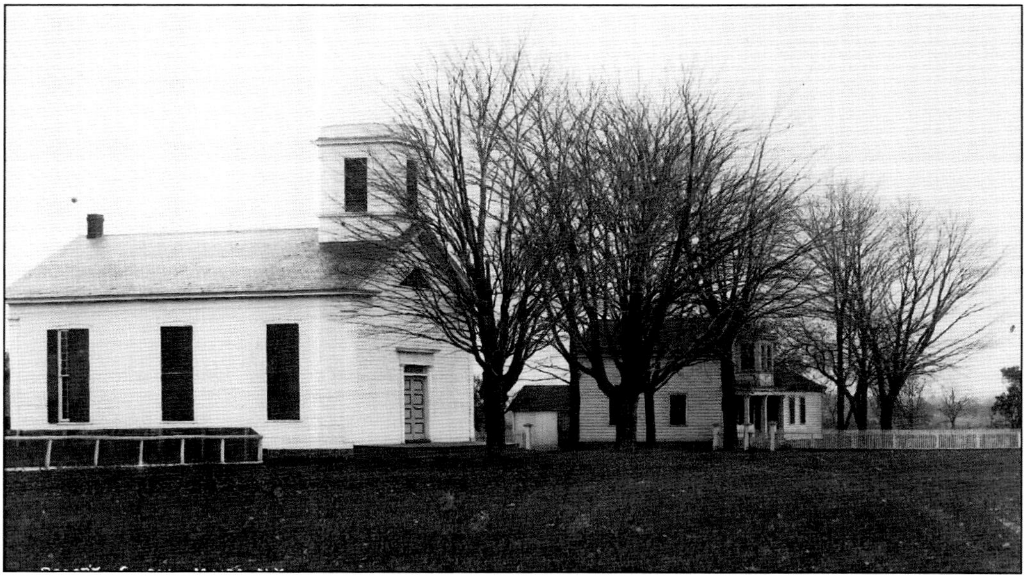

Presbyterian church, *c.* 1910. Situated on the north side of the Parade Ground, the Presbyterian church at Dunning Street was organized in 1845. This church originally grew from the Presbyterian church at Maltaville. The picture was copied from a c. 1910 postcard. The house in the background was the William Selch home and tailor shop (built in 1866). Today this active church is known as the Malta Community Church.

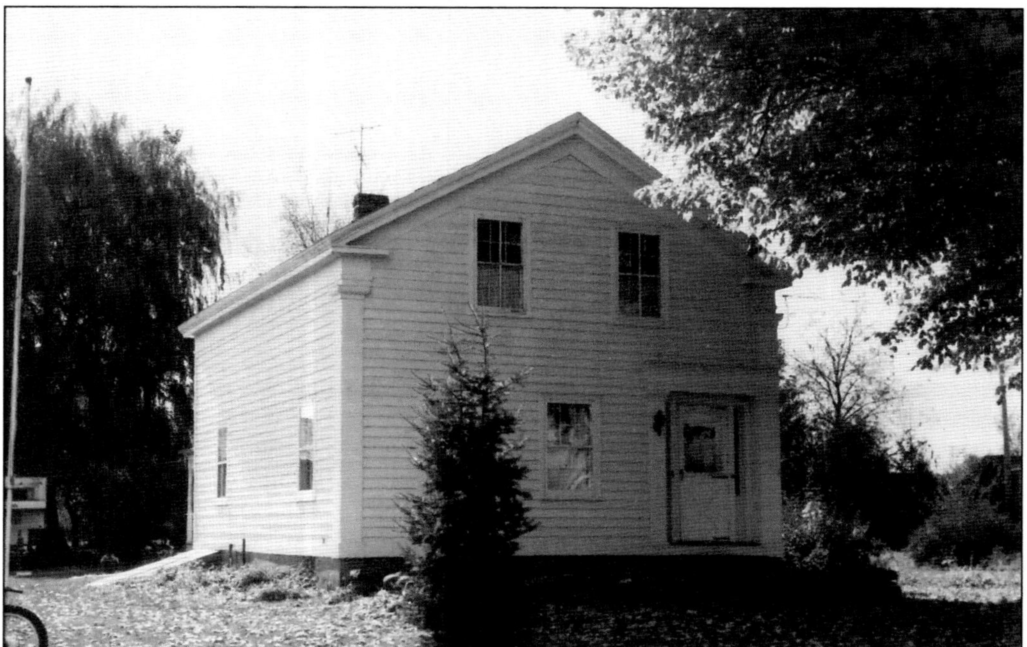

Presbyterian parsonage, *c.* 1840 or 1850. This home was the parsonage of the Presbyterian church at Dunning Street, situated on the south side of the Parade Ground facing north. The church is located across the street on the north side of the Commons. Today this house is the home of the Charles Higley family.

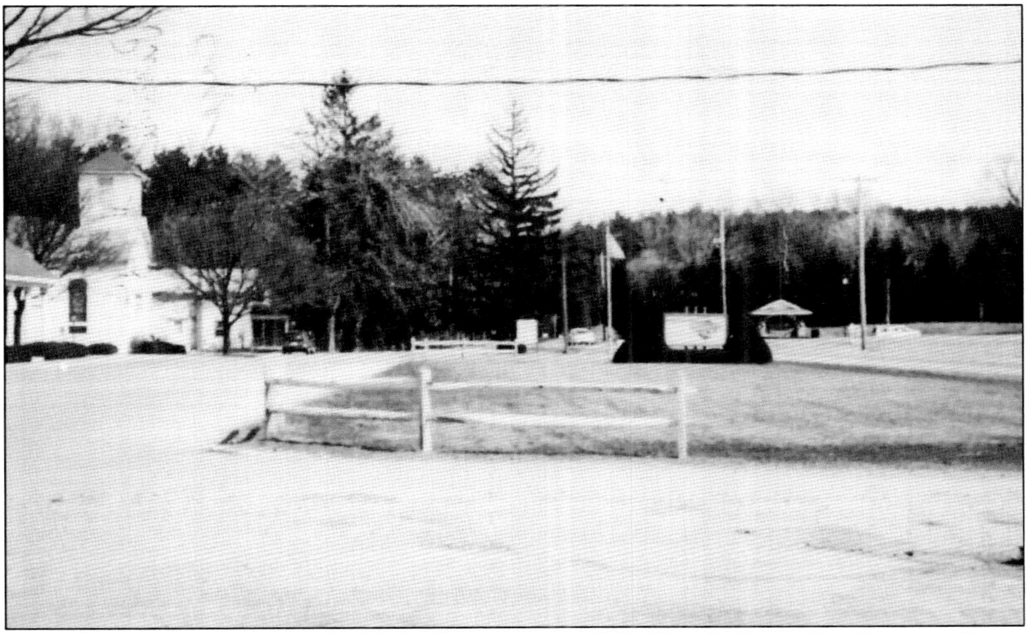

North side of Dunning Street. The northern section of the Parade Ground at Dunning Street is shown here as it appears today, with Luther Forest in the background. A local bank, the community church, and the old home that was once the tailor shop are on the extreme left.

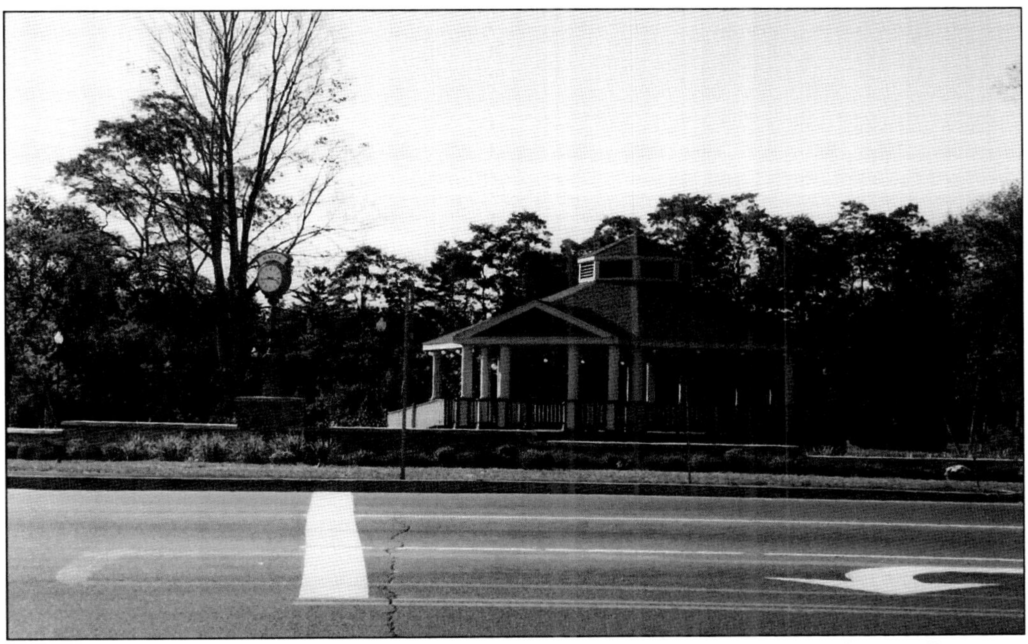

Malta gazebo, 1996. This lovely gazebo is located in today's "Downtown Malta" on Dunning Street and U.S. Route 9. Here residents may gather to enjoy band concerts in the newly built gazebo. The Shops of Malta can be seen in the extreme background. This park and gazebo are on the site of the old Rogers Store.

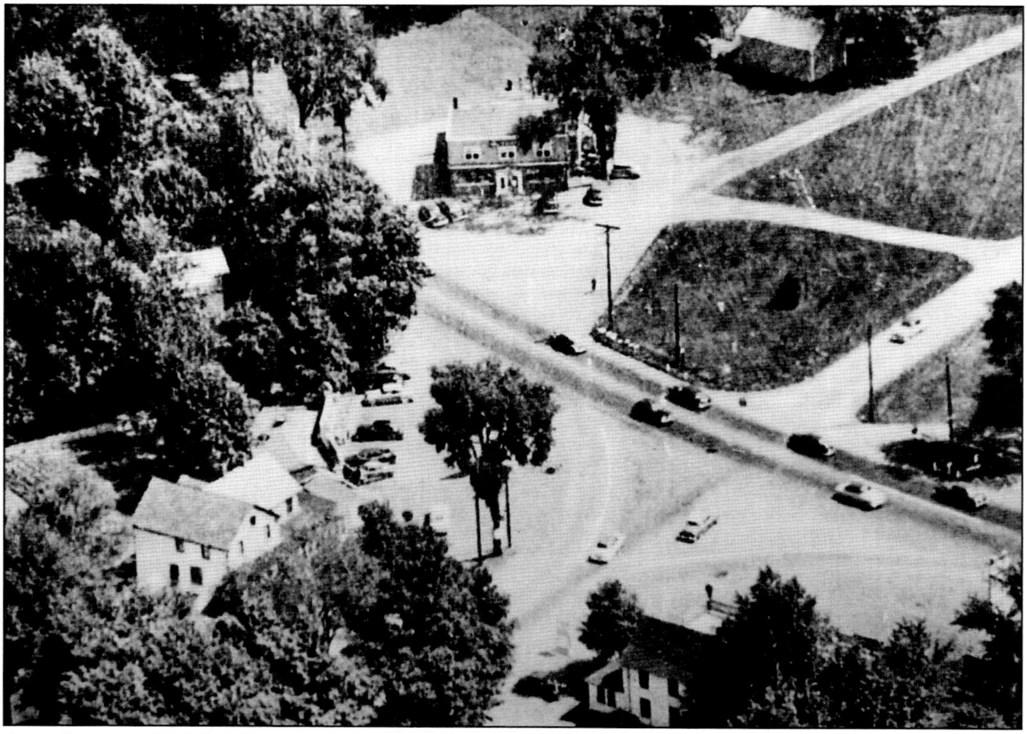

Aerial view of Malta Corners, c. 1952. This image depicts Dunning Street at the intersection of U.S. Route 9. At the top is the old Malta Market, where Stewarts Shop is today. In the left foreground is the home of Harry Barber and the Malta Inn, originally Rogers Store. Today it is the site of the gazebo and the town clock. In the right foreground is what was once Dunsters Restaurant, today the site of the Malta Diner.

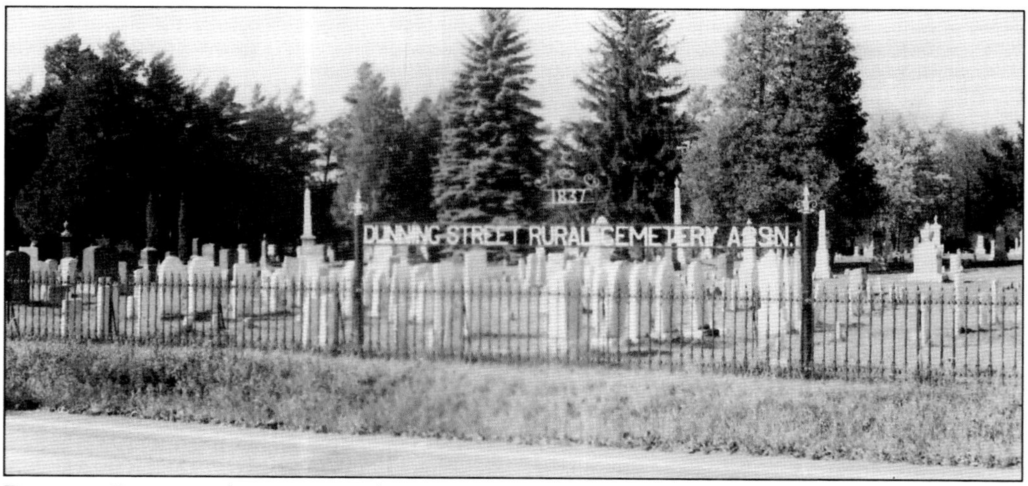

Dunning Street rural cemetery. The Dunning Street cemetery, situated on the north side of Route 67 west of the intersection of Route 9, consists of lands set aside by Michael Dunning for a burying ground. The oldest grave, dug in 1775, belongs to Dunning's wife Hannah. Designated a historic landmark by the Town of Malta in 1990, the cemetery contains the graves of many early settlers.

Colonel Elmer E. Ellsworth. The first Union officer killed in the Civil War in Alexandria, Virginia, was born on Dunning Street on April 11, 1837. His father, Ephraim D. Ellsworth, was a tailor, and his mother was Phebe Denton. He was killed on May 24, 1861, during the invasion of Virginia. His unit was among the first to cross the Potomac. Ellsworth's "Fire Zouaves" (the 11th New York infantry) had been assigned to occupy Alexandria.

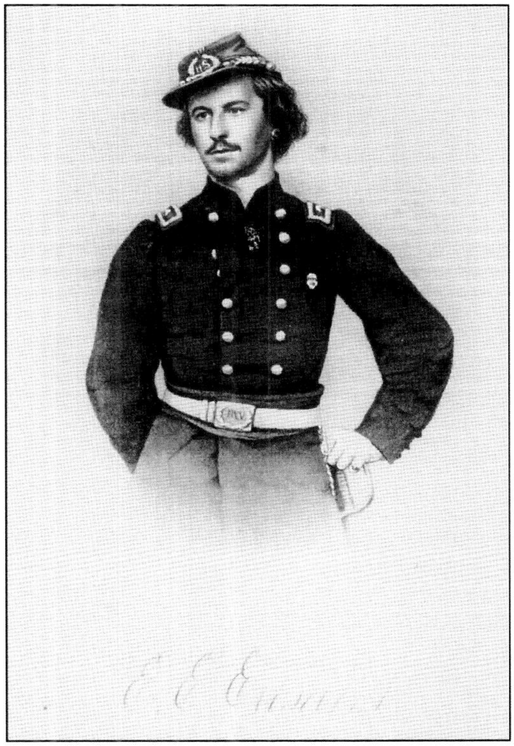

Zouaves in New York City, c. 1860. The postures of the men in the painting would indicate that they were a drill team, and the man with the sword is undoubtedly Elmer Ellsworth. In the rear of the painting is a view of Broadway beginning with the Astor House; probably Central Park opposite the Astor.

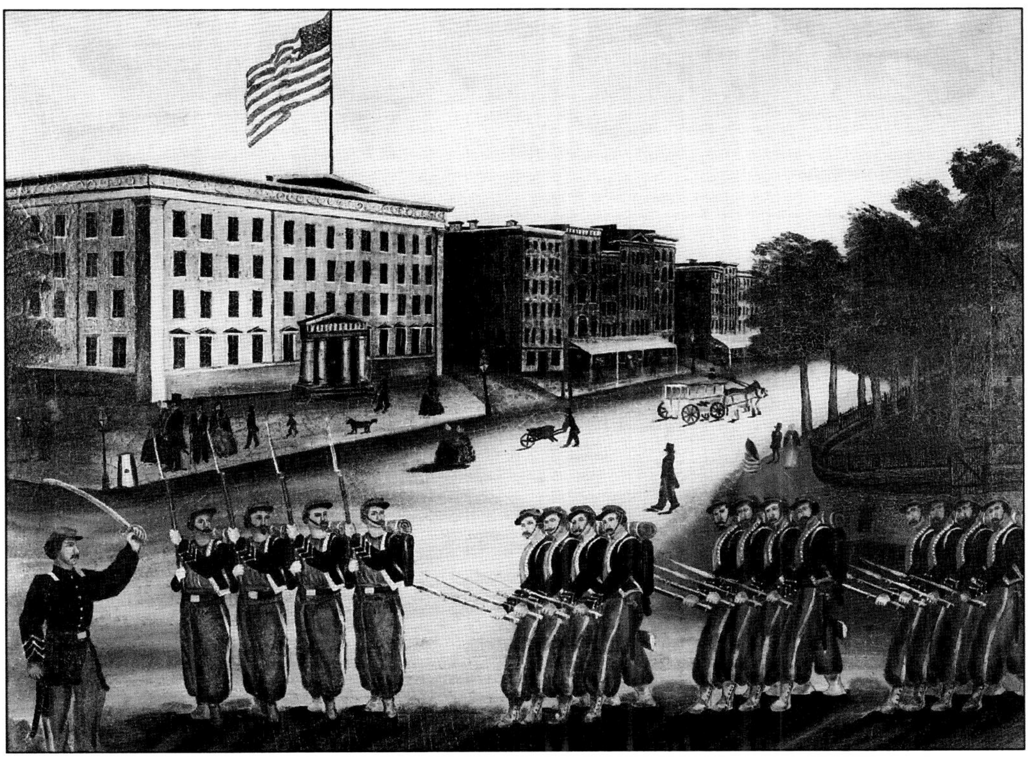

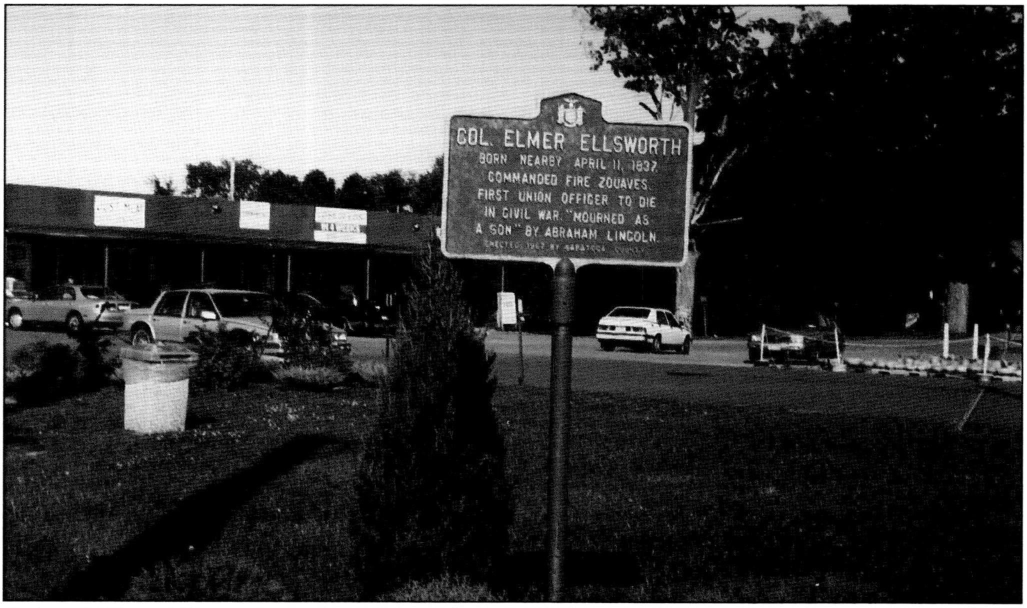

Colonel Elmer Ellsworth marker. Shown here is the town's historical marker commemorating the memory of Colonel Elmer Ellsworth. This marker is on the Common, also known as the Parade Ground.

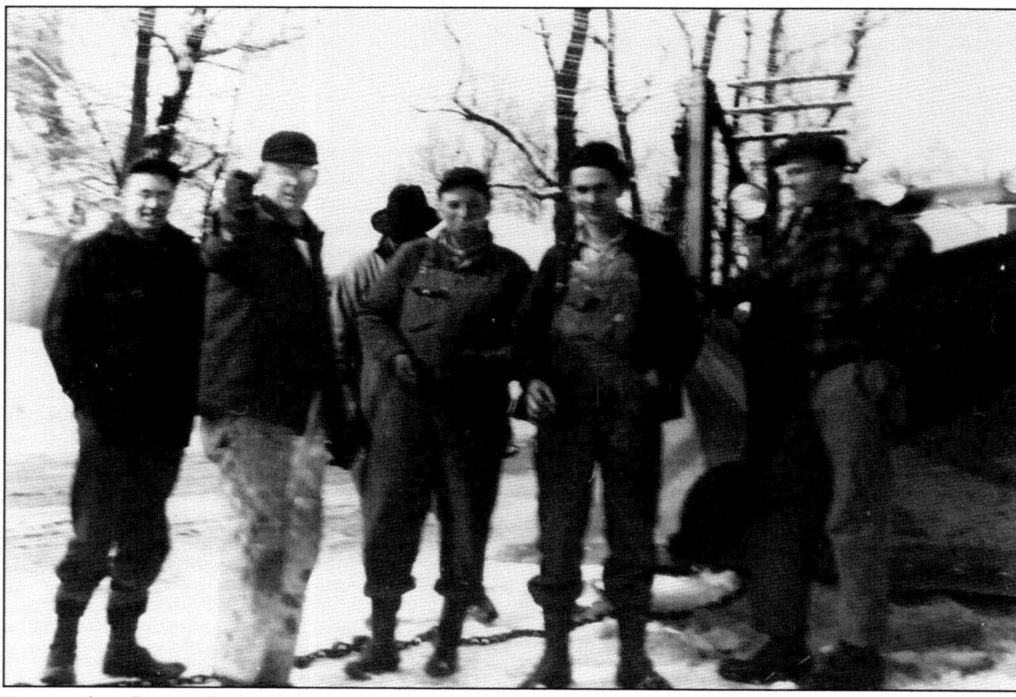

Town of Malta Highway Department. This picture taken on February 28, 1946, shows the Town of Malta Highway Department ready for a day's work. Identified from left to right are Ernest Melander, Howard Knapp, Daniel Arnold (wearing a hat), John Ferris, Royal Arnold, and Ernest Arnold Jr. Note that the winter scene includes a big plow on the far right.

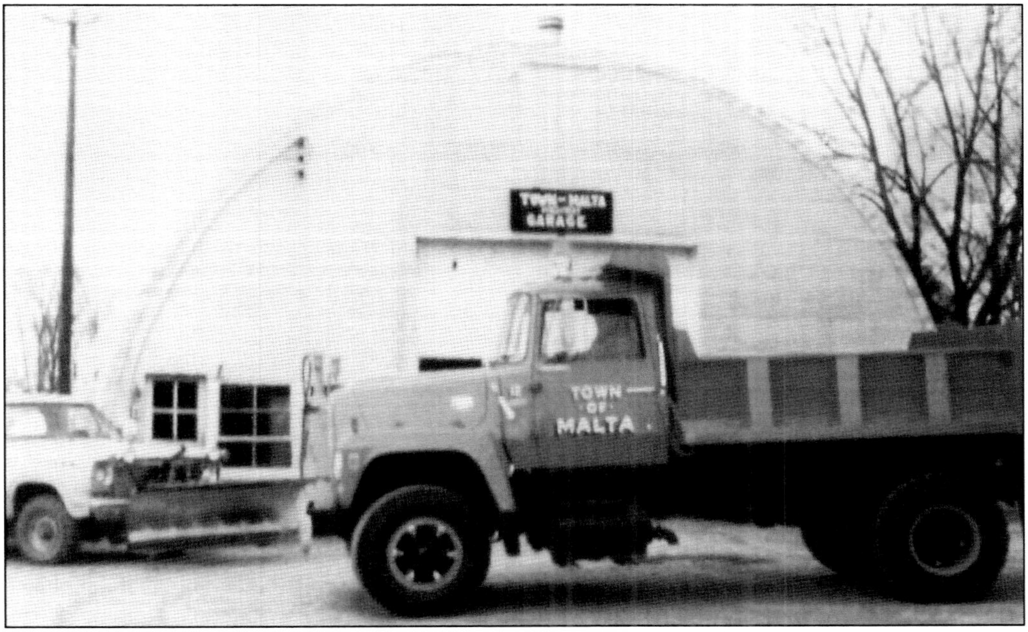

Quonset hut, *c*. 1975–76. This building originally belonged to the Malta Ridge Fire Department. It was purchased by the Town of Malta and moved to the Malta Town Complex site, becoming the original town garage. Pictured also are the new town dump truck and the town's yellow Dodge truck with its snowplow. At this time, Royal T. Arnold was the superintendent of the highway department.

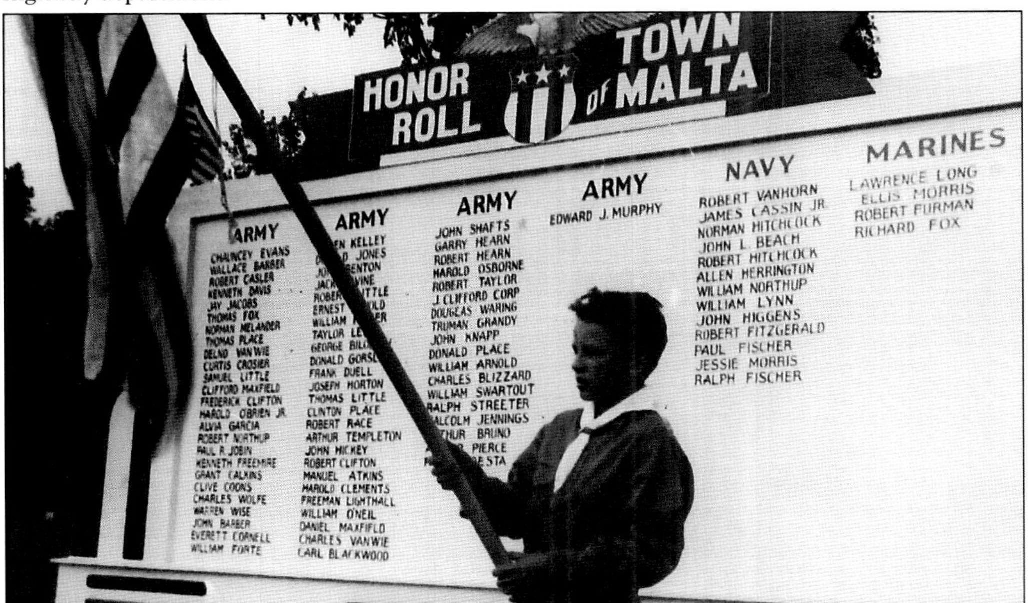

Town of Malta Honor Roll, *c*. 1945. This large sign was erected on the Parade Ground at Dunning Street. It listed many of the names of Malta men serving in the United States Army, Navy, and Marine Corps.

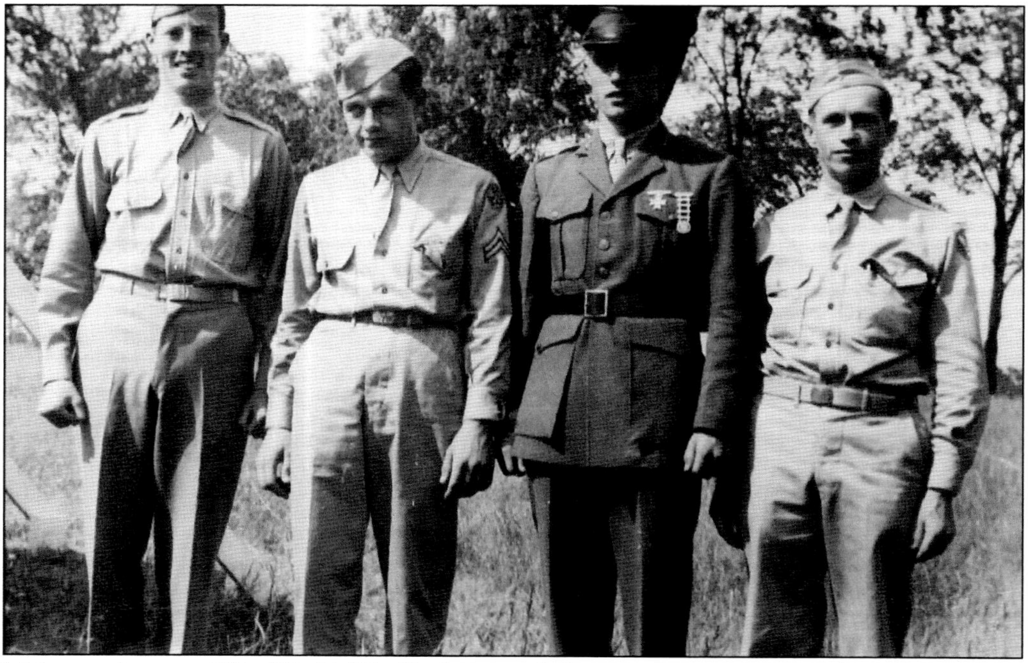

Malta servicemen. This World War II photograph features four servicemen from the town of Malta. They are, from left to right, an unidentified young soldier, Donald Gorsline of the U.S. Army, Richard Fox of the U.S. Marines, and Freeman Lighthall of the U.S. Army. Do you recognize the first soldier? If you do, we would like to learn his name.

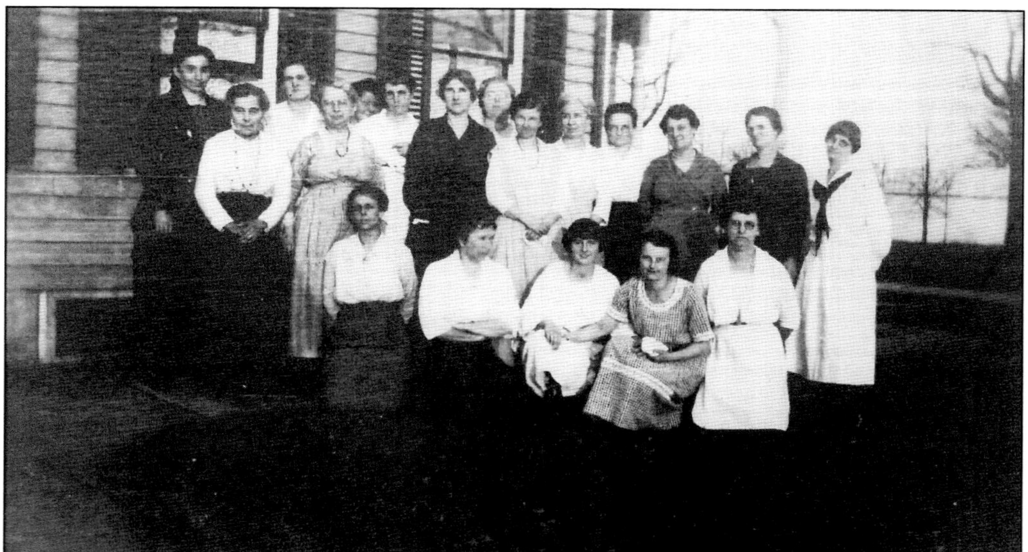

Malta Home Bureau Organization, 1921. There are nineteen ladies in this photograph of the home bureau organization at Dunning Street in 1921. Among them are Etta Knapp, Carrie Brown, Lulu Breen, Myrtle Knapp, Mrs. Wilmot, Myrtle Bathrick, Mrs. Baker, Millie Barber, Lillian Fitch, Clara Curie, Marion Fitch, Estella Cooper, Lillah Bathrick, and Hortense Turpit.

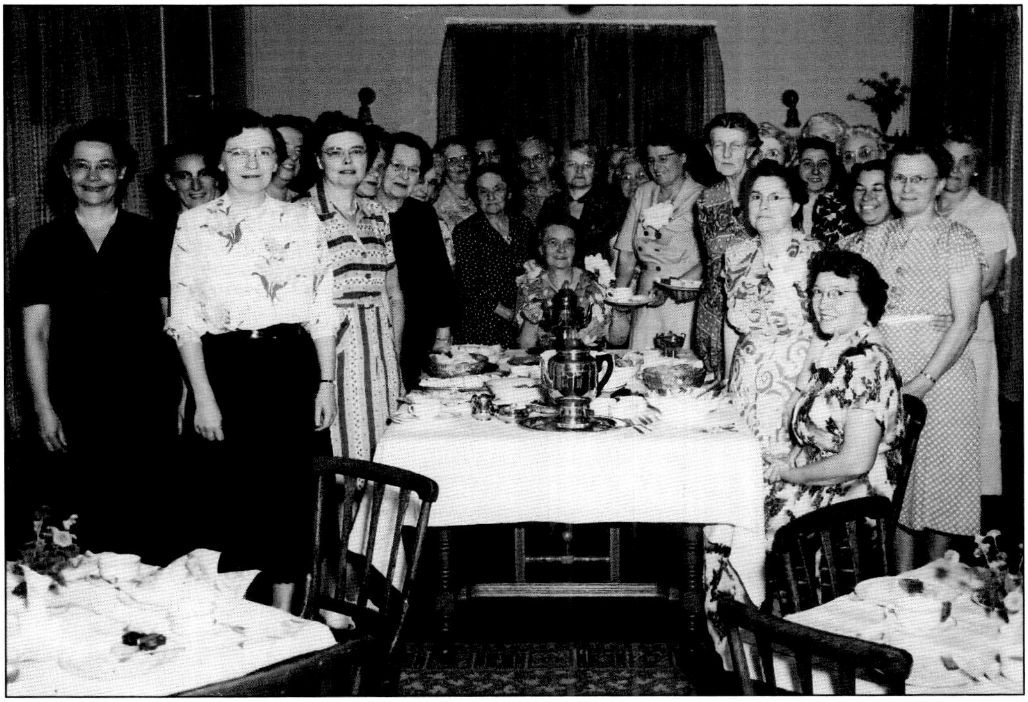

Malta Home Bureau Organization anniversary. The ladies of the home bureau are seen on the occasion of the 30th anniversary of their organization's founding on September 14, 1950. The anniversary event included an all-day meeting at an unidentified location. The entire membership was present—including charter members and several new members.

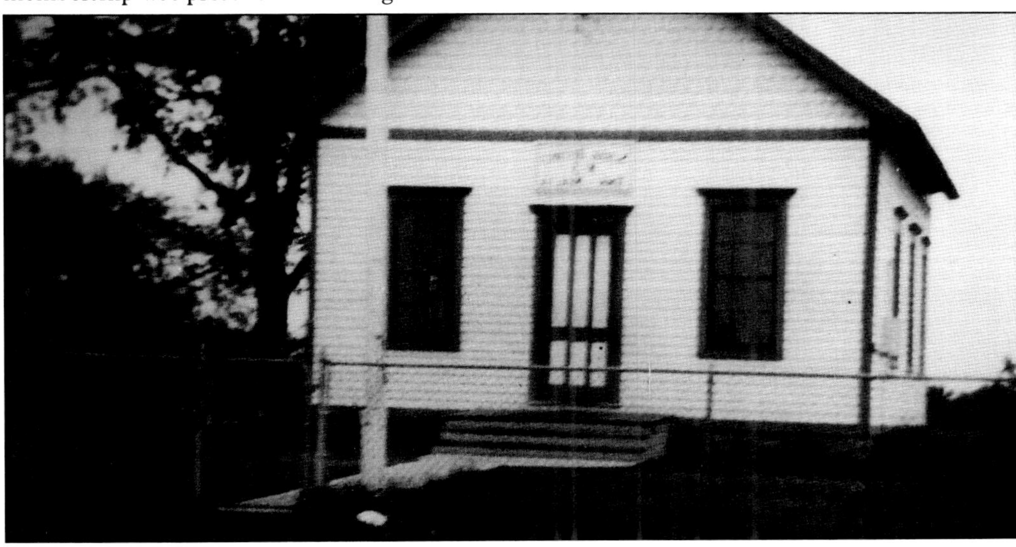

Dunning Street Common School #3. The first meeting of the inhabitants of the district was held at the house of John Swartout in 1813. Melatiah Lathrop, David Powers, and Moses Dunning were elected as trustees. At this same meeting it was resolved that a school would be built on the west side of the road leading from Dunning Street to Round Lake. In July of 1813, a determination was made that the schoolhouse would be made of wood.

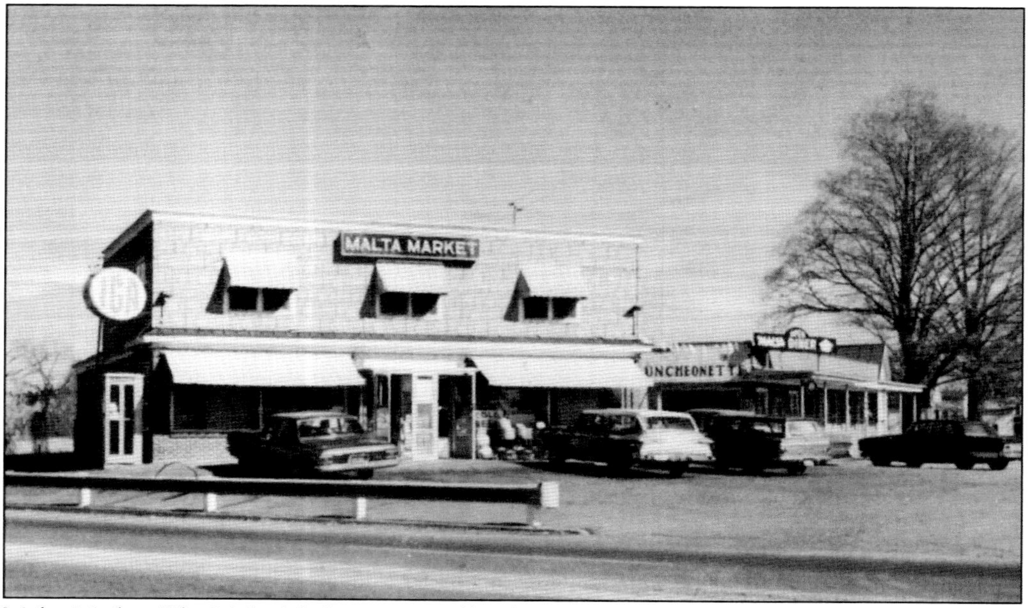

Malta Market. The Malta Market, operated by the Buck family, served the needs of the residents of Dunning Street from the 1940s to the 1960s. It was located on the northeastern corner of the Dunning Street intersection. Today it is the site of Stewarts Shop.

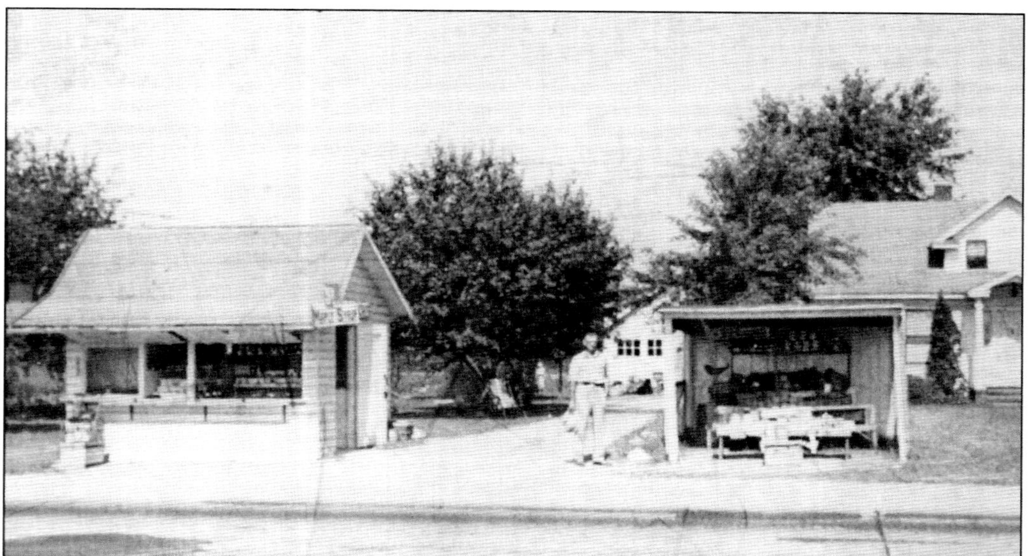

Edgar D. Larkin and Vermont maple products. Mr. Edgar D. Larkin served as supervisor of the town of Malta for several years. He is shown here in front of his home and small market on Route 9, where he sold Vermont maple syrup products. Today this location is the site of the Malta Town Hall and Complex.

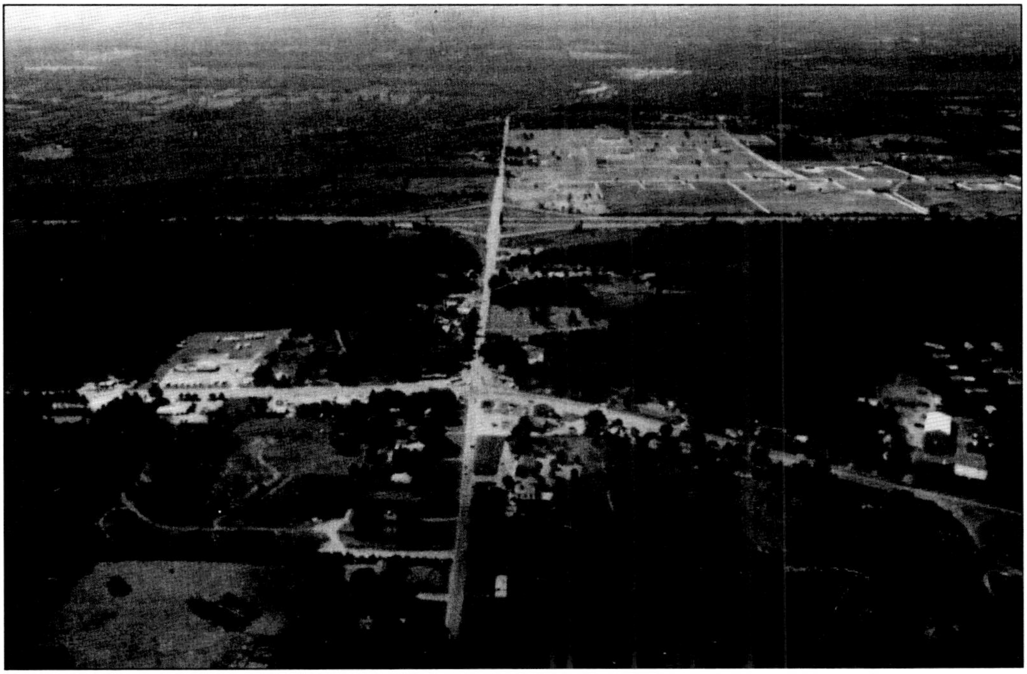

Aerial view of Dunning Street, 1986. This aerial view of Malta was taken in 1986. Exit 12 of the Adirondack Northway (U.S. Route 87) is visible in the background.

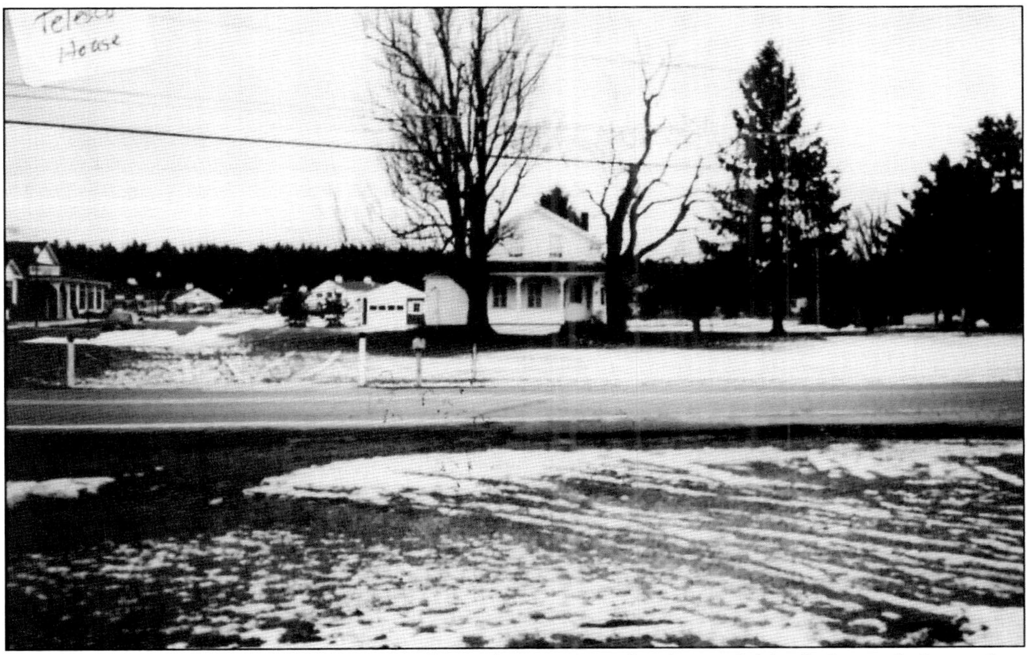

H. Clow residence. The 1866 Beers Atlas indicates that this beautiful little home belonged to H. Clow, about whom little is known. The house is situated on the south side of the Parade Ground at Dunning Street, looking north toward the Presbyterian church. Today this property contains the home of Mrs. Violet R. Ederle.

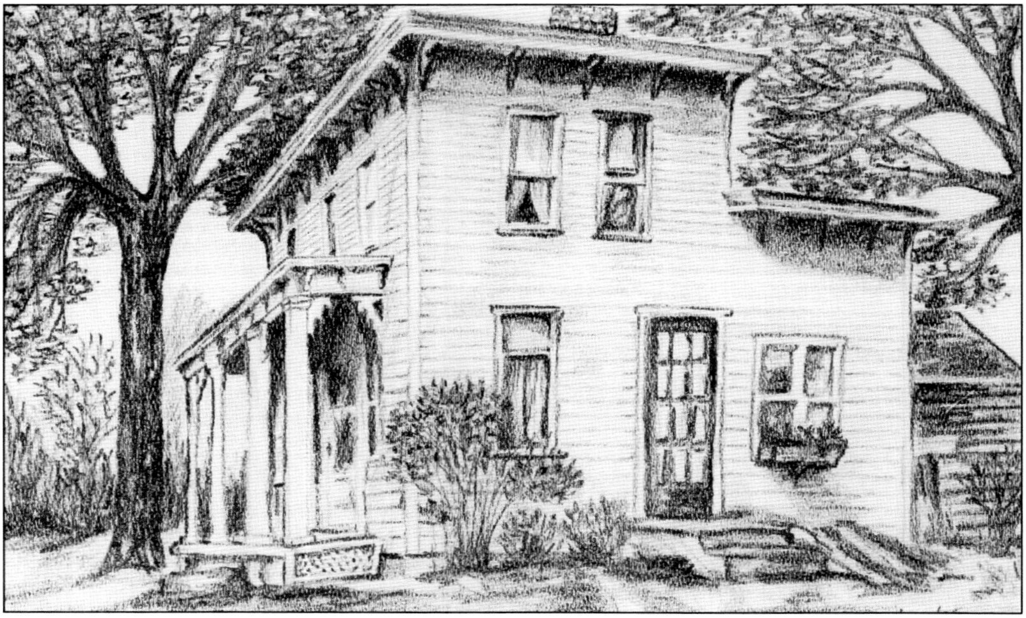

Artist's rendition of the Van Buren/Dunning/Saratoga Standard Farm/Bond Homestead. In the 1840s this home, located on Route 67 west of Dunning Street, belonged to Stephen G. Van Buren. By 1865, it was the property of John Dunning. In 1945, George J. Becktoft purchased the property, and in 1972 it became the home of Clifford and Diane Lange. Later it belonged to Saratoga Standardbred Farms, and at present it is the home of the Bond family.

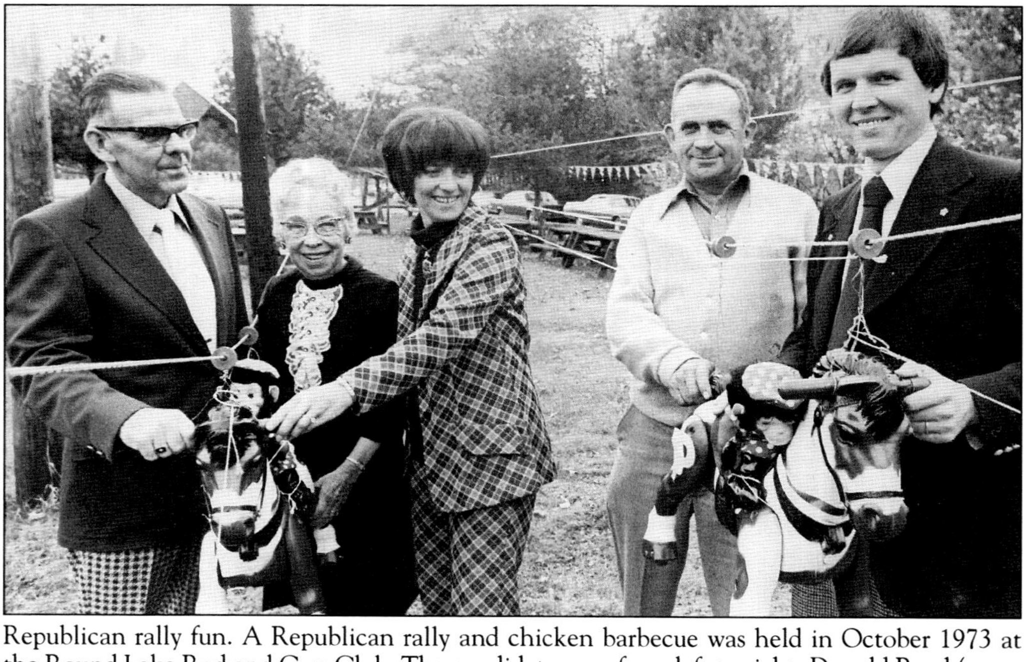

Republican rally fun. A Republican rally and chicken barbecue was held in October 1973 at the Round Lake Rod and Gun Club. The candidates are, from left to right, Donald Reed (town justice), Helen Hirahara (tax collector), Maggi Amodeo (running for town clerk), Royal Arnold (highway superintendent), and David Meager (supervisor).

Two

East Line

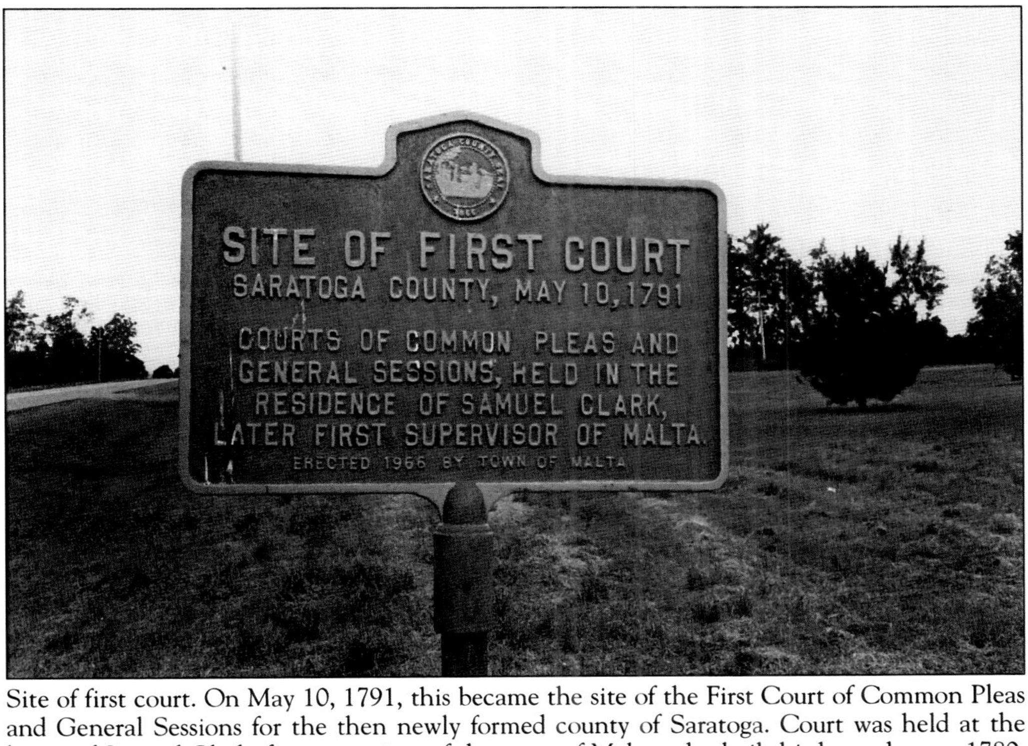

Site of first court. On May 10, 1791, this became the site of the First Court of Common Pleas and General Sessions for the then newly formed county of Saratoga. Court was held at the home of Samuel Clark, first supervisor of the town of Malta, who built his home here c. 1780. The presiding judge was John Thompson, and assisting him were Associate Judges Jacobus Van Schoonhoven, Sidney Berry, James Gordon, and Beriah Palmer. Prisoners were brought to this place from Albany for trial for several years until a new courthouse was built at Court House Hill, town of Milton. This site is located on County Route 82 (East Line Road).

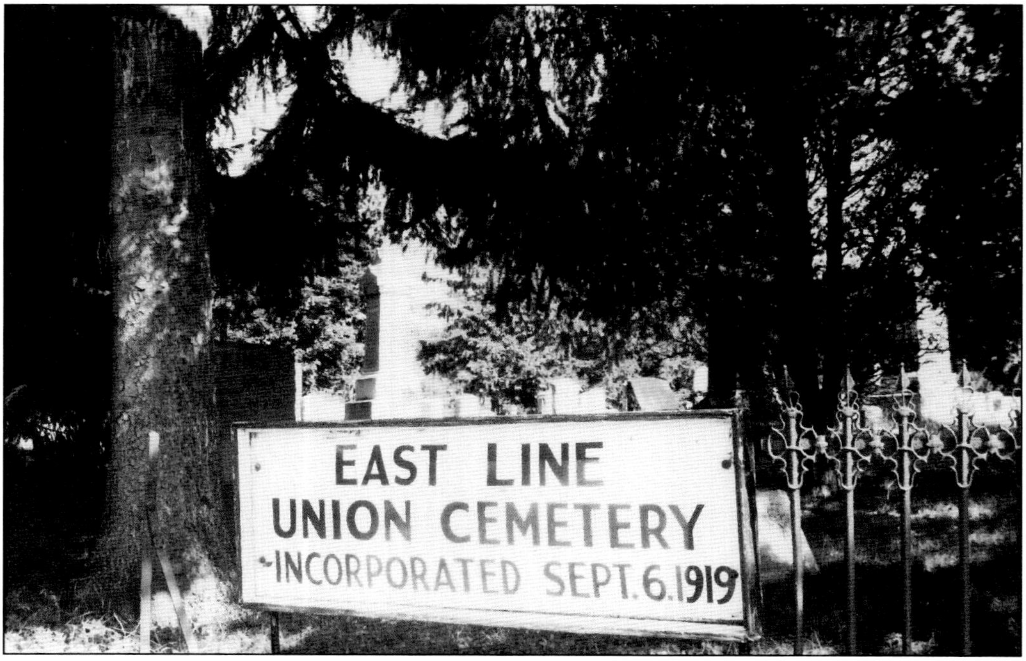

East Line Union Cemetery, incorporated September 6, 1919. The burial ground was once known as the Armstrong's Corners Cemetery. The oldest recorded grave, dug in 1785, belonged to Talcott Morehouse. This small country cemetery contains the graves of twenty veterans of the American Revolution and Samuel Clark, the first supervisor of the town of Malta. It was designated as a historic landmark by the Town of Malta in 1993.

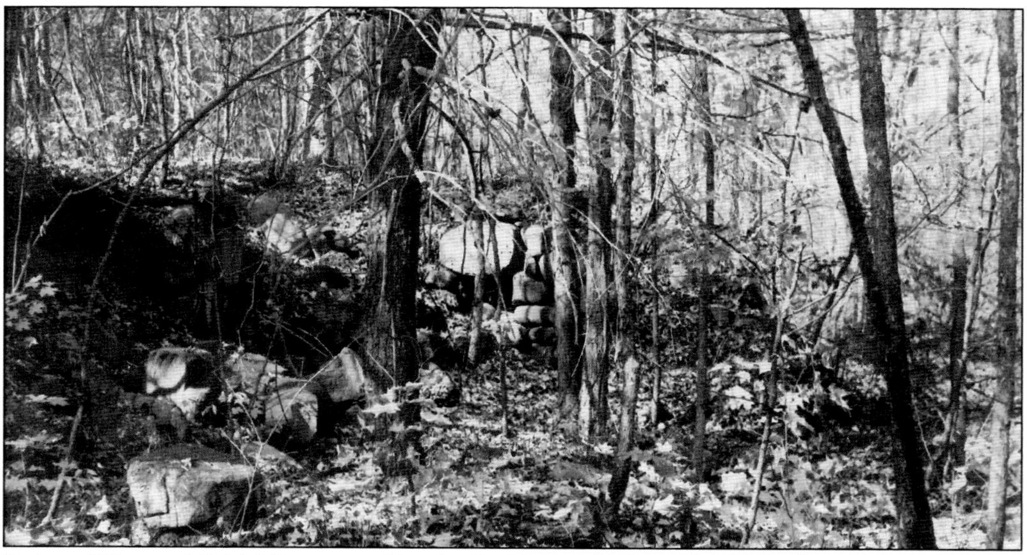

Ruins of Flaxseed Oil Mill, operated by the East Line 1795–1825. This mill was situated on the south bank of the Ballston Creek near Ruhle Road, and was operated by Jonah Starr, who also ran a farm. The mill was later owned by James Clark, who was in business with a Mr. Lindley of Schenectady. Today the site is adjacent to Malta's new Shenantaha Creek Park, on the east side of East Line Road.

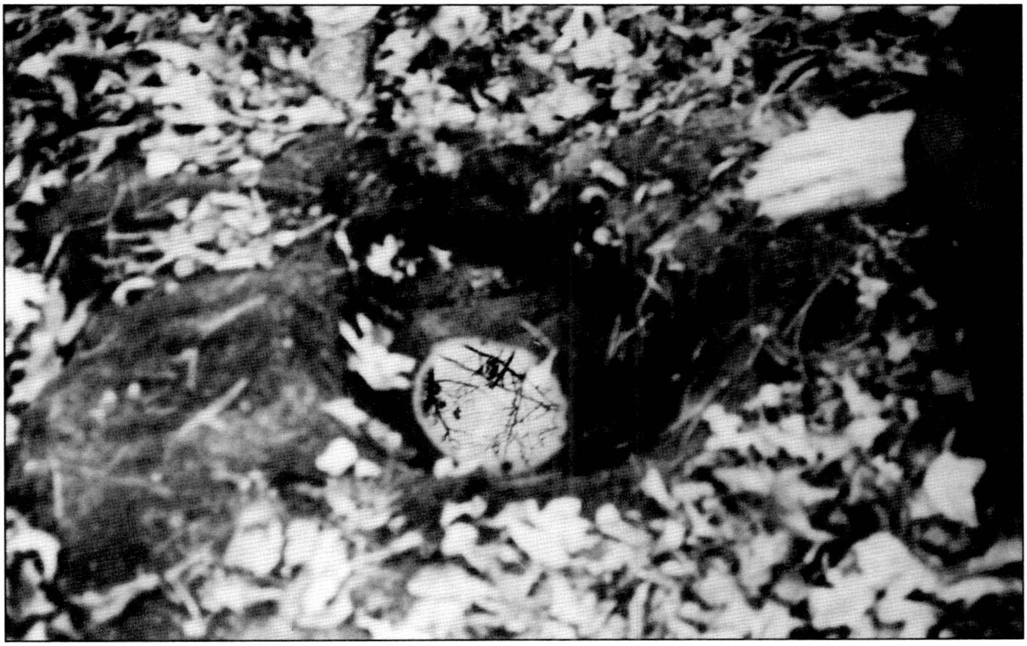

Indian mortars. The Indian Mortars of Malta can be found on the northern bank of Ballston Creek. There are several boulders on the creek bank that have been hollowed out in the shape of mortars either by artificial means or through the action of water. It is believed that the Mohawk Indians used these mortars to crush and grind their corn into meal.

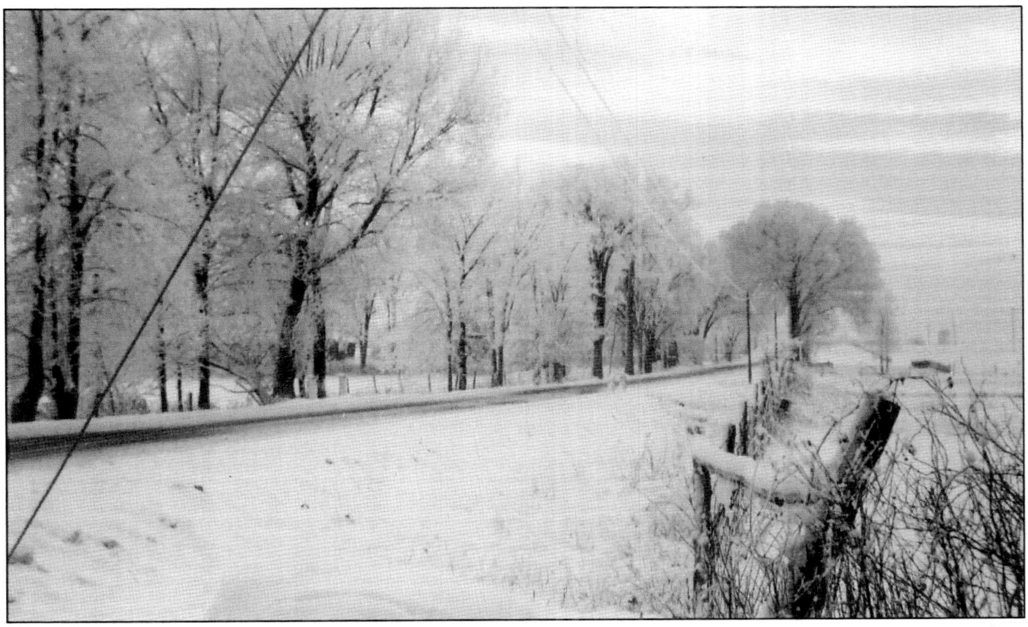

East Line Road winter scene. This photograph was taken on East Line Road on a winter day. East Line Road divides the town of Malta and the town of Ballston (in Saratoga County). This view depicts the most westerly line of the town of Malta, looking to the south. The old Peek Farm can barely be seen in the background among the trees.

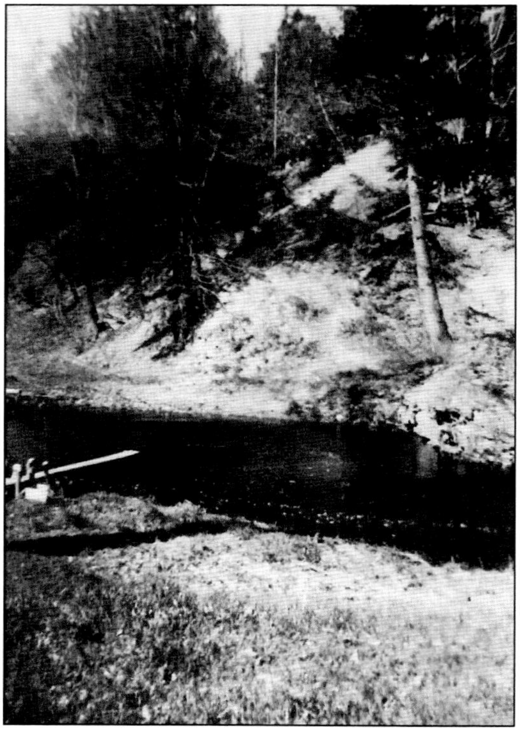

Sheep Hole, *c.* 1850. There were about four thousand sheep in the town *c.* 1860, and Ballston Creek was dug out and properly dammed so that they could be washed prior to shearing. Generally, the washing of the sheep was a social event marked by a "bee." Also, for many years this place was the spot for a great swim for men after a hot day working on the farm.

Stone Arch Bridge, built in 1873 by Elbin Miller. The bridge was built from fieldstone quarried about a 1/4 mile away and hauled to the site by horses. It was listed on the State and National Registers of Historic places in 1988, and is an excellent example of vernacular masonry bridge construction. It was designated as a historic landmark by the Town of Malta in 1984, but collapsed suddenly on April 24, 1993.

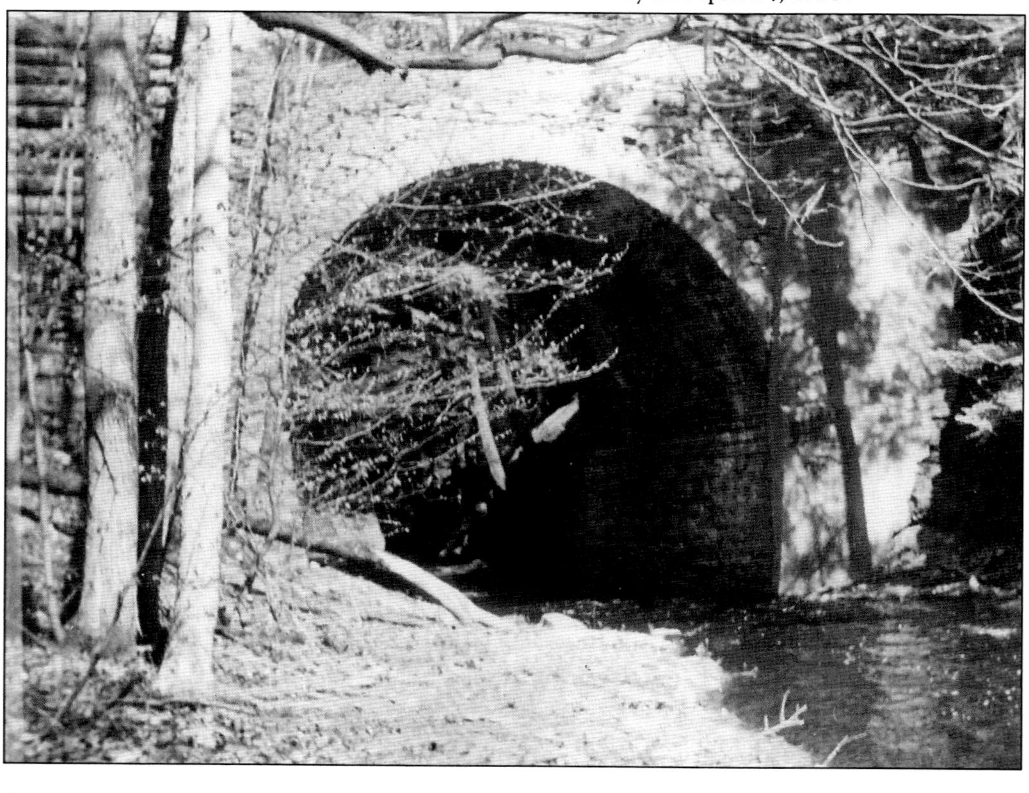

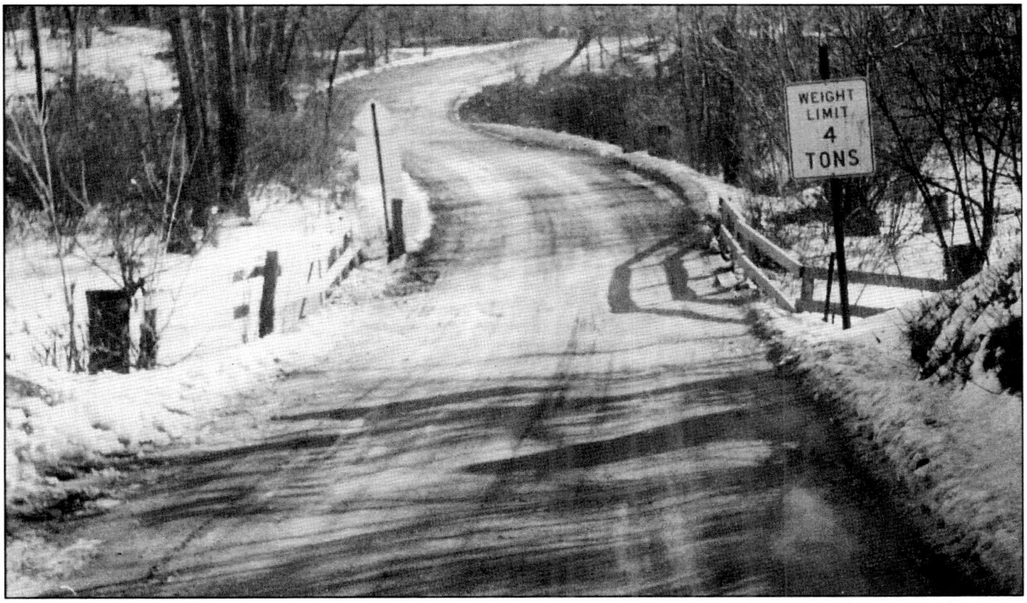

Crossing Stone Arch Bridge in winter. The bridge was narrow enough by modern standards to be considered a one-way span.

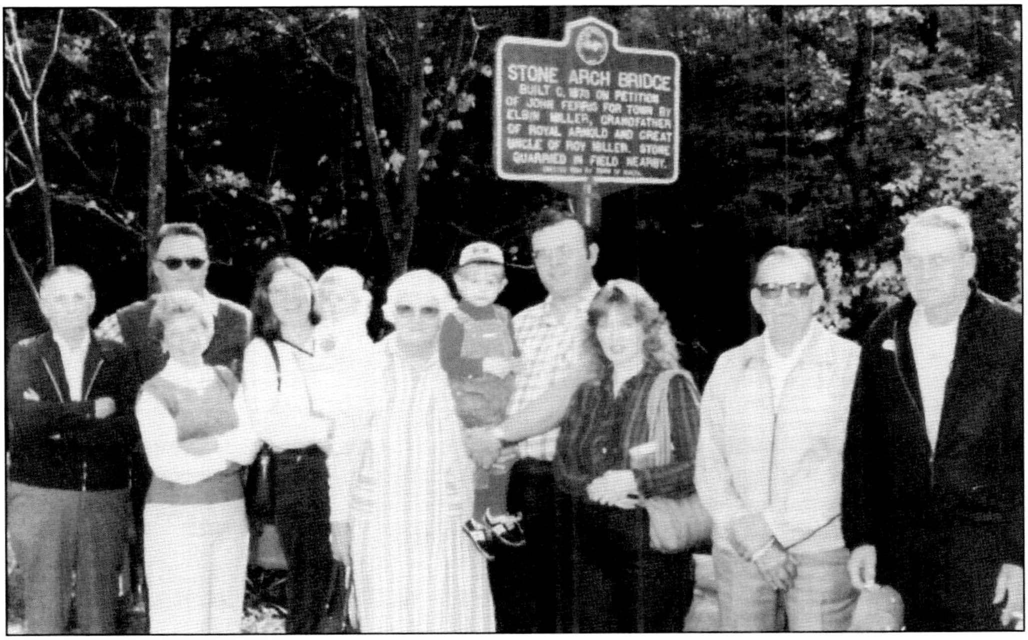

Stone Arch Bridge descendants. The descendants of Elbin Miller, builder of Malta's famous Stone Arch Bridge, are gathered in this photograph beside the historic marker that was presented by the town on October 11, 1984. The marker commemorated the bridge's 111 years of service to the community and honored the Miller, Arnold, and Ferris families, all descendants of Elbin Miller. From left to right are Robert Miller, Harold Arnold, Hazel Miller, Rachel Arnold Clothier, Anne Clothier, Annie Morehouse Arnold, Christopher Arnold, Roy Arnold, Linda Arnold, John Ferris, and Ralph Arnold.

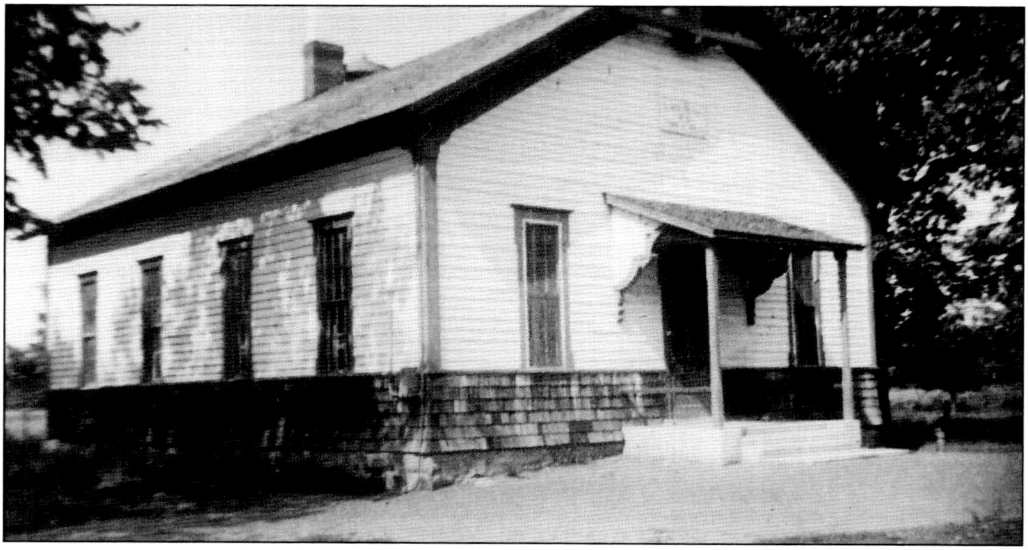

East Line Common School No. 8, situated on the northeast corner of East Line Corners, *c.* 1935. Originally this building was a house of worship, built in 1809 by the Methodist Episcopal church. It was transformed into a schoolhouse *c.* 1870 and for many years operated as the town of Ballston No. 3 and town of Malta No. 8 Common Schools. The school eventually became part of the Malta school system. By 1947, it had closed its doors forever.

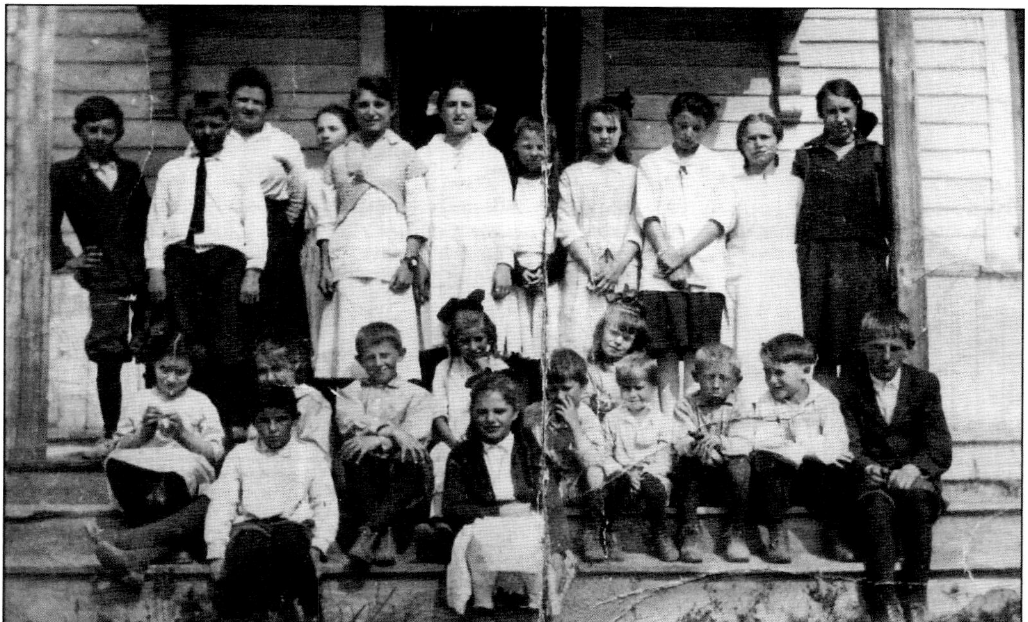

Students from East Line Common School No. 8. Students from the Malta Common No. 8 and Ballston No. 3 Schools, located on the corner of East Line Road and Route 67, are pictured here. This picture was taken before the school was remodeled about 1890, which means that the steps were still made of wood and the original base of the building could still be seen. The school closed and the students became part of the Ballston Spa Centralized School District about 1947.

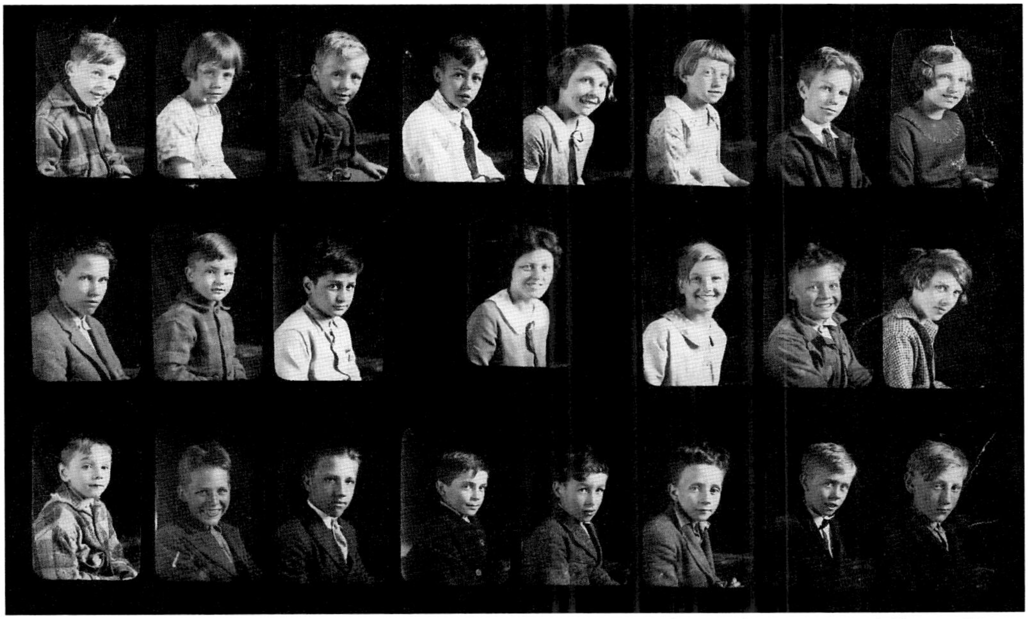

Students of East Line Common School No. 8, c. 1927–30. The students are as follows: (front row) George Relyea, Robert Gower, William Sebasta, George Solotruck, Thomas Malone, Harry Gower, Robert Weed, and Joe Prock; (middle row) Donald Kelley, Paul Sebasta, Eugene Frank, Miss Agnes Noonan (teacher), Frances Sebasta, Herbert Eckstrom, and Alice Weed; (back row) Dudley Malone, Eleanor Gower, Charles Riddervolt, Thomas Clark, Dorothy Weed, Anna Masters, Lawrence Guilfoyle, and Julia Timko.

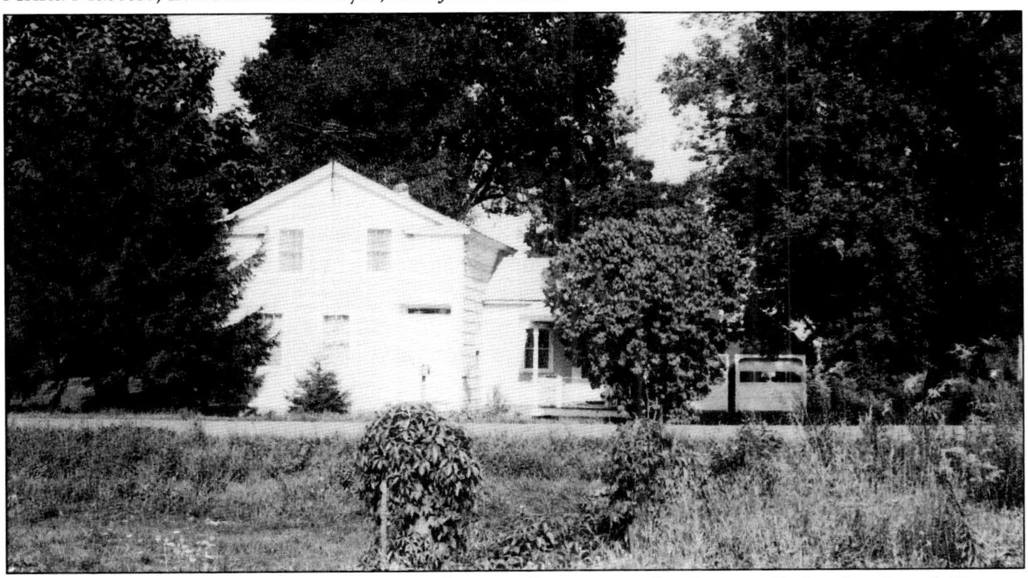

George Vedder home. For many years this residence was the home of the family of George Vedder. On March 8, 1965, it became the parsonage of the Methodist Episcopal church at East Line. The church is situated at northeast corner of the intersection. The parsonage, located on the southeast corner of the intersection, was acquired by the members of the church by public subscription from Benjamin and Catherine Knights.

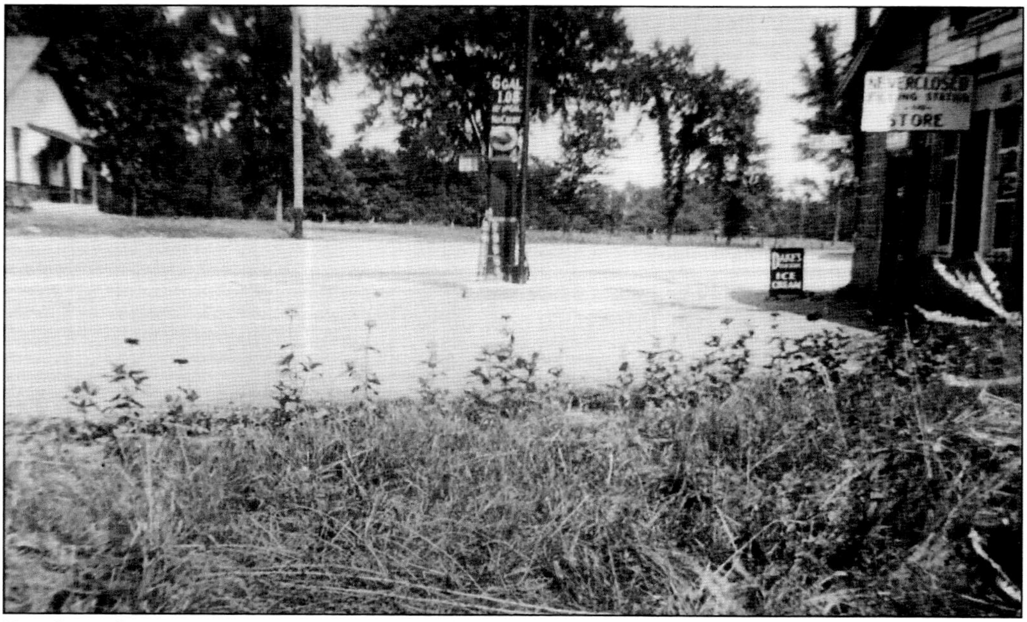

East Line Corners intersection, *c*. 1937. This photograph shows how the East Line intersection looked in the late 1930s. The Neverclosed Filling Station and Store, operated by Robert M. Weed, is on the right. Note the price of gasoline. In the left corner of the photograph, a portion of the Malta Common School No. 8 can be seen. The road that disappears into the background is the road to Dunning Street.

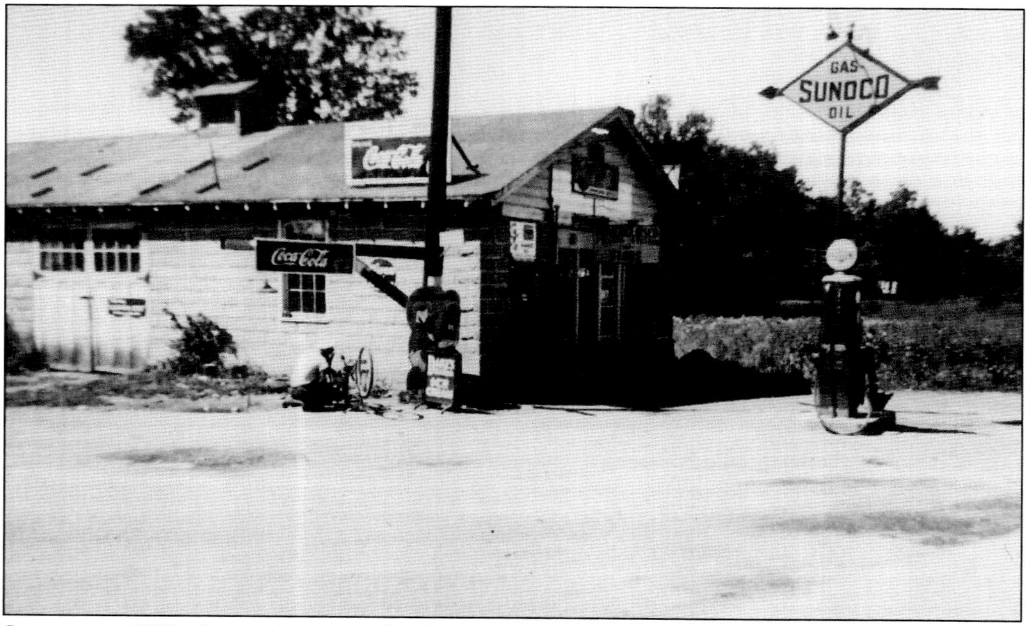

Sunoco, *c*. 1937. Pictured here is the Sunoco Gas Station, garage, and small general store on the southeast corner of the East Line intersection on the Ballston side of East Line Road. The proprietor at this time was Robert M. Weed. The station was originally built *c*. 1930 by William C. Denton and operated as an auto repair garage and gas station by his son, Marshall K. Denton.

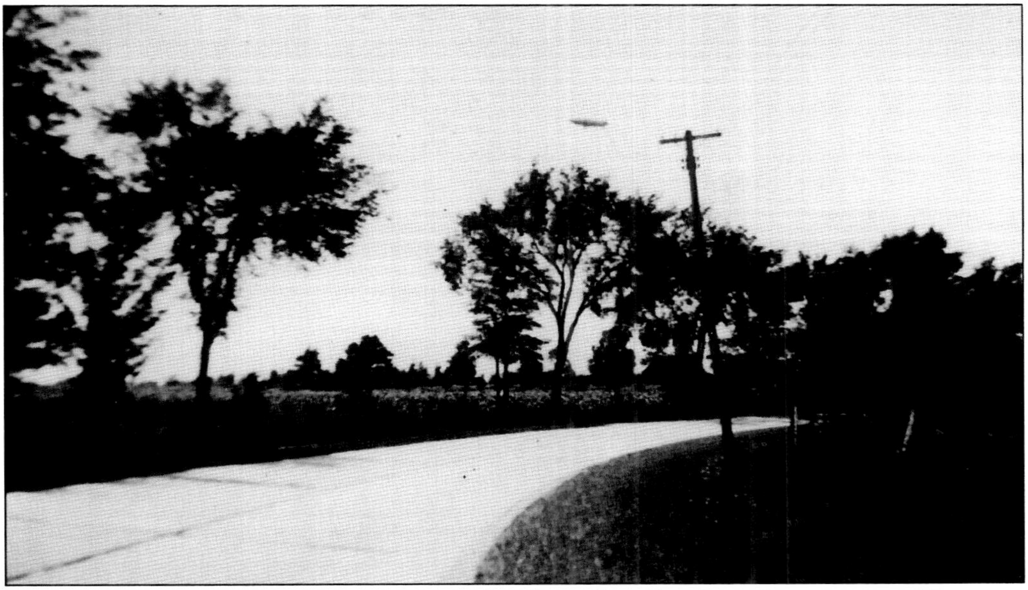

Route 67, c. 1930. This was the view as one faced east from East Line Corners toward Dunning Street. Note the construction and narrowness of Route 67 as it rounds the bend. The open cultivated field in the background is today fully grown, the graceful elms having fallen victim to Dutch Elm Disease.

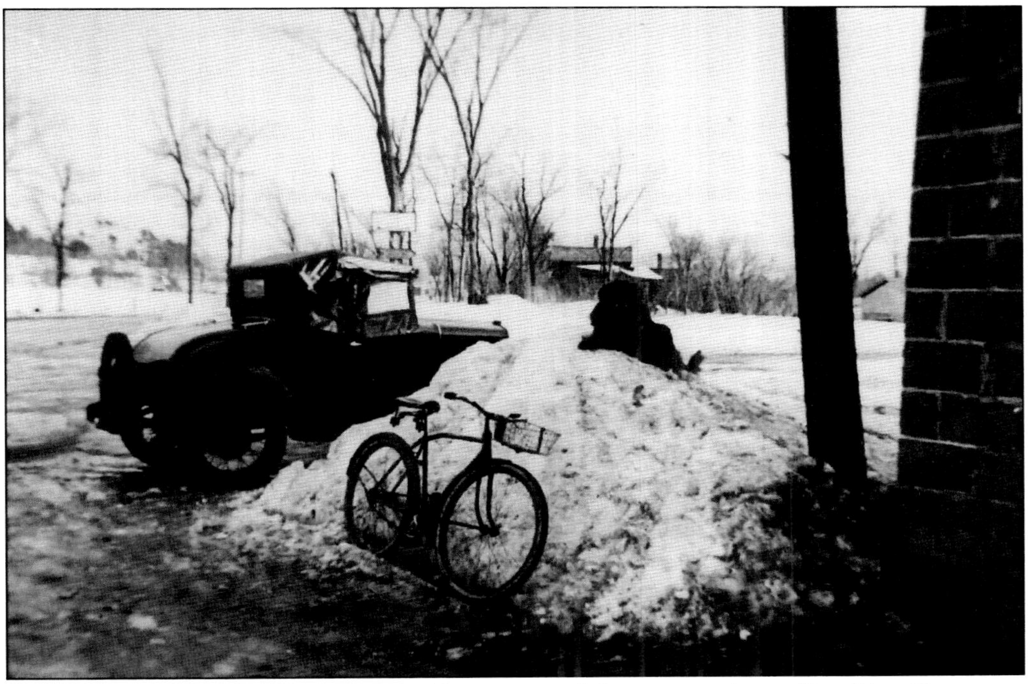

East Line Corners. This winter scene offers a view of the intersection at East Line Corners as it appeared in 1937. The gas station and small general store appear in the foreground; in the background is the building that once housed the East Line Post Office. The large black lump on the snow bank appears to be a dog . . . see the tail on the right?

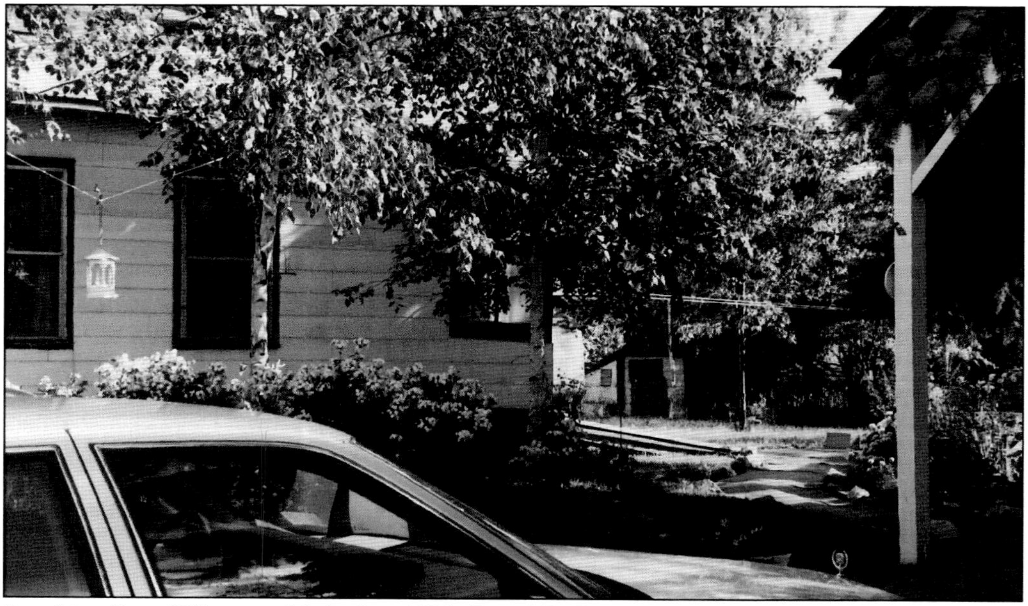

East Line Post Office, established *c.* 1835. David R. Bogart was the first postmaster, and John A. Oliver was the postmaster when, on January 30, 1904, service was finally discontinued. The Delaware and Hudson Railroad passed directly behind this home. Mail was dropped off at the East Line Post Office by the train conductor, who hung the bag of mail on the hook alongside the tracks as the train passed by. Outgoing mail was placed on the hook by the postmaster and the train picked it up as it passed through East Line. Over 129 families were served by this arrangement.

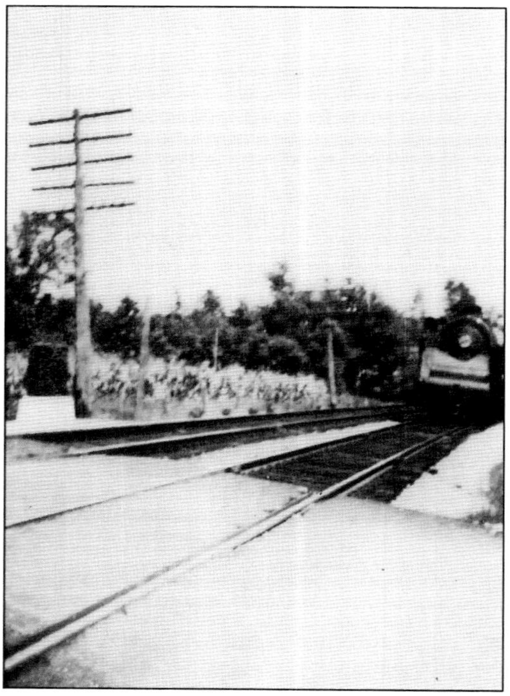

Delaware and Hudson Railroad. Pictured here in the 1930s is the afternoon train of the Delaware and Hudson Railroad coming northwest from Round Lake at the East Line Crossing.

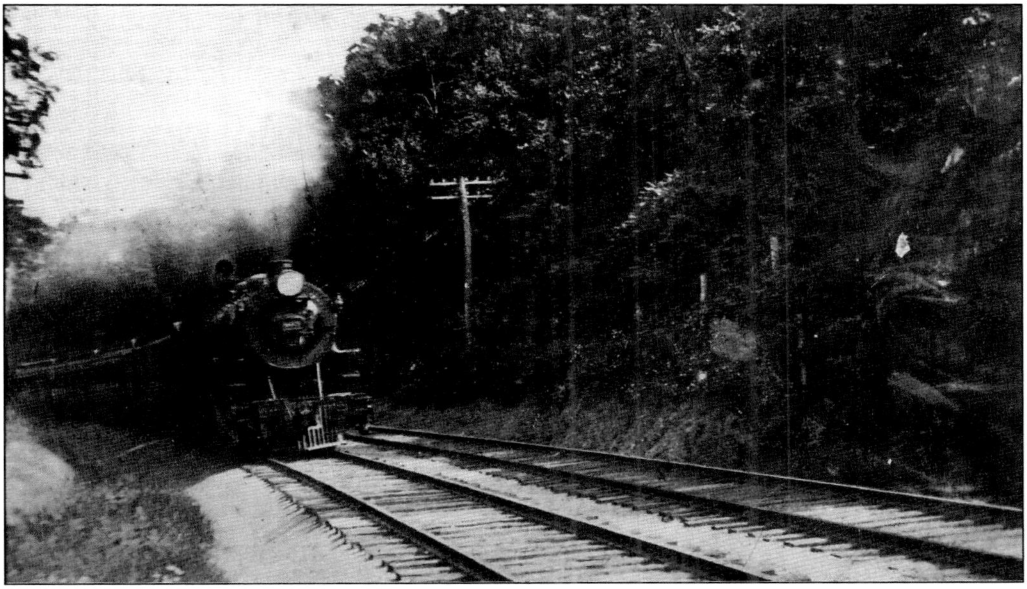

Old Delaware and Hudson train. Pictured here is the Old Delaware and Hudson Railroad making its way from Albany through Round Lake and Ballston Spa to Saratoga Springs and points north. Many older residents of this area can still recall the lonely whistle of the train as it blew its warning at the East Line Crossing. For many years there was a train stop at East Line where produce from local farms was picked up and transported south to New York City. Two products shipped this way were milk and potatoes.

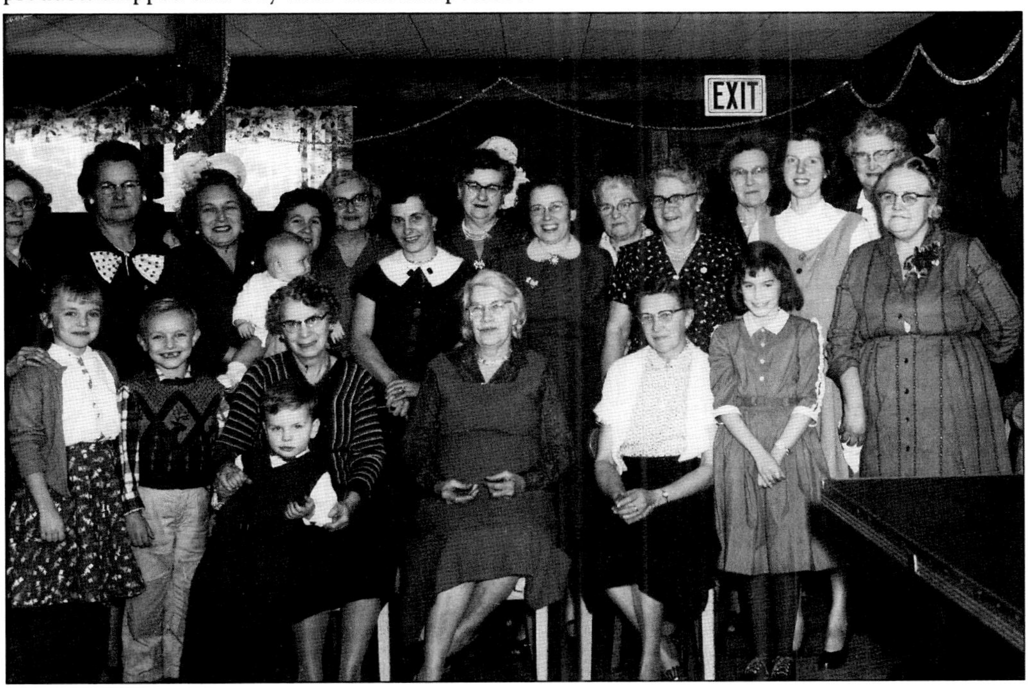

Home bureau party. The ladies of the East Line Home Bureau Organization are shown here at their annual Christmas party at Breyo's Restaurant in 1957.

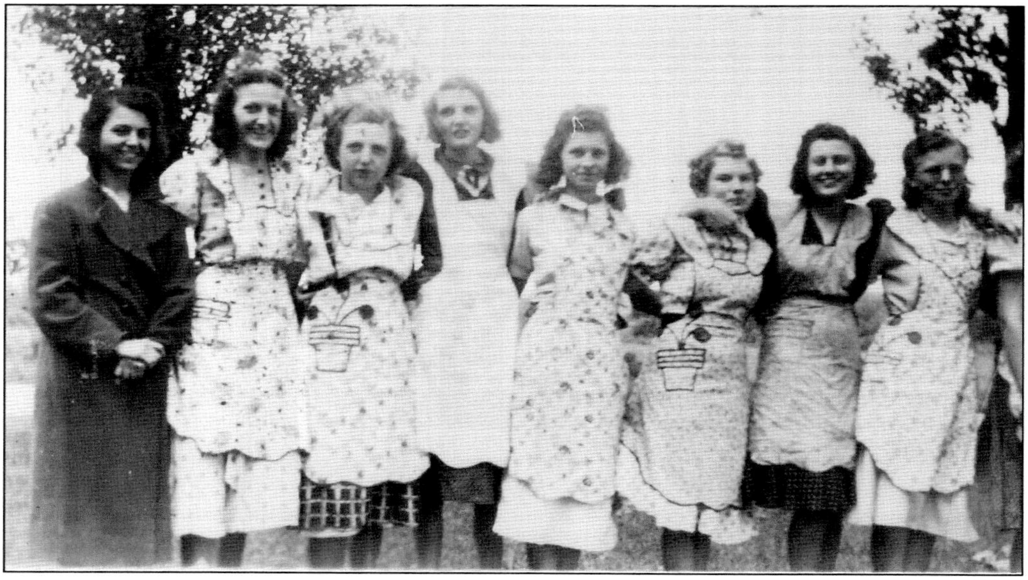

East Line 4-H Club, c. 1940. This photograph shows the ladies of the East Line 4-H Club. For this project everyone made an apron. This picture was taken in the front yard of Mrs. Irving Reed, the 4-H leader, on East Line Road. Identified from left to right are Ruth Mosier, Jane Stewart, Marion Stewart, June Stewart, Pauline Miller, Beatrice Jennings, Climene Relyea, Betty Miller, and Ruth Weed (on the end).

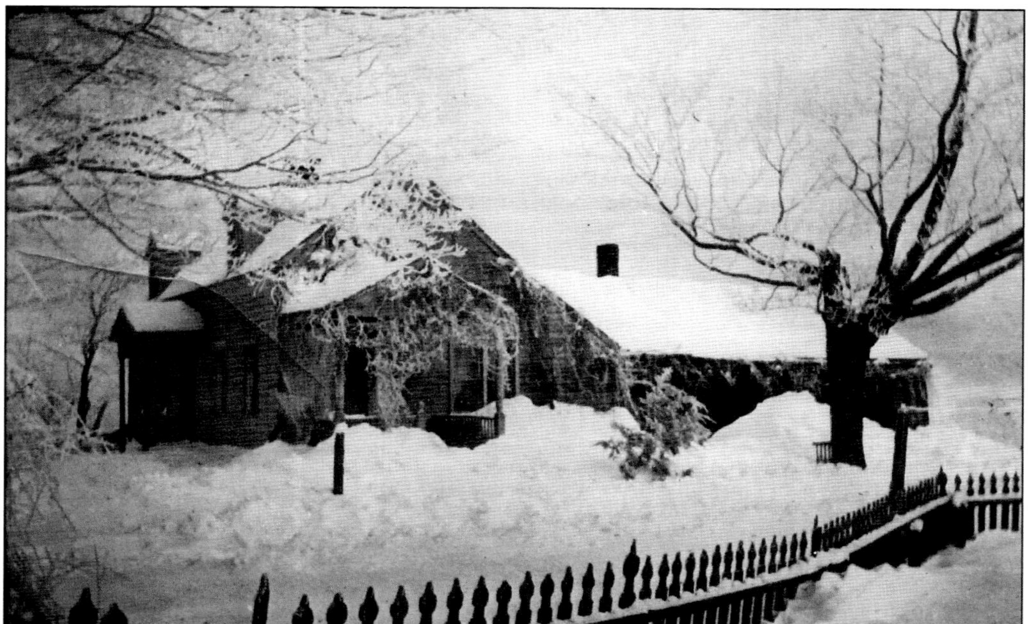

Abner Van Aernem Home, c. 1810–20. A snowy scene shows a house that was the homestead of Abner Van Aernem as indicated in the Beers 1866 atlas of the town of Malta. During the late nineteenth century, the house was also the home of the Abner/William Coon family, followed by the Michael Solotruck family and their descendants. Some summertime pictures of this house show its porch and woodshed areas completely covered by an enormous trumpet vine.

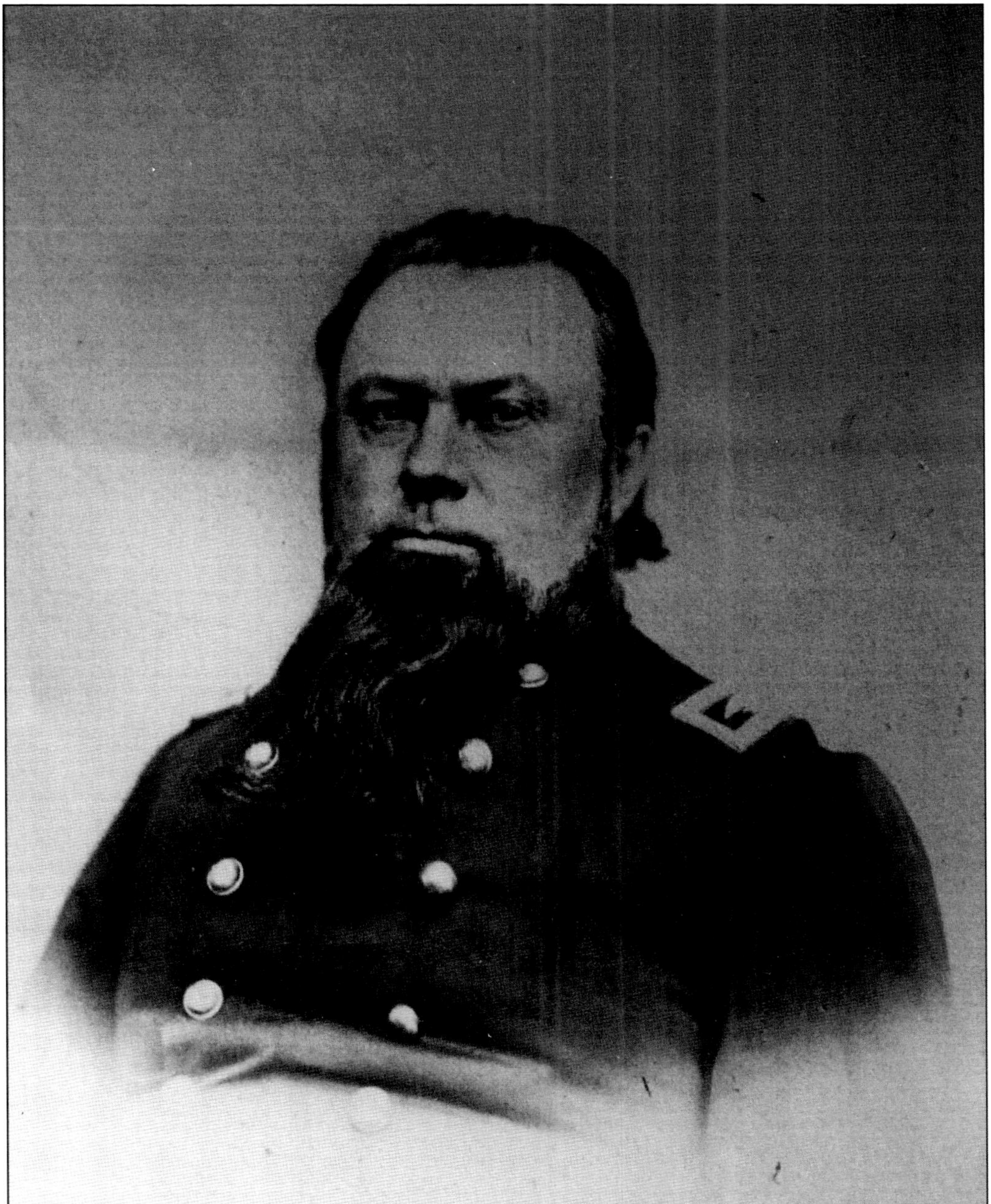

Colonel Calvin T. Peek (1818–1879). Colonel Calvin T. Peek came to live in Saratoga County and the town of Malta in 1838. For many years he operated his farm on East Line Road in the town. After his death in 1879, his Malta farm remained in his family well into the 1900s. Colonel Peek was a prominent man, active in the military, social causes, and farming. He also owned a hotel in the village of Ballston Spa. Colonel Peek organized the 29th Regiment of the New York State National Guard in 1857 and served as its colonel for several years. In 1858, he took an active roll in the building of the armory in the village of Ballston Spa. He married Elizabeth L'Amoreaux on February 21, 1838.

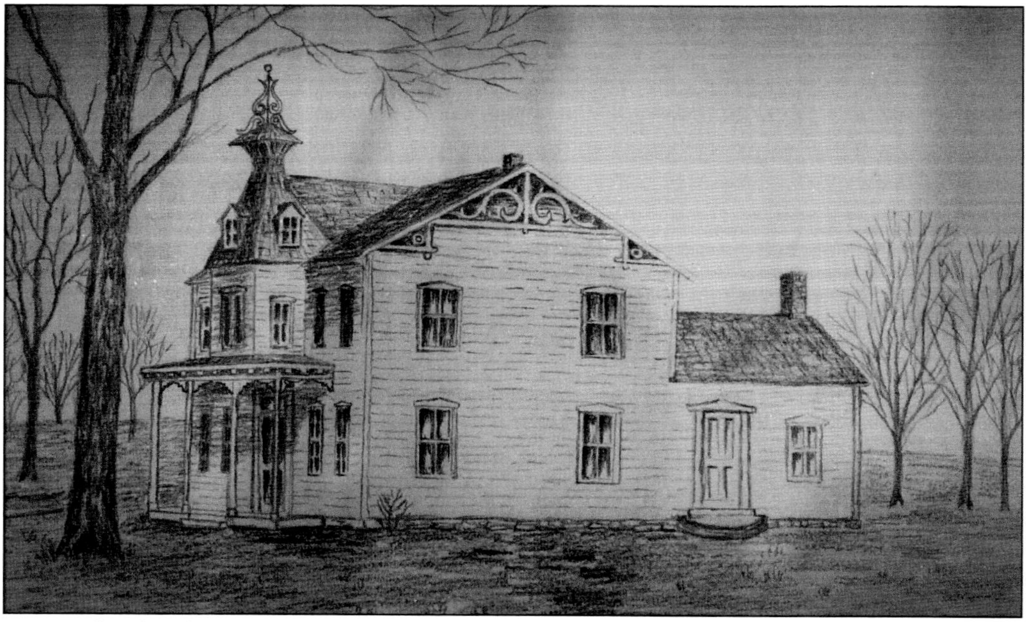

Home of Colonel Calvin T. Peek, built *c.* 1800. This homestead was originally built by or for pioneer settler James Clark, and is one of the very few Victorian-style farmhouses left in Malta. Through the years the owners of this homestead have been Clark, Peek, Hall, Bliss, Denton, Whinnery, and Howansky. Today it is the farm of David J. Howansky at 330 East Line Road in Ballston Lake.

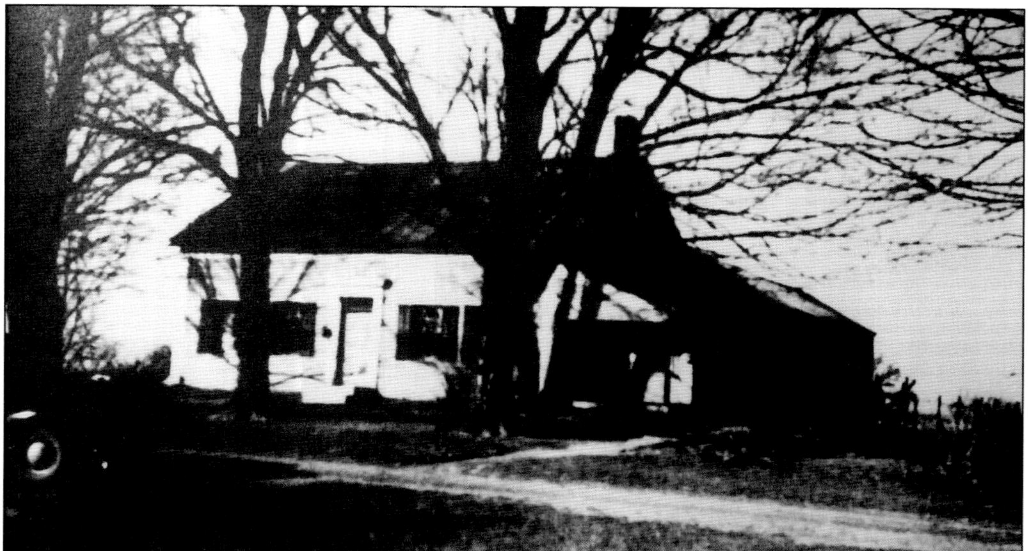

Coon family home. The homestead of the Coon family once stood on the west side of Raymond Road in the town of Malta. The names of the original owners of this old farm, taken from old deeds held by the family, are Phineas Thompson (1827) and Daniel Briggs (1863). Jonas Coon bought the farm in 1866, and William H. Coon was the owner by 1882. The farm then belonged to George H. Coon in 1907 and finally was the home of Olive B. Coon in 1935. The homestead burned in 1942 (see p.128).

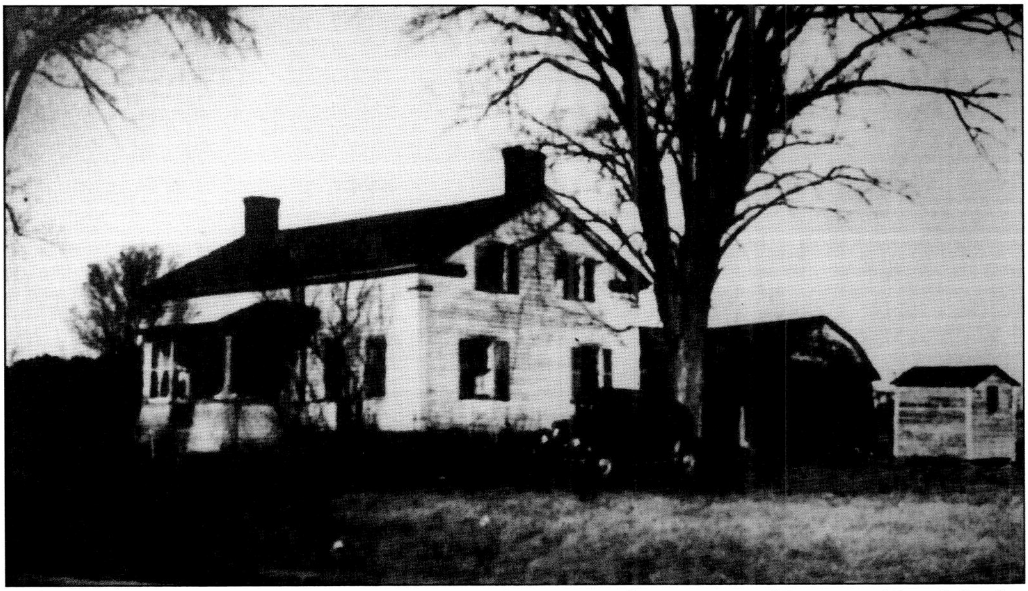

Raymond Homestead, located at East Line on the corner of Route 67 and Raymond Road. In the days of early East Line, the Raymond family members were large landholders, with their lands extending across East Line Road into the town of Ballston. Several generations of the Raymond family lived here; it is believed that the house was sold after the demise of the Raymonds and the building moved to Massachusetts.

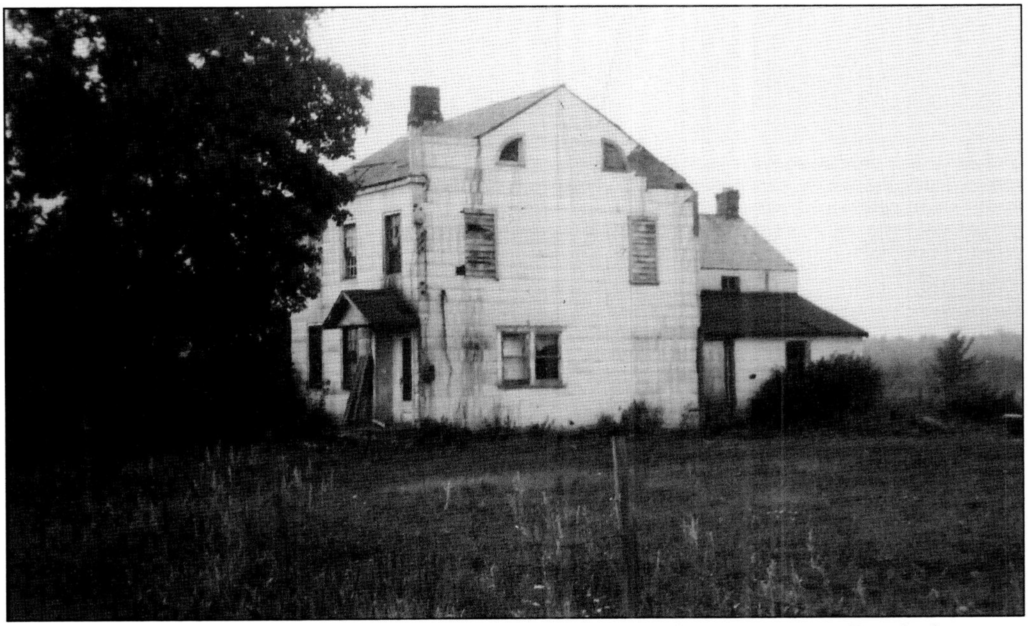

The Hill place. This farmhouse was located in the town of Malta on East Line Road where it is joined by Lake Road. The house was labeled the Hill place on an 1856 map of Saratoga County. Other known owners were Vanderwerker, Hillner, Gonya, Masters, and Solotruck. The front stairway was said to have been extremely graceful and elegant. The house was destroyed by fire on September 7, 1969.

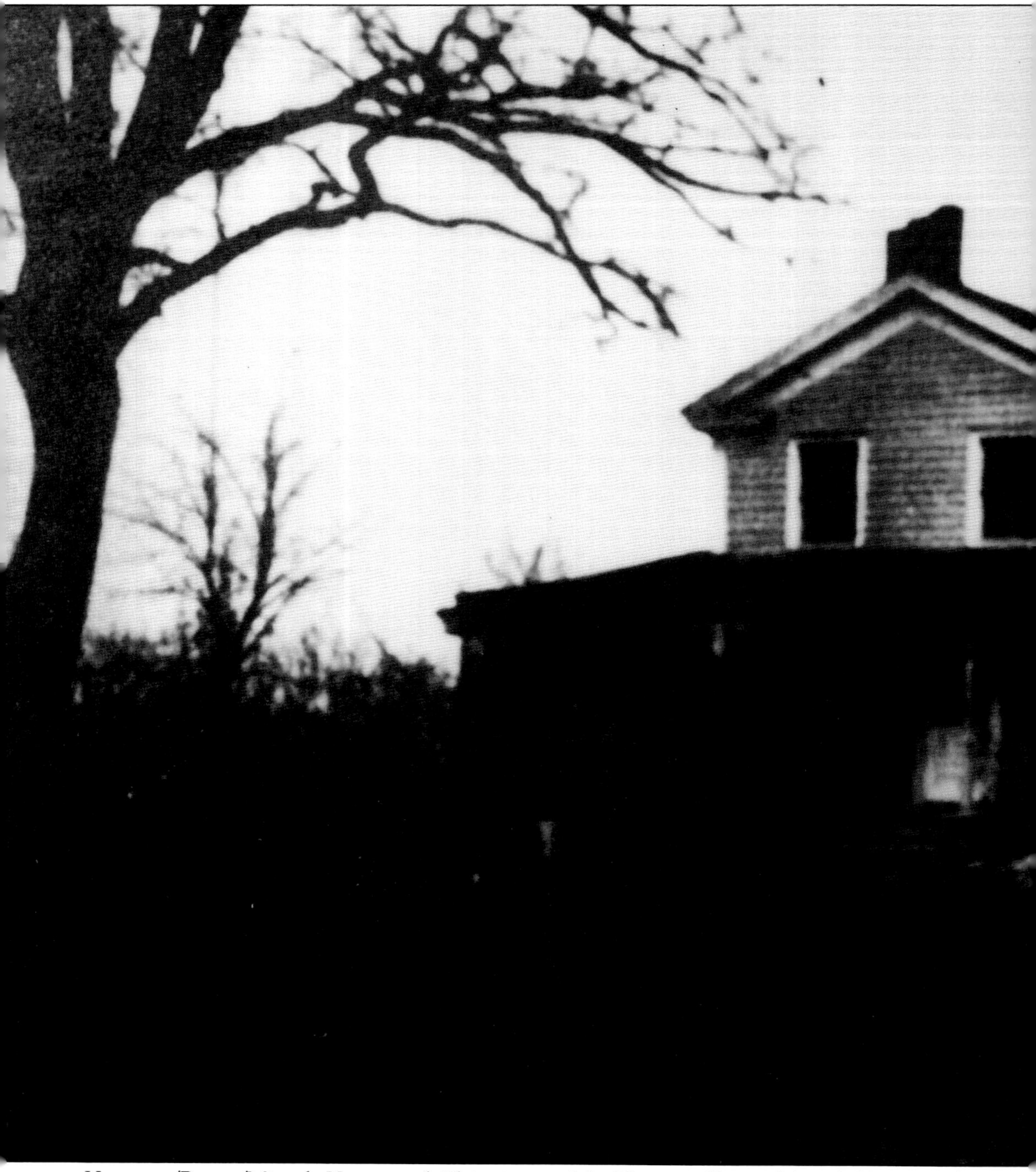

Hennessy/Brown/Minerly Homestead. This picture of the Hennessy/Brown/Minerly Homestead was taken in the early 1930s. A road once existed between East High Street and Malta Avenue. The southern tip of this road was just beyond today's Spa Brauhaus Restaurant on East High Street at the big bend in the road. The north end of this extinct road intersected Malta Avenue at the old Pompa residence and the home of Alexander Weed. This house stood on the corner

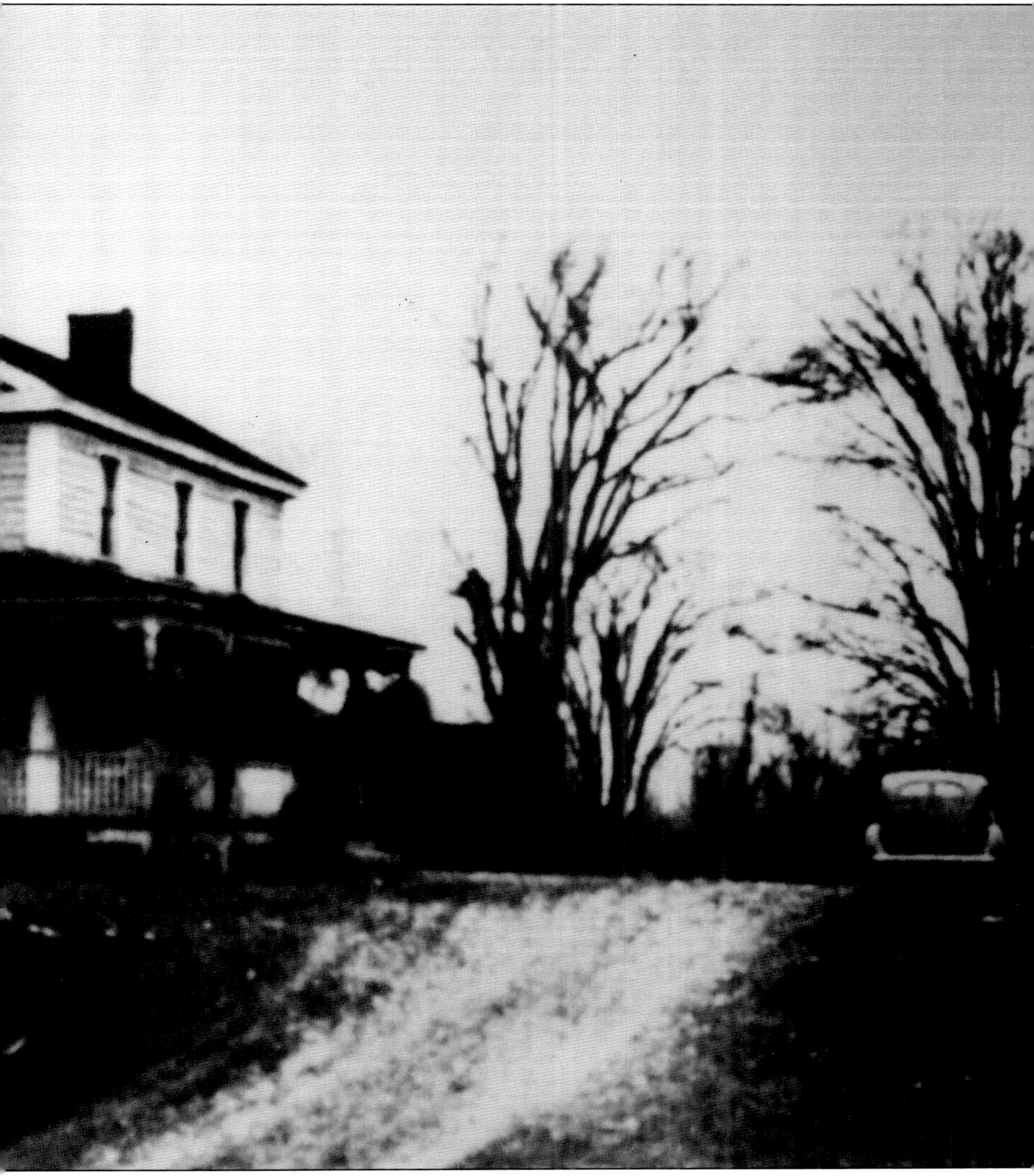

of East High and the south end of the old road and was the home of David Hennessy in the 1850s–60s. Orvis Brown lived here in the 1920s–30s, and the home was later occupied by Edward Minerly, still remembered for the horse and wagon he drove as he traveled the town collecting rags and paper. The house no longer stands.

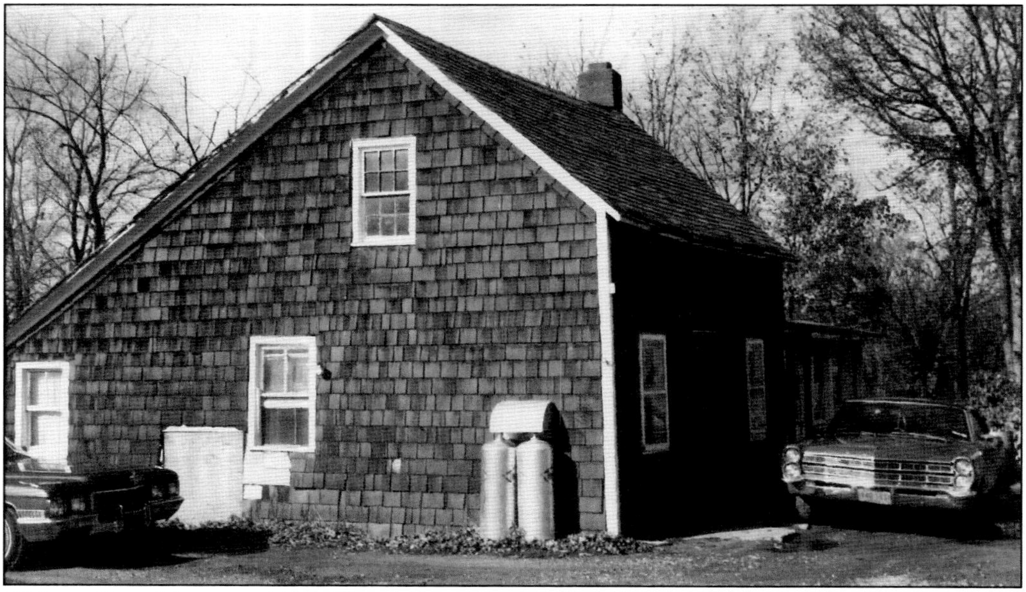

William Ryan Home, *c*. 1830. This old New England saltbox was the home of William Ryan, an early settler in East Line. It is probable that the house had a fireplace when it was first built. In later years, it was the home of the Kelly family for several generations, followed by the family of Raymond E. Barnes. It stands today on Route 67 just east of the East Line intersection.

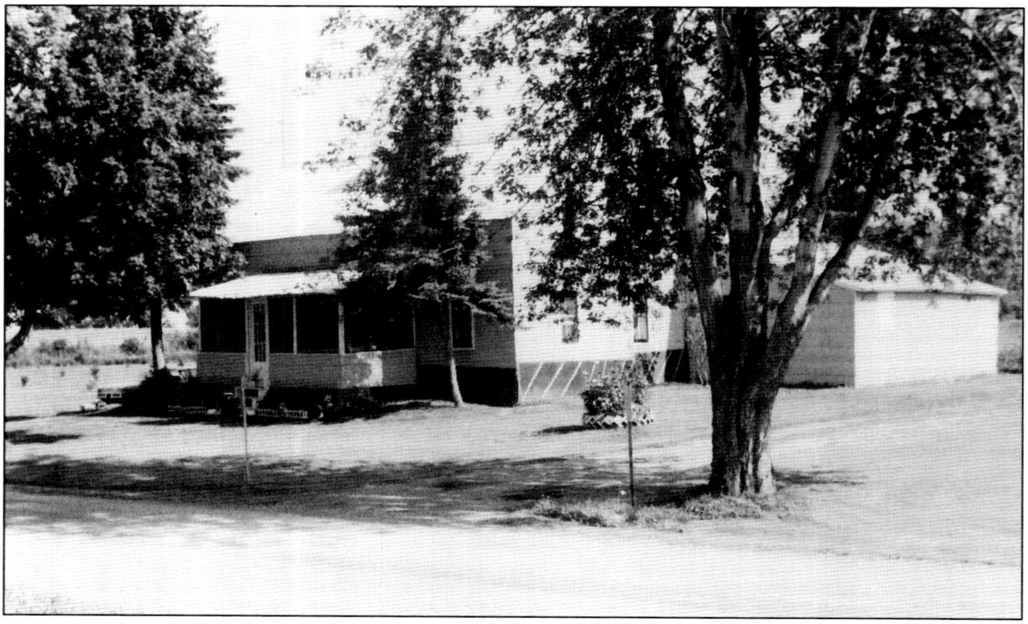

Harvey Doolittle Home, *c*. 1800. This old homestead and an adjoining tannery and cobbler shop were built well before 1800. Mr. Doolittle crushed his own bark and mixed his own tanning solution. The only traces of this early business are remnants of the bark-crushing areas and a few foundation stones where the tannery building once stood. The house still stands on the south side of Miller Road between Ruhle Road and East Line Road.

Three

Malta Ridge

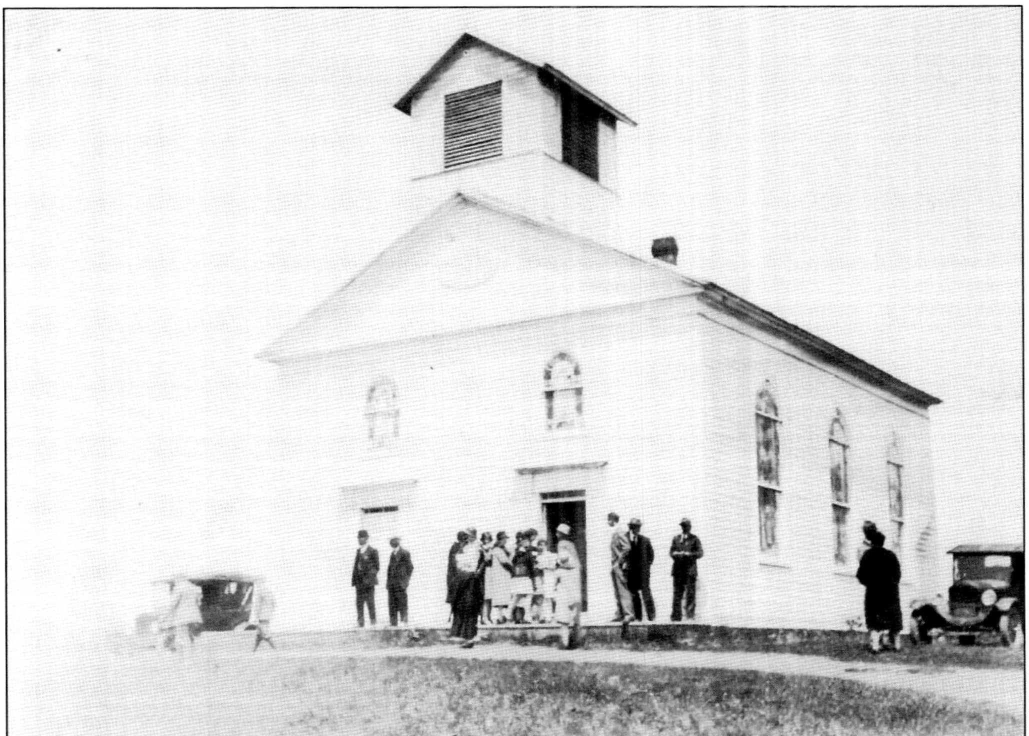

Malta Ridge Methodist Church. This picture of the Malta Ridge Methodist Church was taken about 1921. This Methodist society was formed in 1814, and the church building was erected in 1831. By 1929, the congregation made the decision to build a new church. The old church was demolished and that same year a beautiful new church was erected.

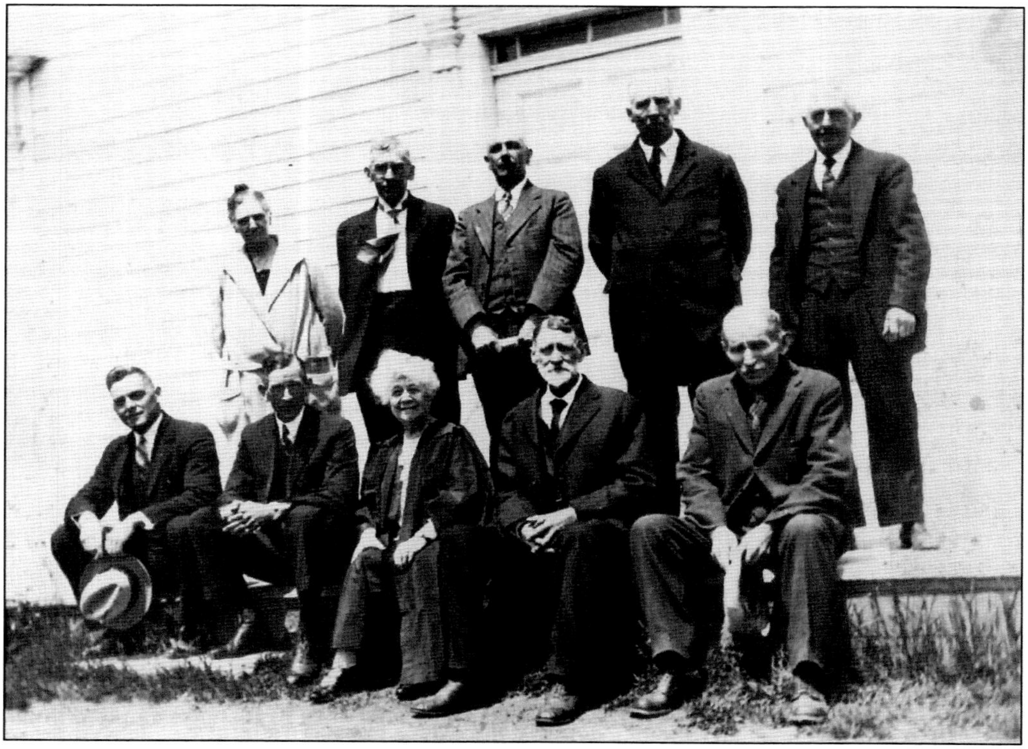

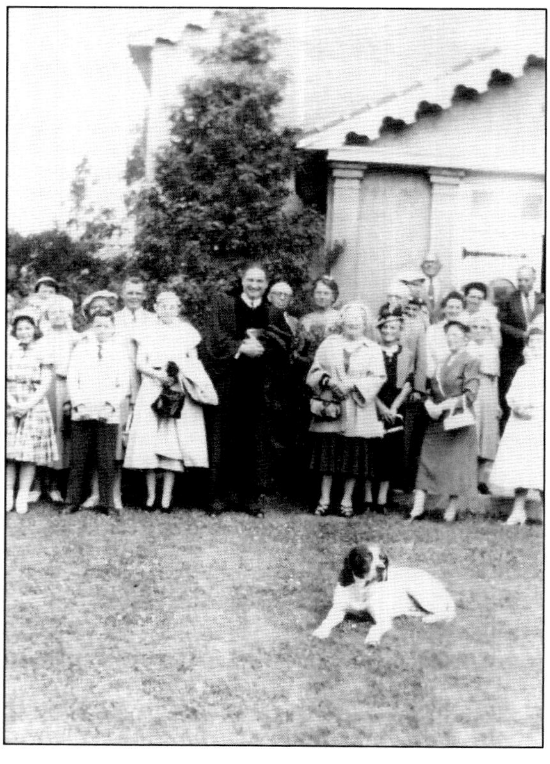

Trustees of Malta Ridge Methodist Church, spring 1929. From left to right are as follows: (front row) Lee Graves, Robert Taylor, Reverend Eliza Duffield, Ferdinand Carr, and George Franklin Ramsdill; (back row) Grace Hegeman, Frank Reno, Albert Stoddard, Simeon Morehouse, and Guy Fitch. In the center of the picture is Reverend Eliza Duffield, the first woman to be ordained as a local preacher in the Troy Conference.

New Malta Ridge Methodist Church. This photograph taken in 1954 shows the new Methodist church at Malta Ridge, which was built in 1929. The new church edifice was donated by Mr. and Mrs. Benjamin C. Riley and was dedicated on December 1, 1929. Pictured is the lovely new church, the congregation, and the minister, Reverend Fred B. Jones, who served the congregation from 1951 to 1955.

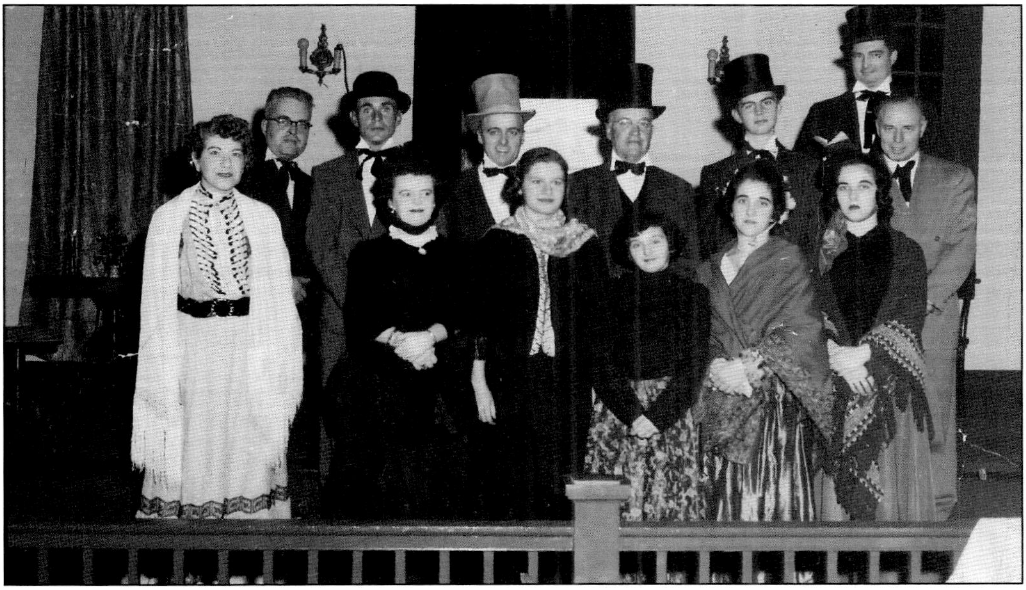

Malta Ridge Methodist Church 150th anniversary, November 29, 1964. These congregants standing at the altar depicting old-time dress are identified as follows: (front row) Ruth Gates, Olive Tobin David, Naomi Hettrich, Pauline Remmington, Janet Remmington Hearsh, and Joyce Remmington; (back row) Jack Davis, Ed Jackson, David Carr, Lester Davis, John Dewey, and Earl Gates. The gentleman at the top right is not identified.

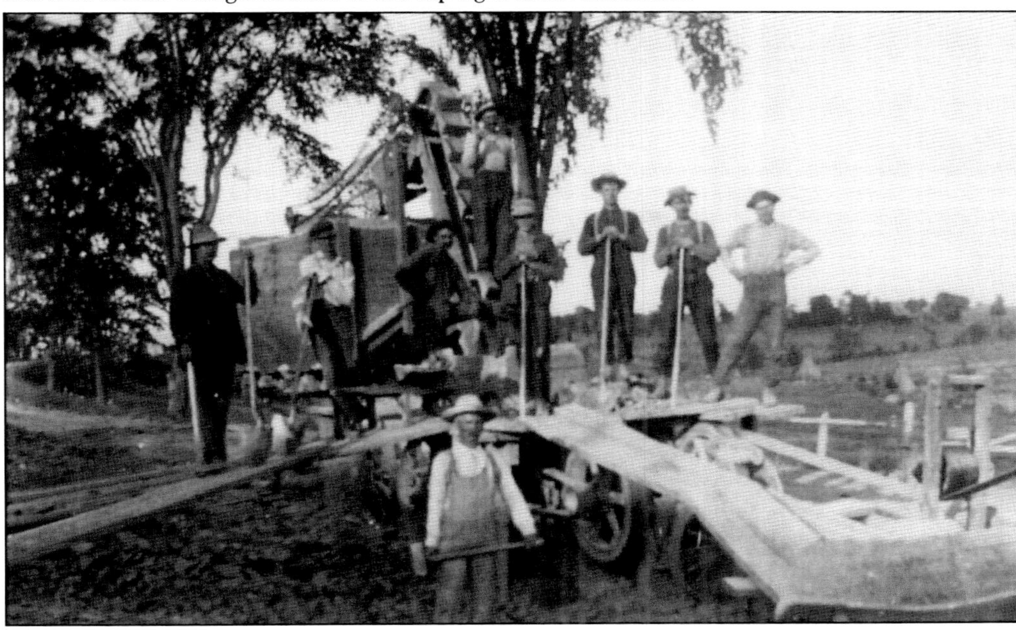

U.S. Route 9, *c.* 1911. In this picture stone crushers take a break to pose while they are at work building U.S. Route 9 at Malta Ridge. The labor required to build this road was performed by men, horses, and simple, non-motorized earth-moving equipment such as shovels and scrapers. Quoting Earl F. Gates in his history of Malta, "Construction of the road from Dunning Street to Kayaderosseras Creek required a hundred men and nearly as many horses."

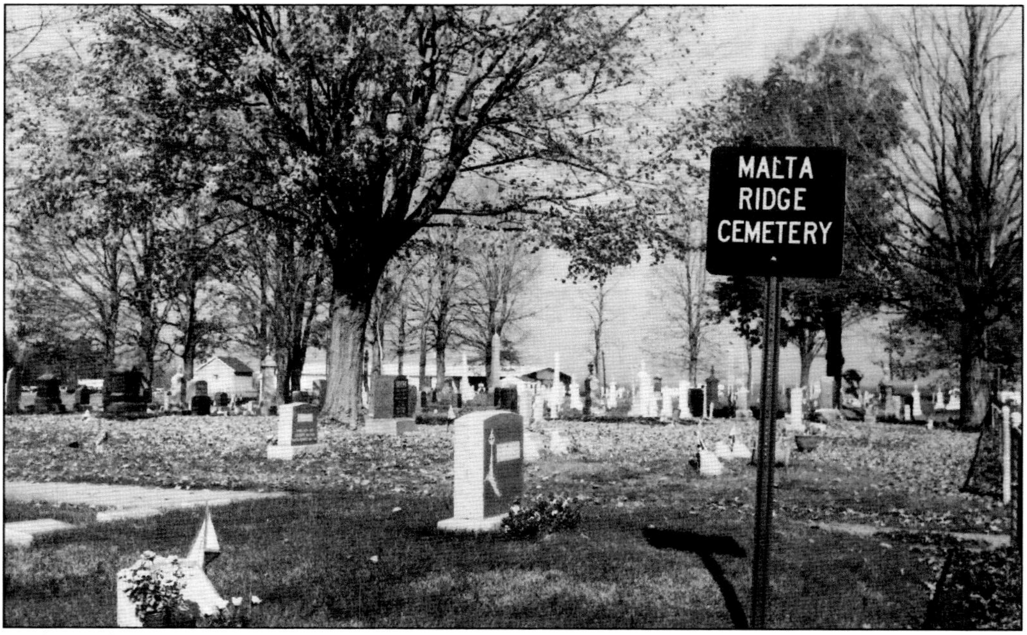

Malta Ridge Cemetery. The Malta Ridge Cemetery is situated on Route 9 south of Exit 13 on the Adirondack Northway in the northern part of the town. The earliest recorded grave is dated 1805. Some of the early family lines buried here are Arnold, Baker, Brown, Chase, Crouch, Fish, Hill, Ireland, Millard, Phillips, Ramsdale, Reno, Riley, Rowley, and Wiggins. The cemetery was granted landmark status by the Town of Malta in 1993.

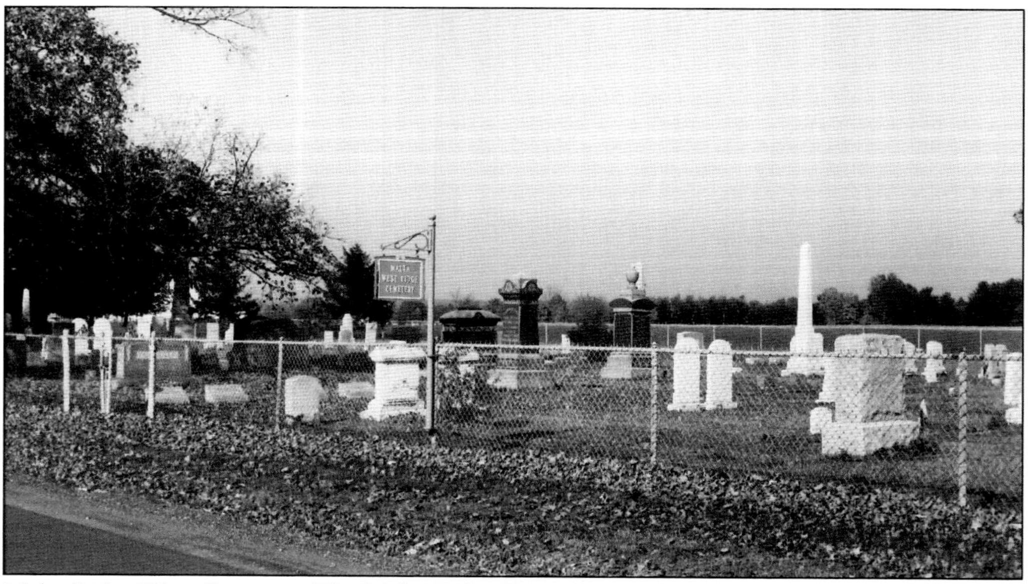

Malta Ridge West Cemetery. The Malta Ridge West Cemetery is located at Hall's Corners at the intersection of East High Street and Brownell Road. Formerly known as the Collamer Cemetery, the oldest recorded grave here is 1796. There are also soldier's graves from the Revolutionary War, the War of 1812, the Civil War, World War I, and World War II. The burial ground was granted landmark status by the Malta Town Board in 1993.

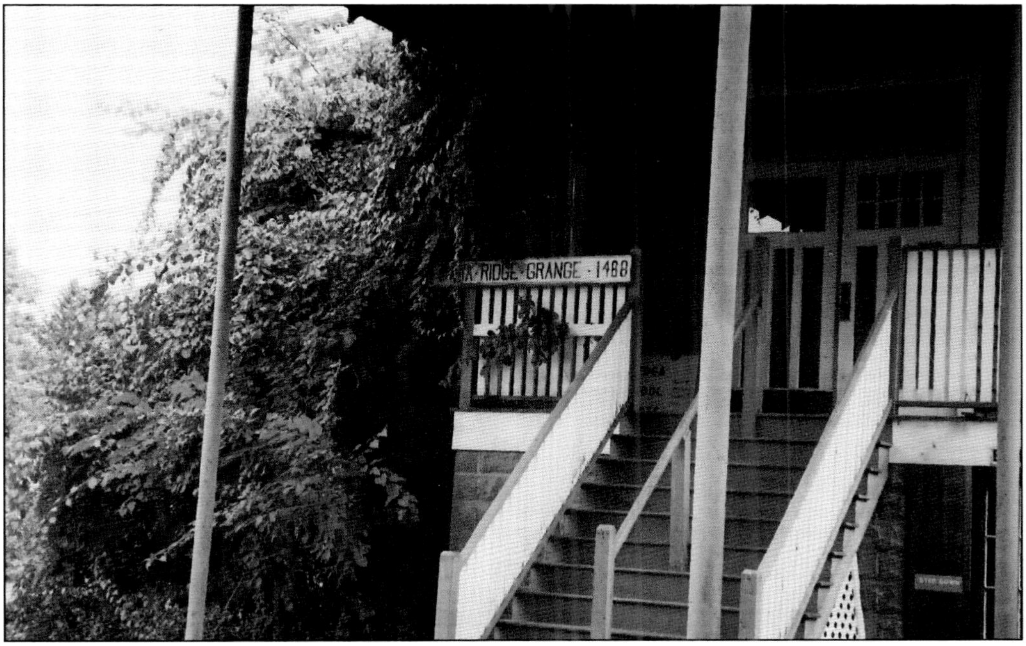

Malta Grange #1488. Pictured here is the entrance to the Malta Grange at Malta Ridge. For many years this organization played an important part in the lives of the farming families in the area. The grange was also an important community institution, since it was responsible for scheduling many social activities.

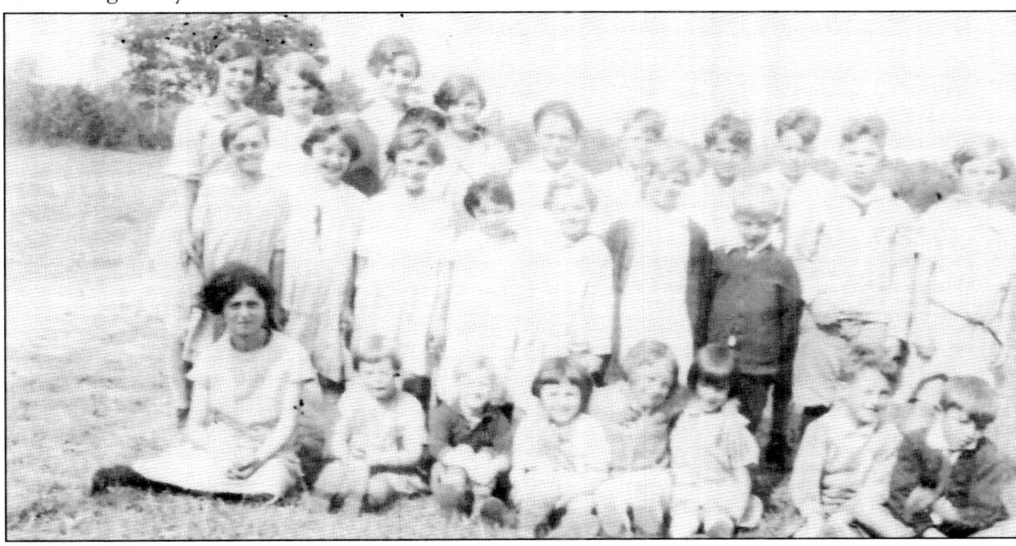

End-of-the-year school picnic, 1927. The children pictured are from several schools; some attended Eddy's Corners School, located on Nelson Avenue near Crescent Avenue in Saratoga, while others attended Malta Ridge School. The Arnold children and Jack Davis attended Eddy's Corners; the Graves girls lived at Manning Cove; the Arnold, Carr, Blackwood, and Davis families lived on Nelson Avenue Extension; the Czupil family lived at Saratoga Lake; the Melander family lived on Malta Avenue Extension just east of Route 9; and Doug Graves, a cousin to the Graves girls, lived on Malta Avenue just west of Route 9.

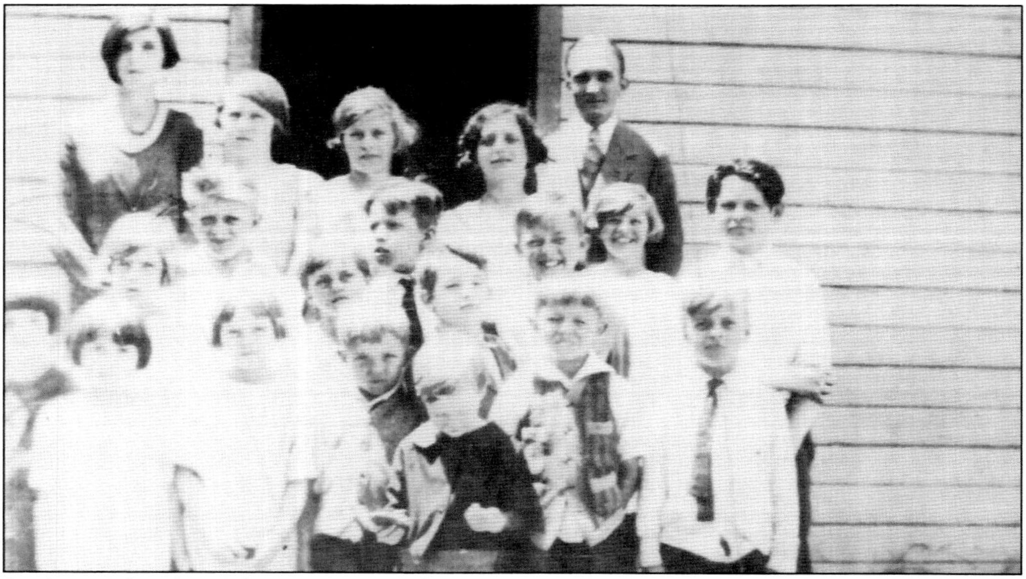

Students of Malta Ridge Common School No. 1, 1927–28. Identified in this school picture, from left to right, are the following: (front row) Eleanor Birkbeck, Ella Mae Carr, Mike Czupil, Paul Quinn, Walt Czupil, and David Carr; (middle row) Dorothy Taylor, Helen Blackwood, Ruth Melander, Doug Graves, Paul Blackwood, Lawrence Birkbeck, Norman Melander, Helen Czupil, and Bill Birkbeck; (back row) Annie Morehouse, Gladys Brown, Mabel Carr, Gertrude Goldberg, and Mr. Thorman Nelson (teacher). Most of the students in this picture are alive today.

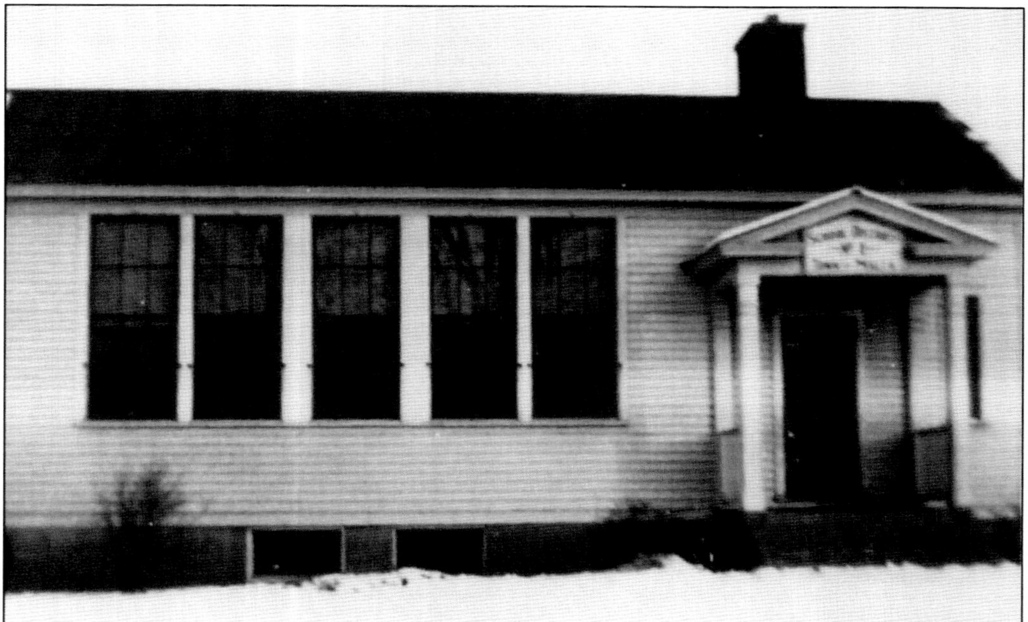

Malta Ridge Common School No. 1, *c.* 1939–40. This school was located on County Highway 63, east of Route 9. The photograph depicts a newly remodeled school that was the pride of the neighborhood.

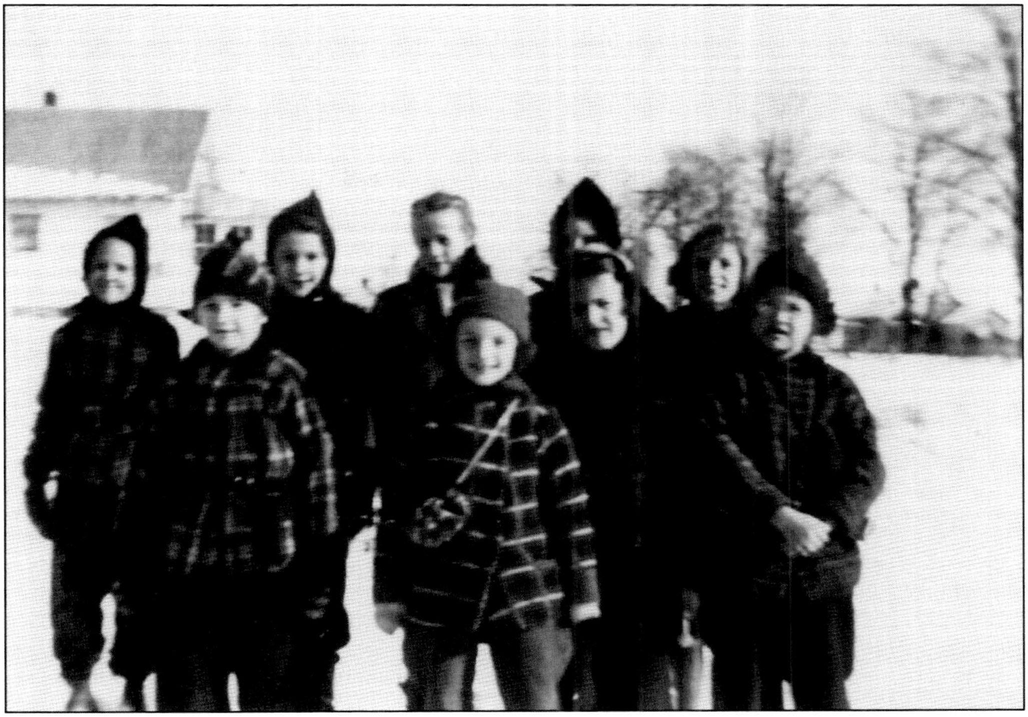

Students of Malta Ridge Common School No. 1, 1939–40. These children were students in the newly rebuilt school and are identified as follows: Evelyn Yager, Annie Francis, Aleta Arnold, Nancy Waring, Peggy Strang, Helen Strang, Jeanne Flinton, Virginia Place, and Margaret Francis. Their teacher was Annie Morehouse.

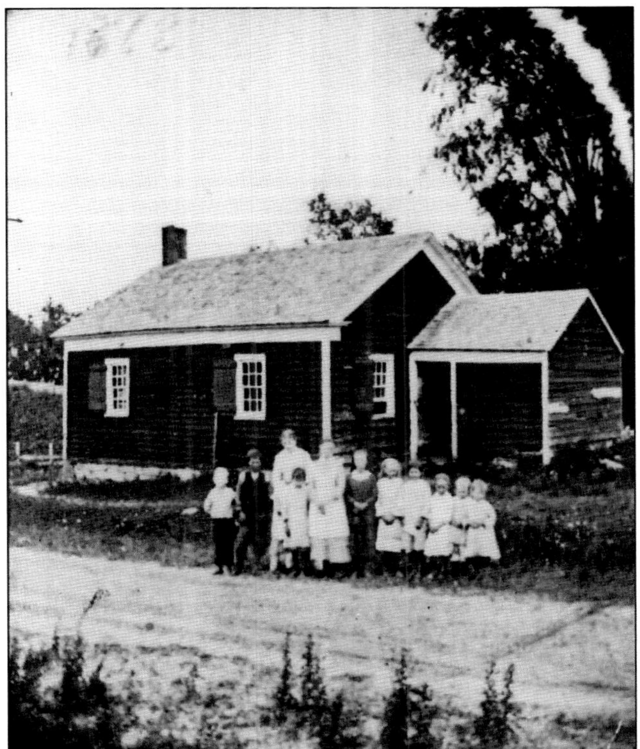

Cramer Road Common School No. 2, 1888. This school was located on the corner of Cramer Road and U.S. Route 9 in Malta.

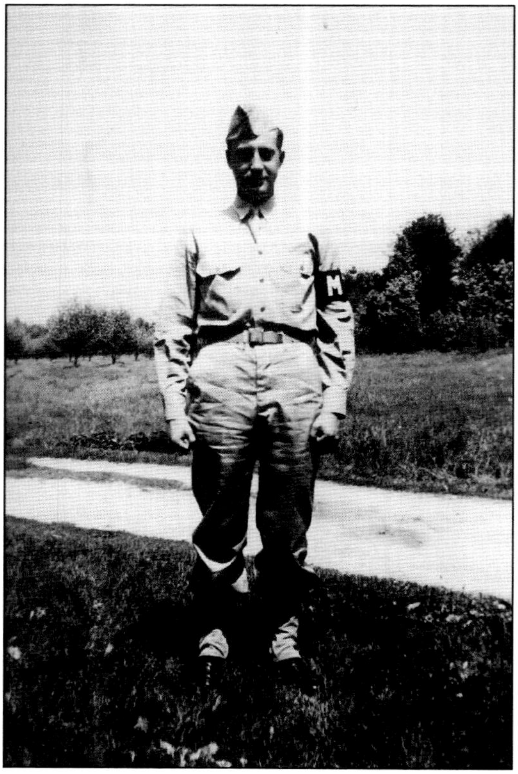

Serviceman Manuel Atkins, *c.* 1940s. This photograph is of Manuel "Pat" Atkins as he stands roadside in front of his home on Malta Avenue, now called Atkins Hill Road. The son of William and Edith Green Atkins, Manuel was born on January 13, 1915. He served in World War II with the military police. He died on October 27, 1984.

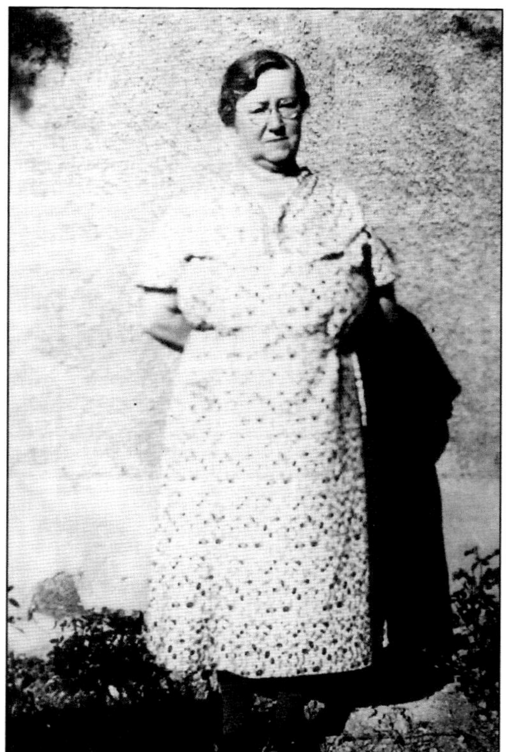

Edith Green Atkins. Known to her family and friends as "Grandma Atkins," Edith lived much of her life on Atkins Hill Road. She was the wife of William E. Atkins, whose ancestors were also Malta pioneers. They were the parents of three sons, William, Manuel, and Milton, and one daughter, Mabel Atkins Venefron. Their son, Manuel "Pat" Atkins, served in the military police, and is pictured above.

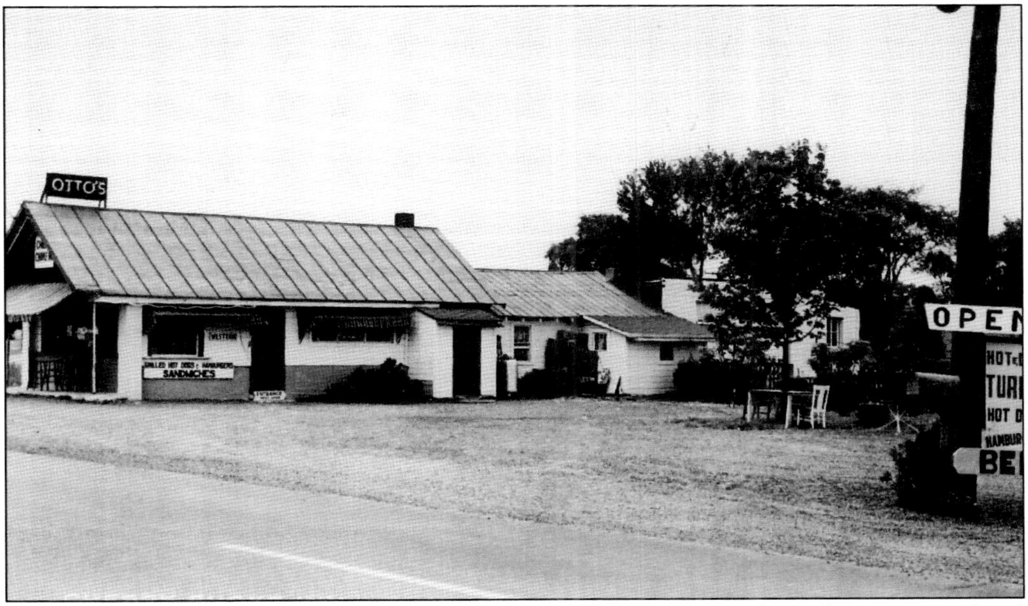

Cherry Choke Inn, *c.* 1949. The Cherry Choke Inn on Route 9 at Malta Ridge was owned and operated by Mr. Otto Haenal, who came to this country after World War I. As you can see by the photograph, the specialty of the house was turkey. The restaurant was well known in the area for its excellent preparation of roast turkey dishes, as well as some fast foods.

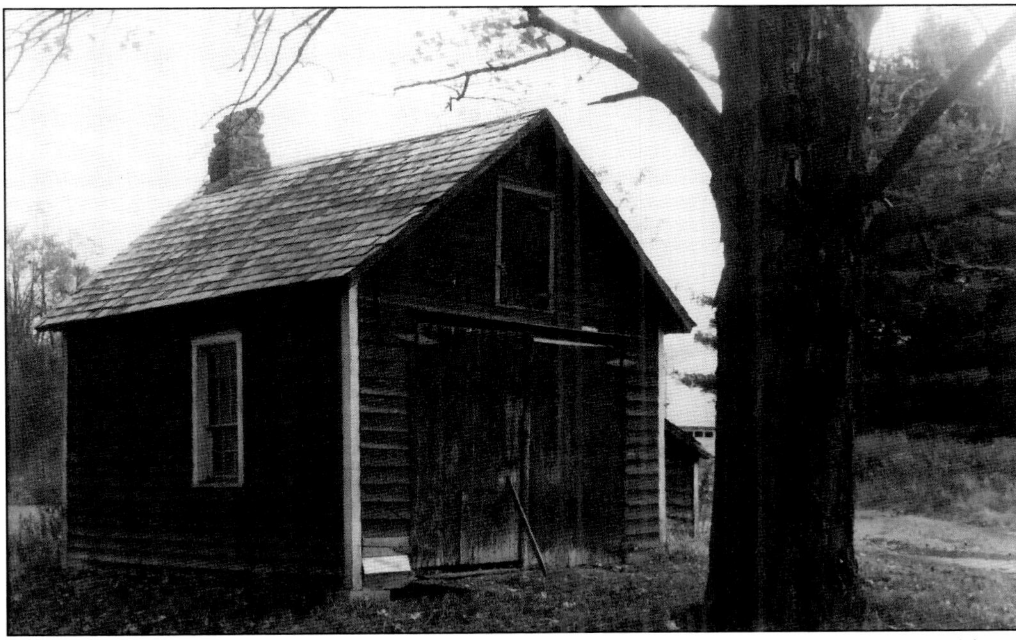

Van Hyning Broom Factory, 150 Cramer Road, *c.* 1835. In the nineteenth century, Alvaro Van Hyning and his son James grew broom corn and manufactured brooms, which were sold in nearby Saratoga Springs. The site is important because it is one of the few remaining reminders of cottage industry in the town. It was designated as a historic landmark by the Town of Malta in 1991 and received a historical marker.

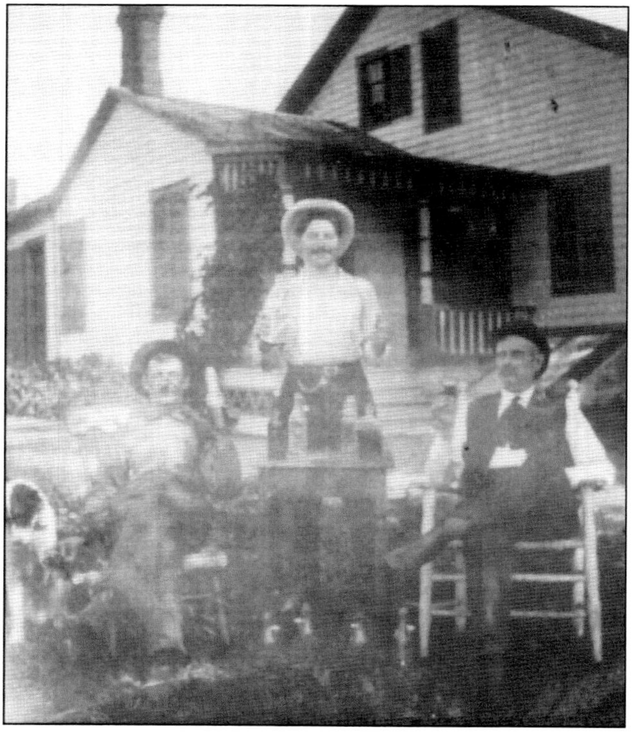

Blackburn/Slade/Bartlett House, c. 1913. This house on Malta Avenue was the tenant house of C.W. Bryan probably before 1913. In the left foreground is Cyrus W. Bryan, and in the middle is probably Phil Bryan. On the right is Daniel Sullivan from New York City, who spent his summers at the big white farm.

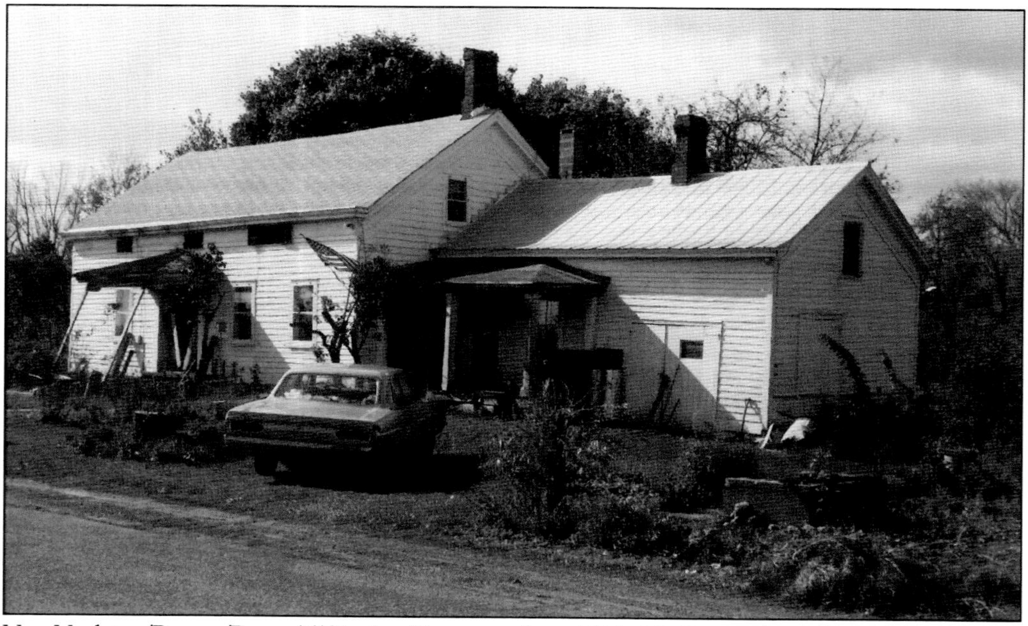

Van Vechten/Brown/Ramsdill/Seeley Homestead, c. 1815–20. Situated on the Nelson Avenue Extension in Saratoga Springs, this property originally consisted of 93 acres. The home was built between 1815 and 1820, and L. Van Vechten was the owner listed in the 1866 Beers atlas. Rosa Brown and her descendants lived here until 1944, when the property was purchased by Mary and Malcolm Ramsdill. Today this is the home of George and Margaret Seeley.

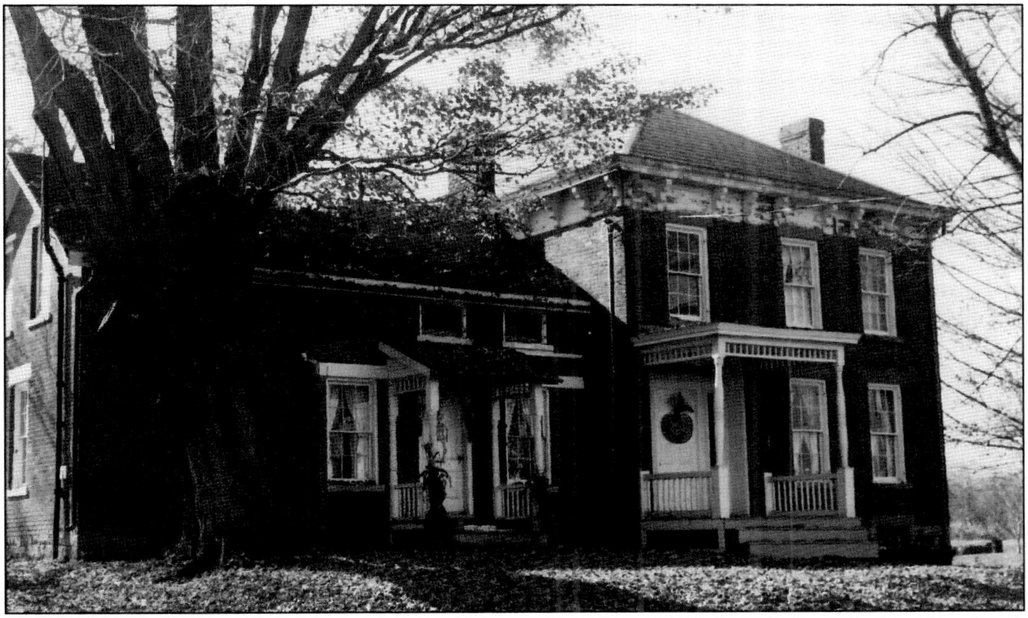

Ramsdale/Downs/Morelock Homestead, Old Post Road, *c.* 1850. It is believed that this brick house was built *c.* 1850 by William Ramsdale. It is presently the home of Nancy Morelock.

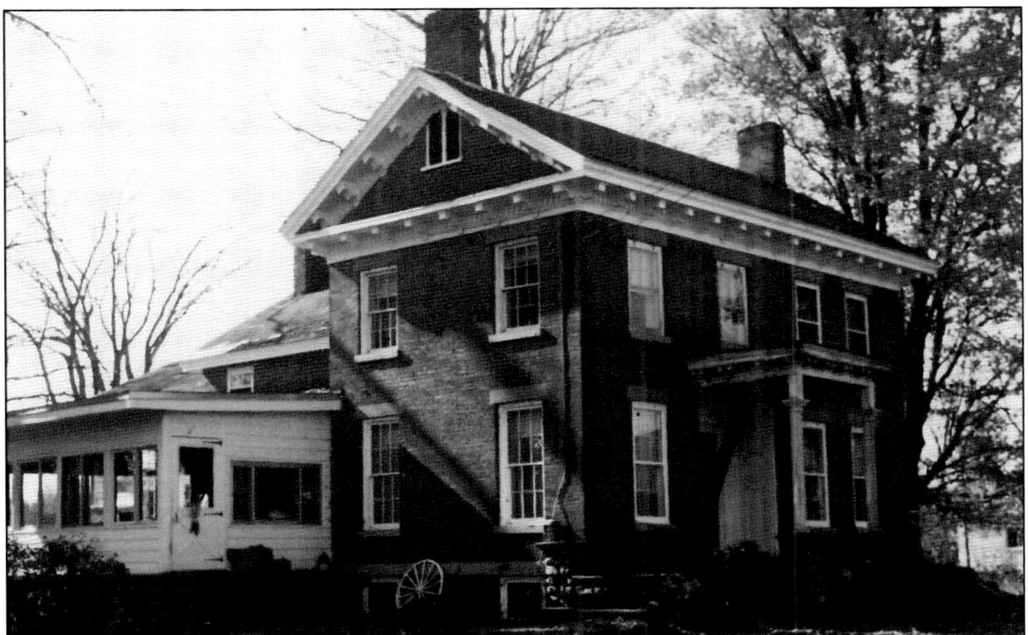

Ramsdale/Waring/Vandish Homestead, 195 Old Post Road, *c.* 1850. The house was built *c.* 1850 by Zachariah Ramsdale. Today it is the home of Thomas W. Vandish Sr.

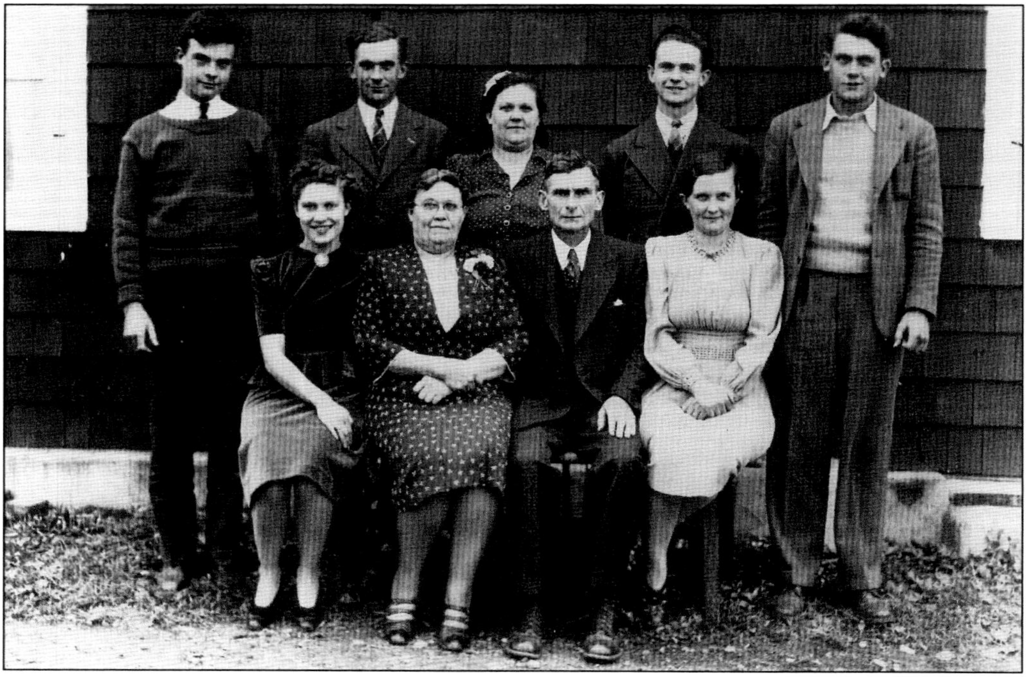

Ernest P. Arnold Sr. family, c. 1943. The Arnolds originally came to Malta from the town of Wilton about 1927. Seated are Ernest P. Sr. and his wife, Edith Miller Arnold, a descendant of Elisha Miller of Ballston. To their right is their daughter Edith, and to their left is another daughter, Georgia. Standing are Harold, Royal, Helen, Sonny, and Ralph. Their other son, Ernest P. Jr., is missing from the picture because he was in military service at the time.

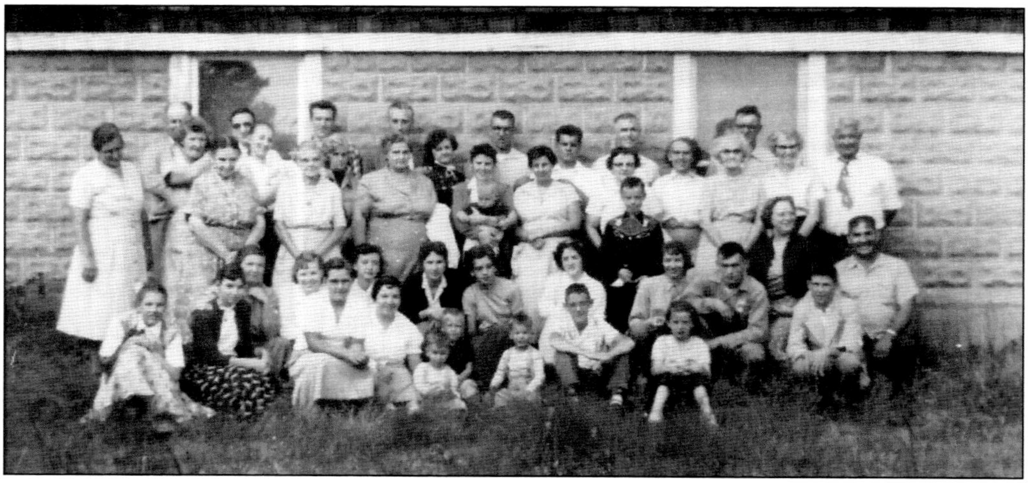

Morehouse/Ramsdill reunion, Malta Ridge Grange Hall, 1955. Sixty-two annual reunions have been held in Malta by the descendants of these families. Identified family members are as follows: standing on the far left are Margaret Melander and Annie Morehouse Arnold, with Mary Gates in front of Annie; Gladys Noyes Seeley and her four daughters are kneeling on the far left; at the top center of the picture is Ernest Melander with his wife, Irene; and on the far right kneeling in the second row is Malcolm Ramsdill with his wife, Mary Seeley Ramsdill, to his right.

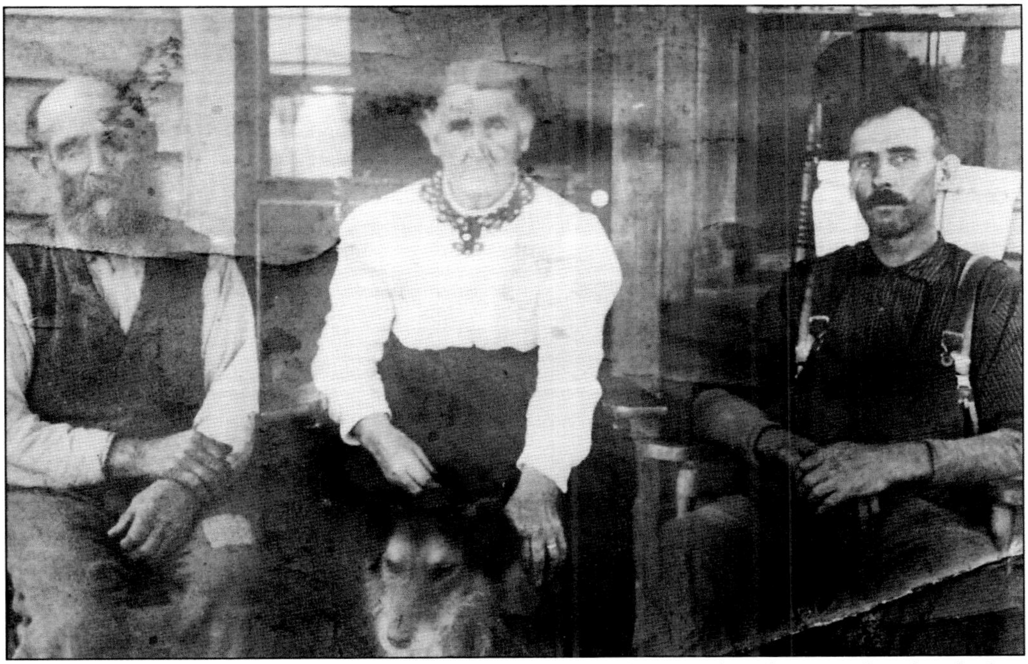

John and Elizabeth Ramsdill with their son, Simeon Morehouse. This photograph, taken before the turn of the century, shows the family seated on the front porch of their home at Malta Ridge.

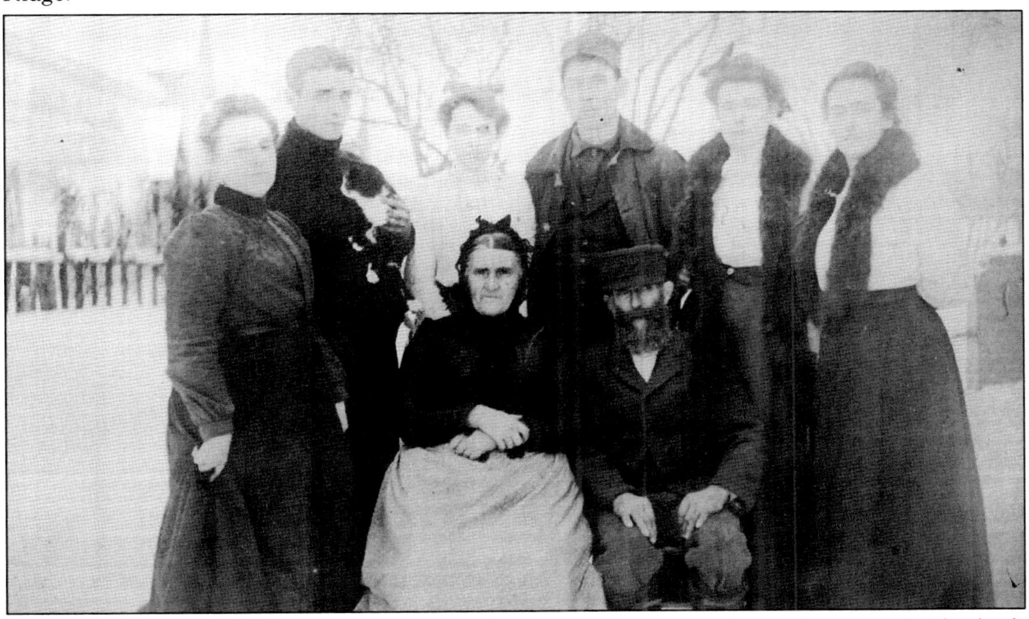

Ramsdill/Morehouse family, *c.* 1905. From left to right are as follows: (front row) Elizabeth Thrall (Morehouse) Ramsdill and John J. Ramsdill; (back row) Florence Morehouse (Seeley), John Ramsdill, Martha Ramsdill (Boyce), Simeon Morehouse, Mary Ramsdill (Gates), and Eugene (Jean) Ramsdill (Boyce). The Ramsdill family has lived in Malta since *c.* 1880. The descendants of these pioneer families of the town of Malta have a family reunion annually.

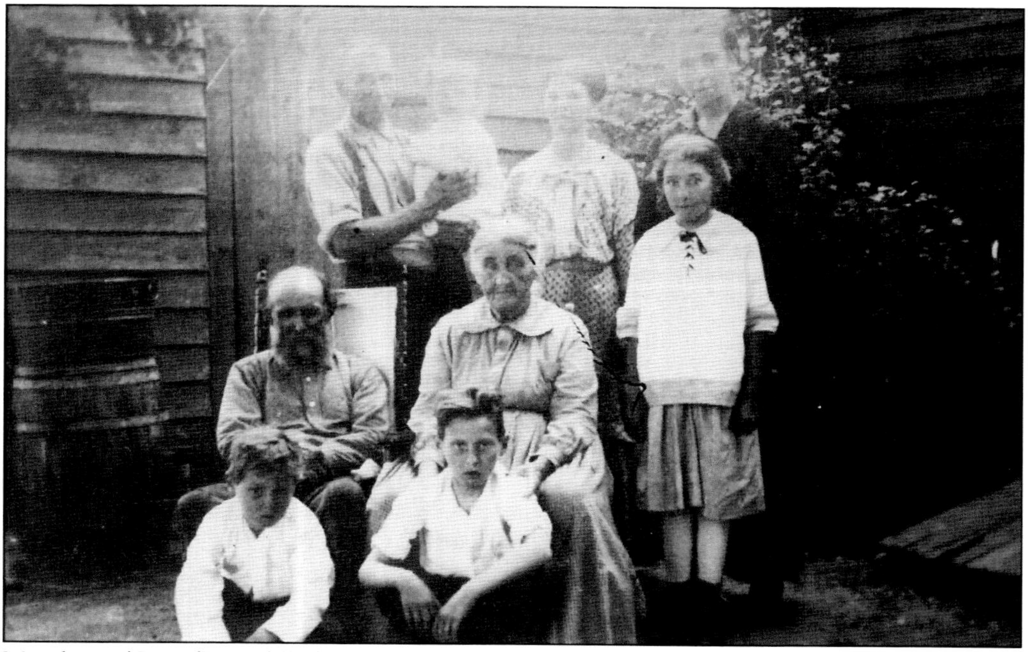

Morehouse/Gates/Ramsdill family, c. 1900. This photograph was taken at the Ramsdill Homestead at Malta Ridge. Family members are identified as follows: (front) John and Elizabeth Ramsdill, with grandchildren James and Kenneth Boyce; (back) Simeon Morehouse (holding his baby daughter, Annie) and, standing to the right, Emma Morehouse and Mary and Margaret Gates.

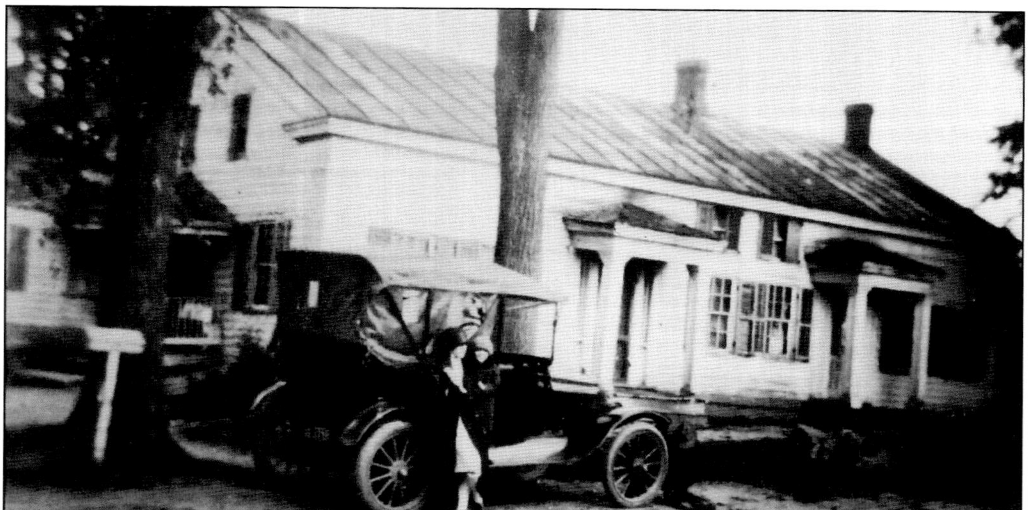

Brown Homestead, c. 1920s. The Brown Homestead at 136 Van Aernem Road, Malta, was the home of John and Florence Brown. In the photograph is Florence Brown holding her small daughter, Dorothy Brown Johnson, in front of the house. Florence Brown was the mother of retired Town of Malta Councilman Alfred Brown. For many years this house was also the home of Attorney Harold N. Van Aernem and his wife, Ann. Today this is the home of Mr. and Mrs. Karl Avenarius.

Brown Homestead. This picture of the Brown Homestead at 136 Van Aernem Road was taken in the mid-1920s. The two young gentlemen shown in the picture are Alfred and Gilbert Brown, with their favorite heifer. Al and Gilbert Brown are the sons of John and Florence Brown. Al Brown once served as a councilman for the town of Malta.

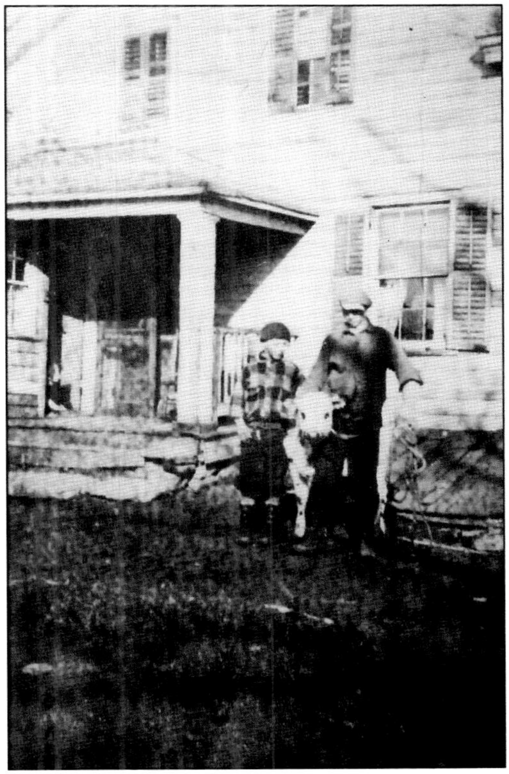

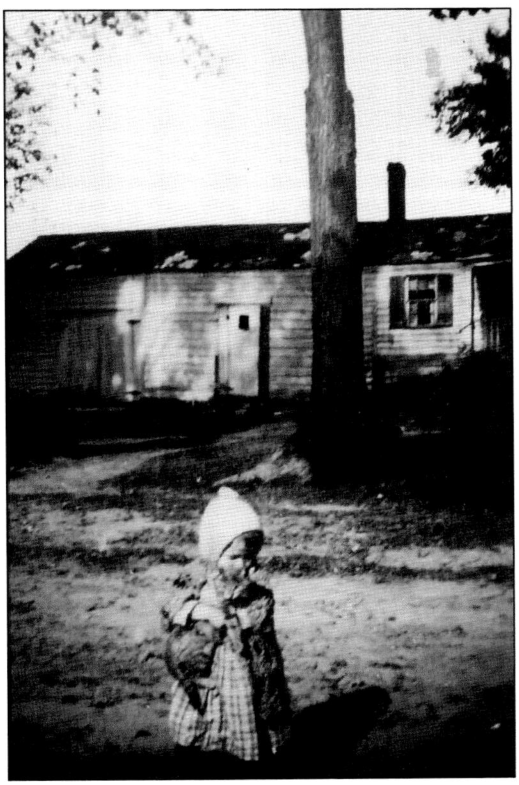

Dorothy Brown and cat. This photograph of little Dorothy Brown (Johnson) with her cat was taken in front of the Brown Homestead. She is the daughter of John and Florence Brown and the sister of the Al and Gilbert Brown.

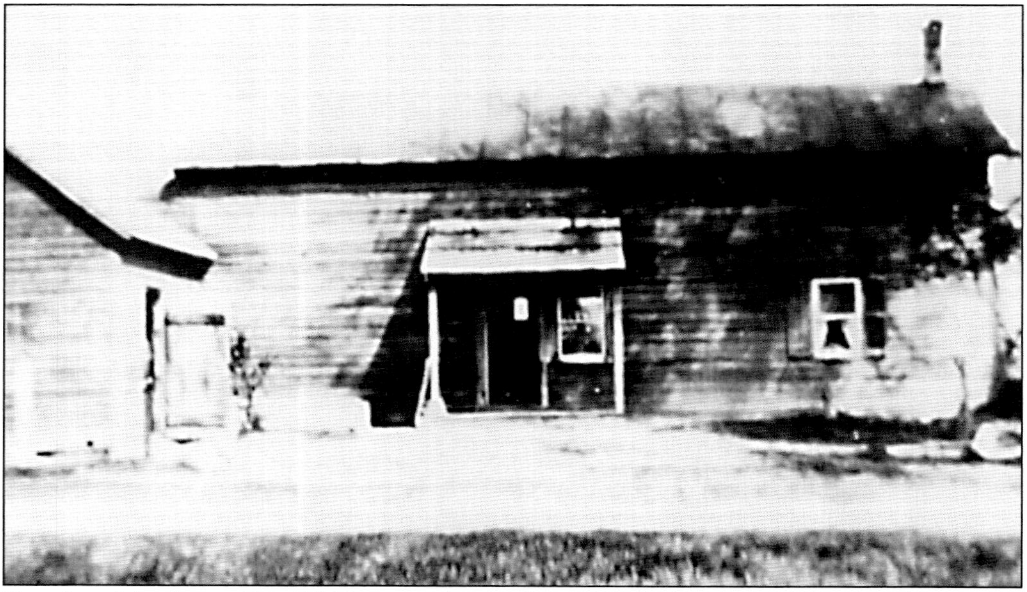

Tompkins/Morehouse/Arnold Homestead at Malta Ridge, built *c*. 1840 (photograph *c*. 1910). The house stood at the intersection of Arnold Road and Malta Avenue. In 1866 this residence was the home of William Tompkins, and around 1907 the property was purchased by Simeon Morehouse, grandfather to the Royal T. Arnold family.

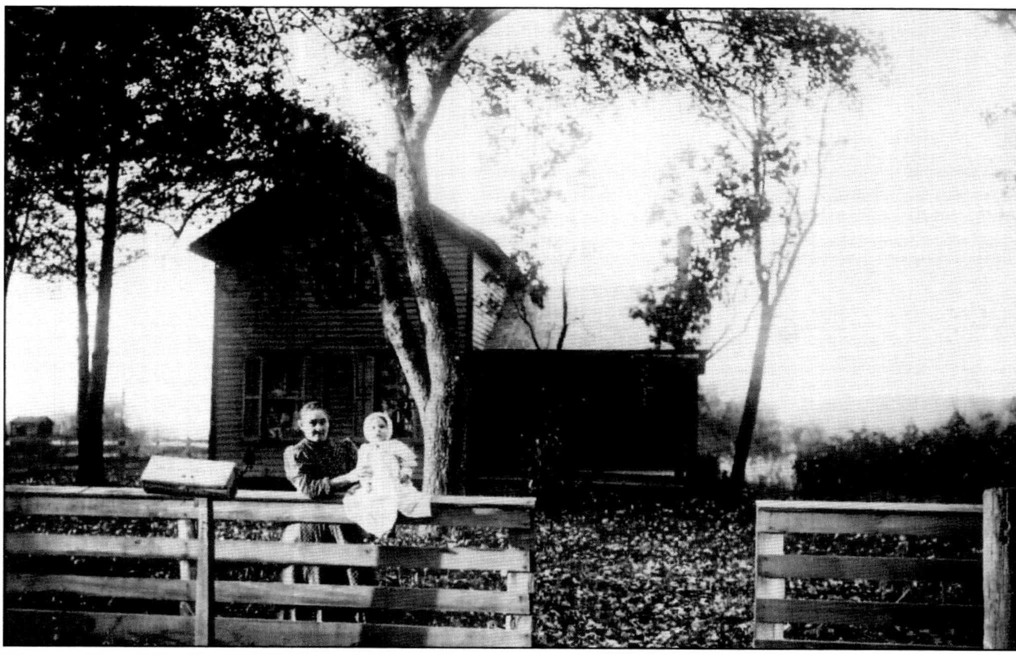

George Franklin Ramsdill Home. This photograph of Lottie Reno Ramsdill and Baby Malcom Ramsdill was taken in front of the George Franklin Ramsdill Home on the Malta Avenue Extension. This is the also the former home of Chris Morrell, who served the town of Malta as councilman, and also as deputy sheriff in Saratoga County. Mr. Morrell presently resides in Vermont.

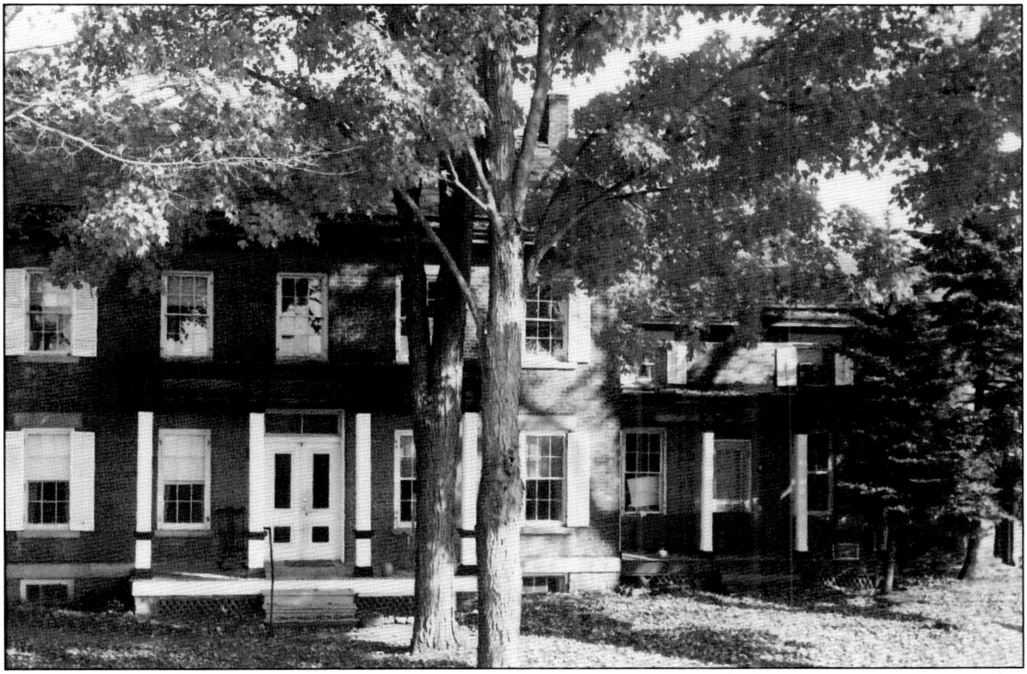

Collamer/Baker Homestead, *c*. 1860. Pictured here is the Collamer/Baker Homestead on Malta Avenue at Malta Ridge, built *c*. 1860 by David N. Collamer.

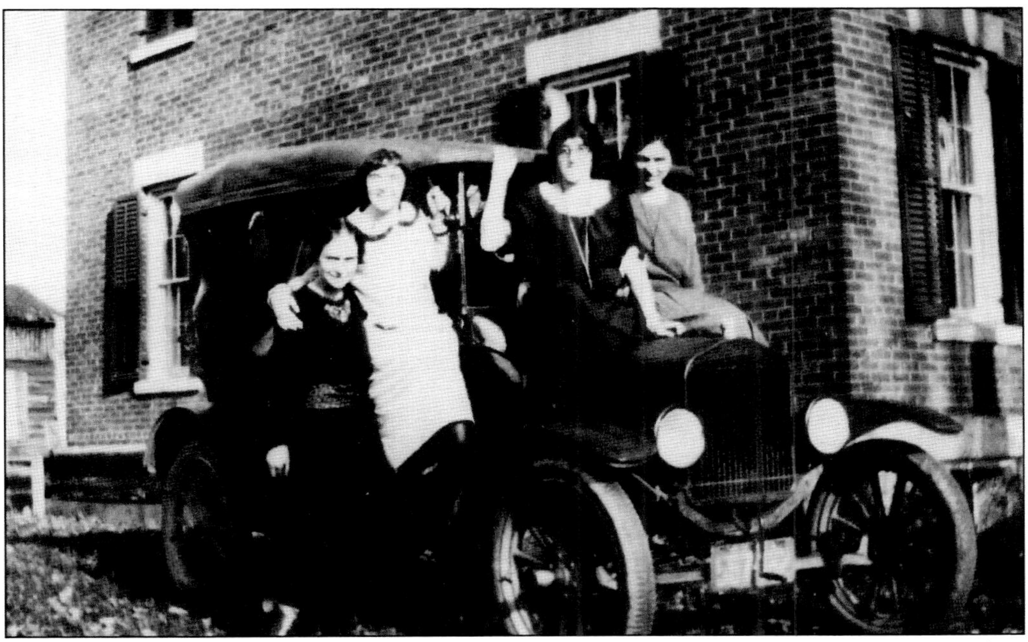

"Henry" the Model T. This photograph of the granddaughters of David N. Collamer was taken at the Collamer/Baker Homestead on Malta Avenue in the early 1920s as they posed with "Henry" the Model T. On the far left is Dora Baker (1887–1966) and on the far right is Matie Baker (1989–1965). The two young ladies in the center are unknown.

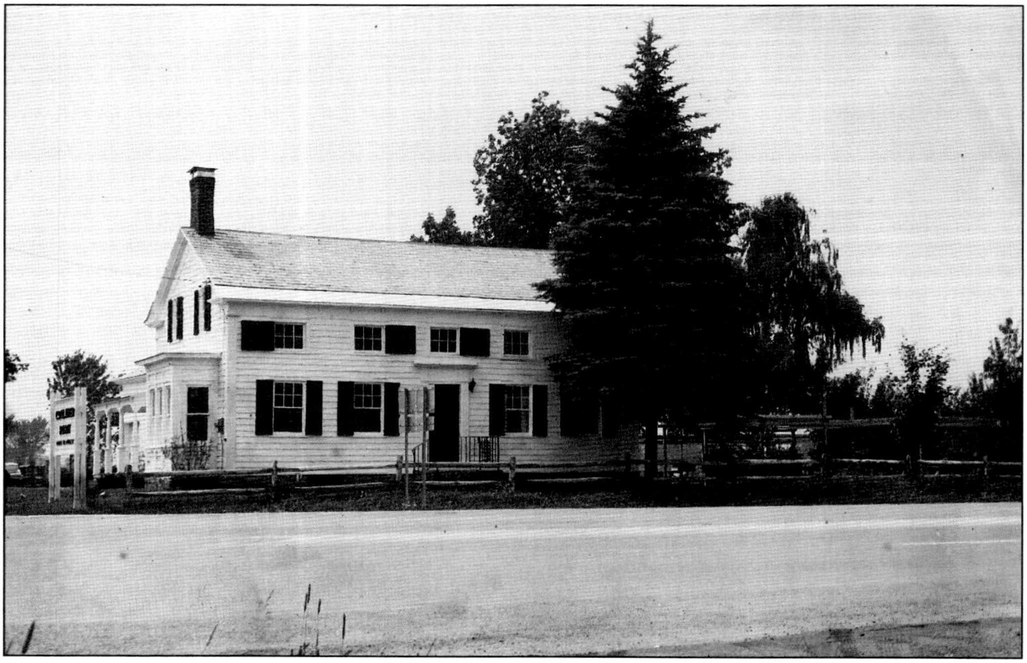

Wiggins/Collamer Homestead, *c.* 1835. The Wiggins/Collamer Homestead was built *c.* 1835 by George Wiggins on land that had been purchased in 1821. The property remained in the Wiggins family until 1883, when upon the death of John and Paula Wiggins, the property was inherited by their daughter, Harriet Wiggins Collamer, wife of William A. Collamer Jr. This homestead then stayed in the Collamer family until 1972, when Nelson P. Collamer, the great-great-grandson of George Wiggins, deeded the house and the land to the town of Malta. It was designated as a historic landmark by the Town of Malta in 1980.

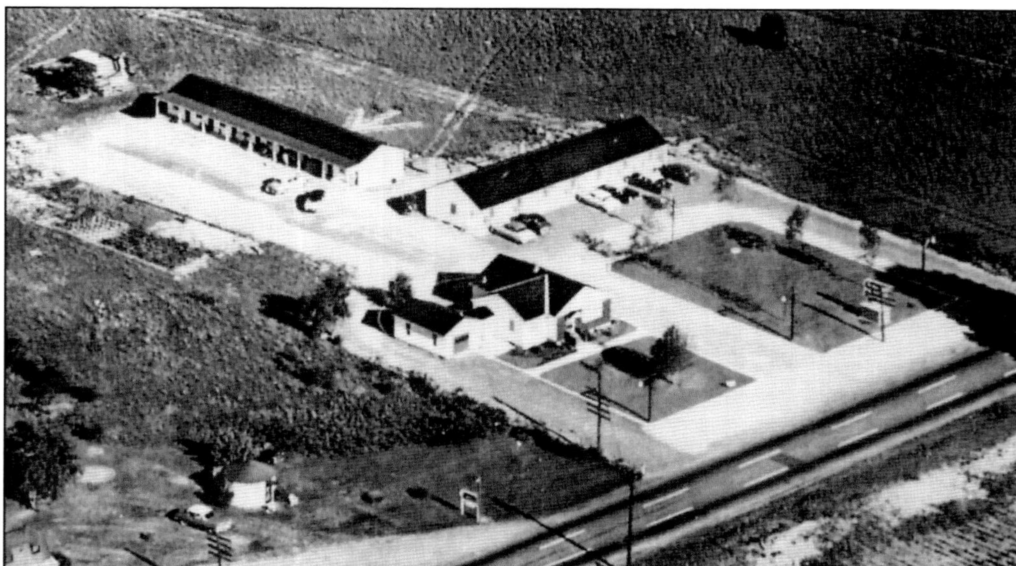

Malta Ridge Motel. The Malta Ridge Motel on Route 9 is located 4 miles south of Saratoga Springs.

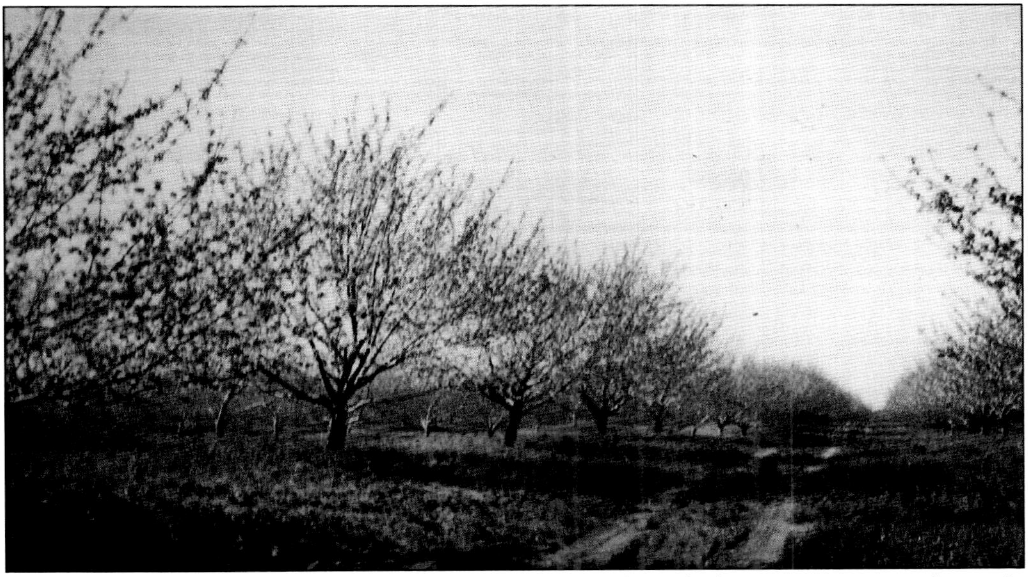

Melander's Apple Orchard. Mr. Clarence Melander planted about 20 acres in the early 1920s, and the orchard grew to 100 acres. The rows are planted in a perfect north-to-south arrangement. Although Mr. Melander was advised that the soil conditions were not correct for an orchard, he persevered and faithfully mulched and attended his trees year after year. The mulch was a product of the Saratoga Racetrack nearby. The varieties of apples grown here were MacIntosh, Cortland, Red Delicious, Red Spy, and Northern Spys, and many of these trees are still producing.

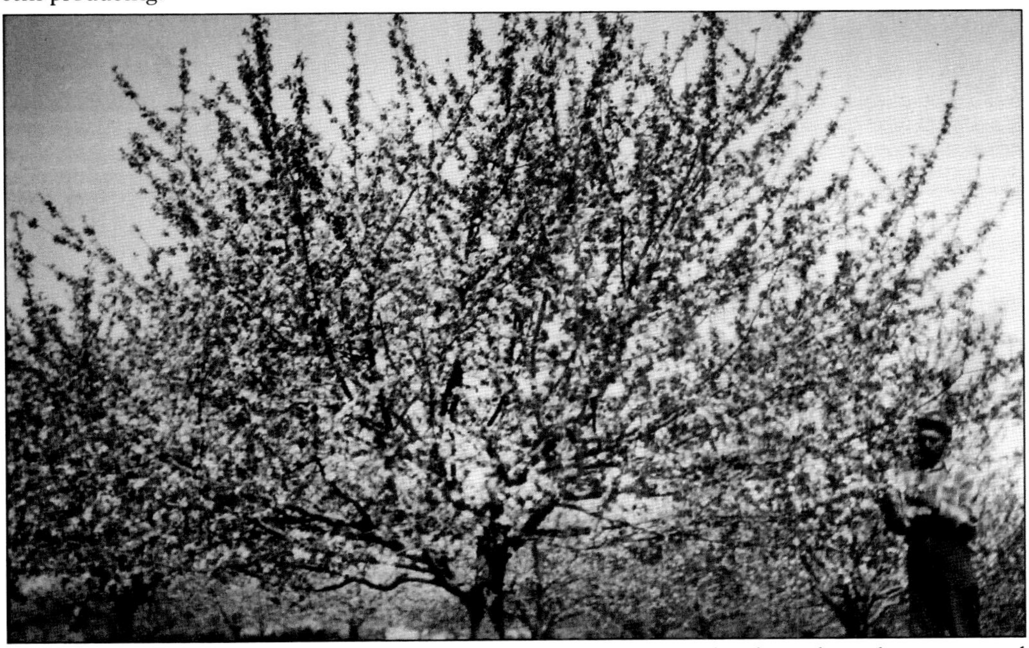

Ernest Melander in his Malta Ridge orchard. Melander's Apple Orchard was the only commercial apple orchard in Malta, and it is still in operation today. The orchard is presently known as Bowman's Orchard, owned by the Dave Bowman family.

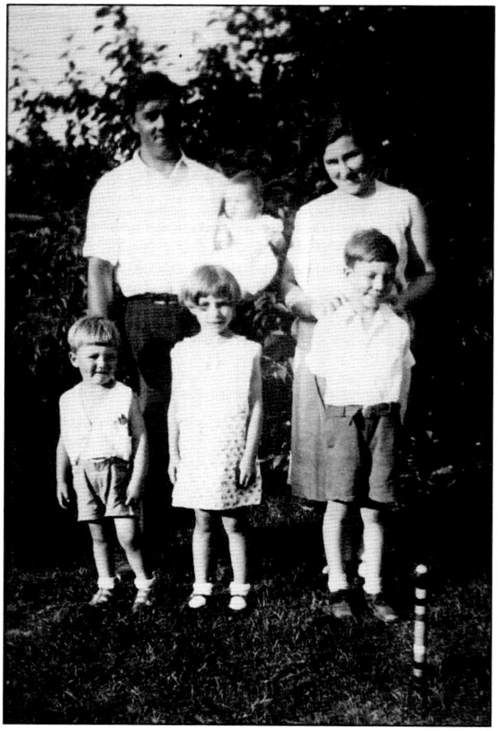

Melander family portrait, 1931. This photograph shows Clarence Melander with baby Eleanor held in the crook of his arm. Next to him is his wife, Margaret, and in the front are Ernest, Doris, and Raymond. Robert, their youngest child, was not yet born.

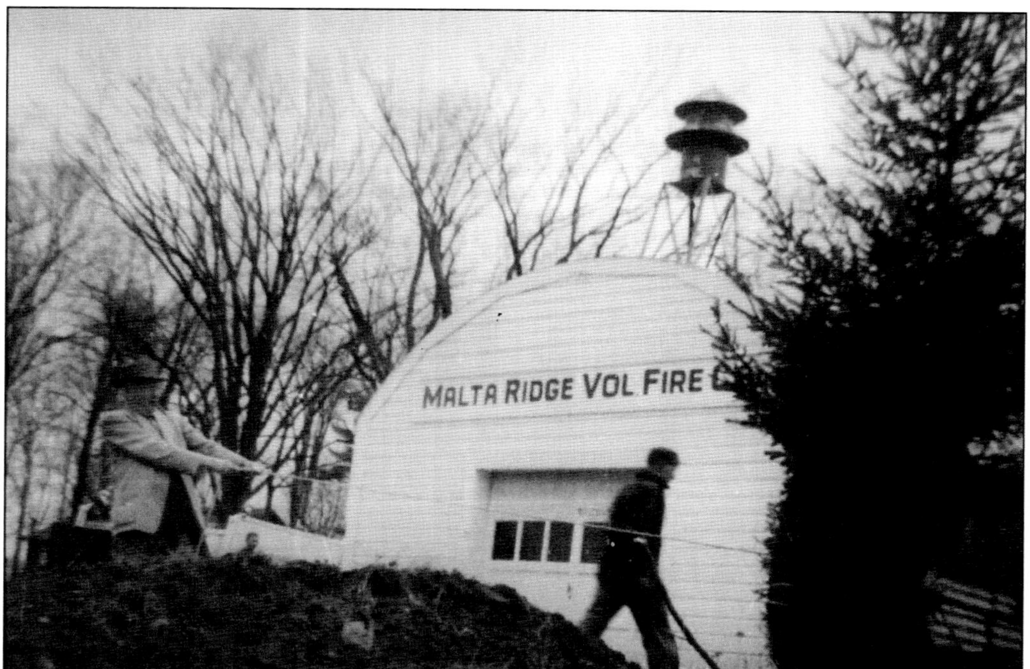

Malta Ridge Volunteer Fire Company, 1957. Pictured here is the Malta Ridge Volunteer Fire Company on Route 9. The annual Christmas tree is being planted by the local 4-H Club, while "Mayor" Gary Hearn holds the rope to steady the tree.

Four

Maltaville

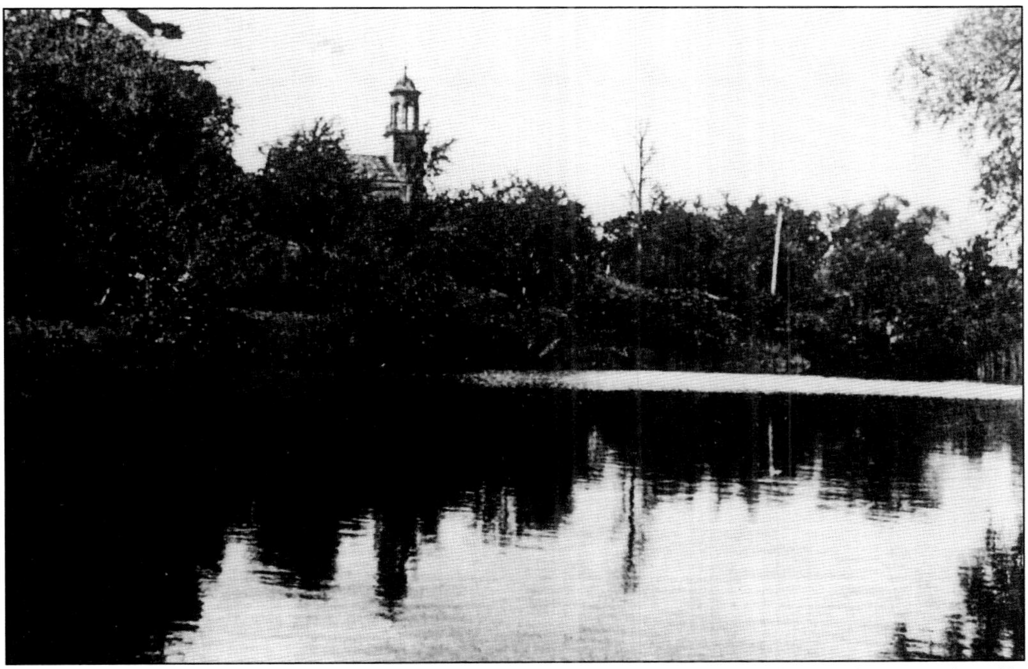

Presbyterian-Congregational church. The Presbyterian-Congregational church at Maltaville was organized as early as 1785 and was dedicated in 1806. It stood for more than one hundred years and the last recorded meeting of its society was held on July 7, 1852. During the years 1834 through 1840, the church became exclusively Congregational and then exclusively Presbyterian. In its final years the church was used by Methodists. The congregation was finally absorbed into the Presbyterian church at Dunning Street, and the church became extinct. The building was razed in 1903.

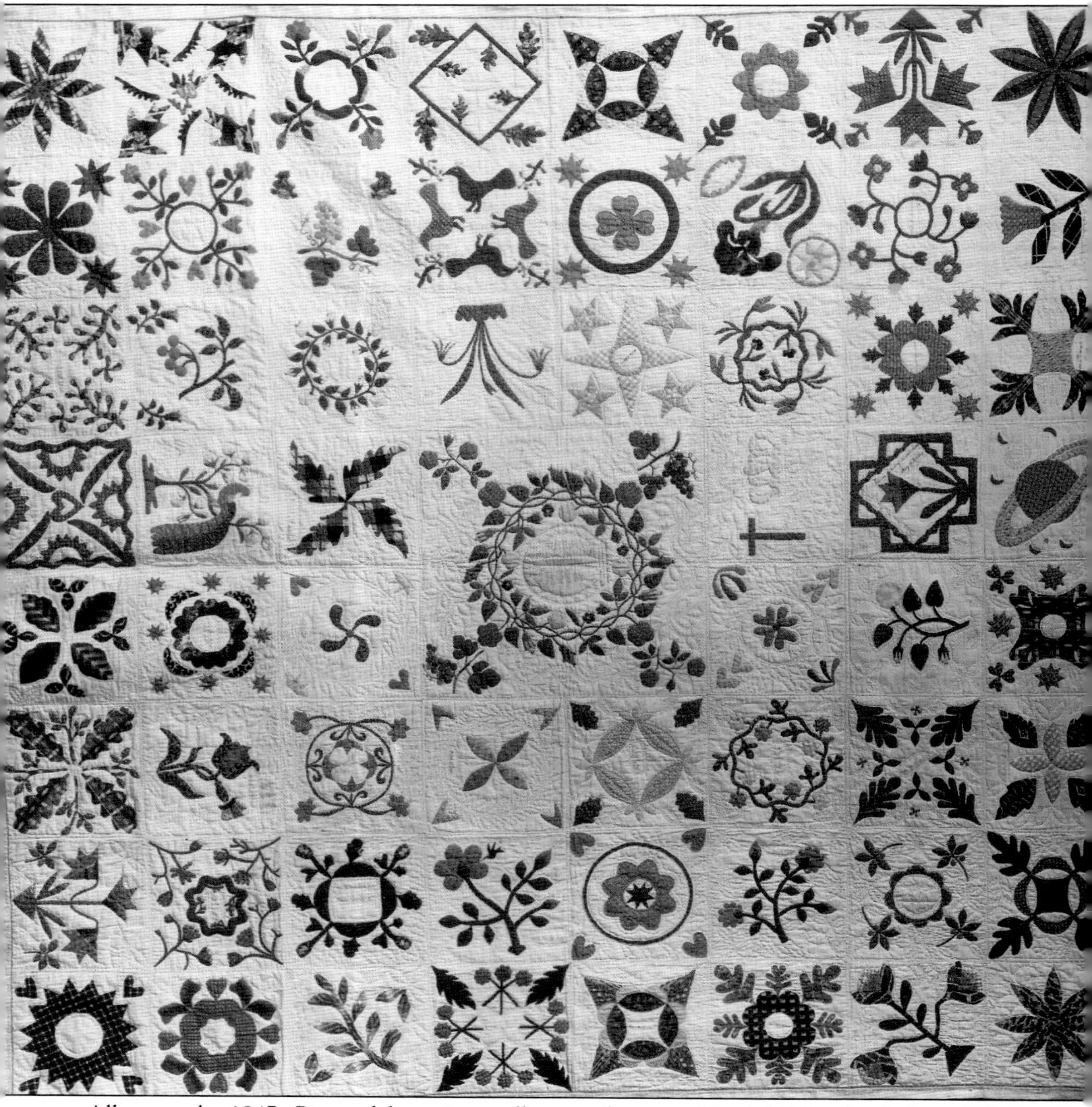

Album quilt, 1847. Pictured here is an album quilt created in 1847 by the ladies of the Presbyterian church of Maltaville for the pastor's wife, Mary Benton Barnard Hill, whom they held in the highest esteem. Mary Hill was the wife of the Reverend William Hill, who served that church for several years. This appliqué quilt, embroidered and dated 1847, has a large center square containing a dedicatory poem, and each quilt square bears the name of the woman who created it. The quilt was given to the Museum of American History in Washington, D.C., by Mrs. Isaac Carrington Morton, the granddaughter of Reverend and Mary Hill. It was put on display by the museum at an exhibition of quilts from July 1990 through 1991.

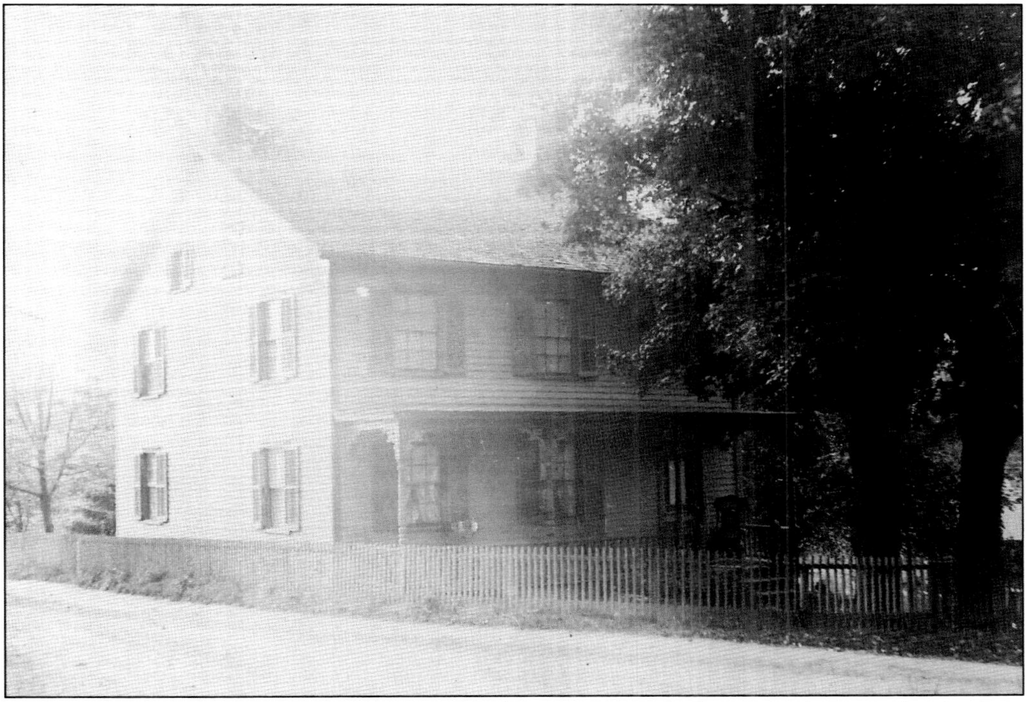

Andrew Scotland Homestead. This picture taken sometime before 1901 features the Andrew Scotland Homestead at Maltaville. The house stood on the southwest corner of the intersection of Route 67 and the Maltaville-Round Lake Road.

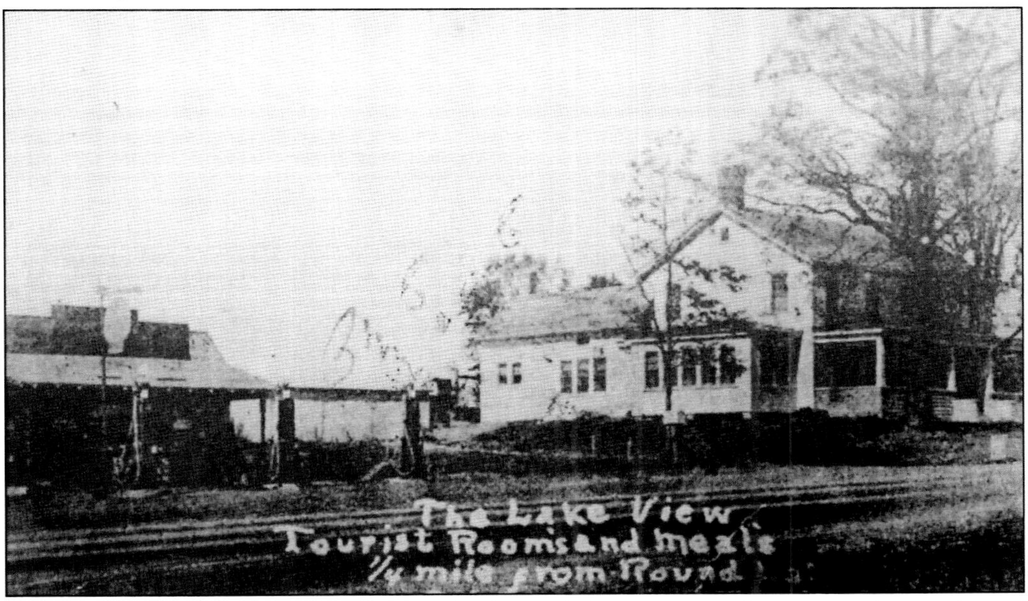

Wiley's Lake View, 1936. This photograph obtained from a postcard promotes the services of the Lake View, which was operated by the Wiley family. The Wileys provided rooms and meals, and operated a small gas station and store. Today the place is operated as the Starting Gate Cottages by the McDonough family.

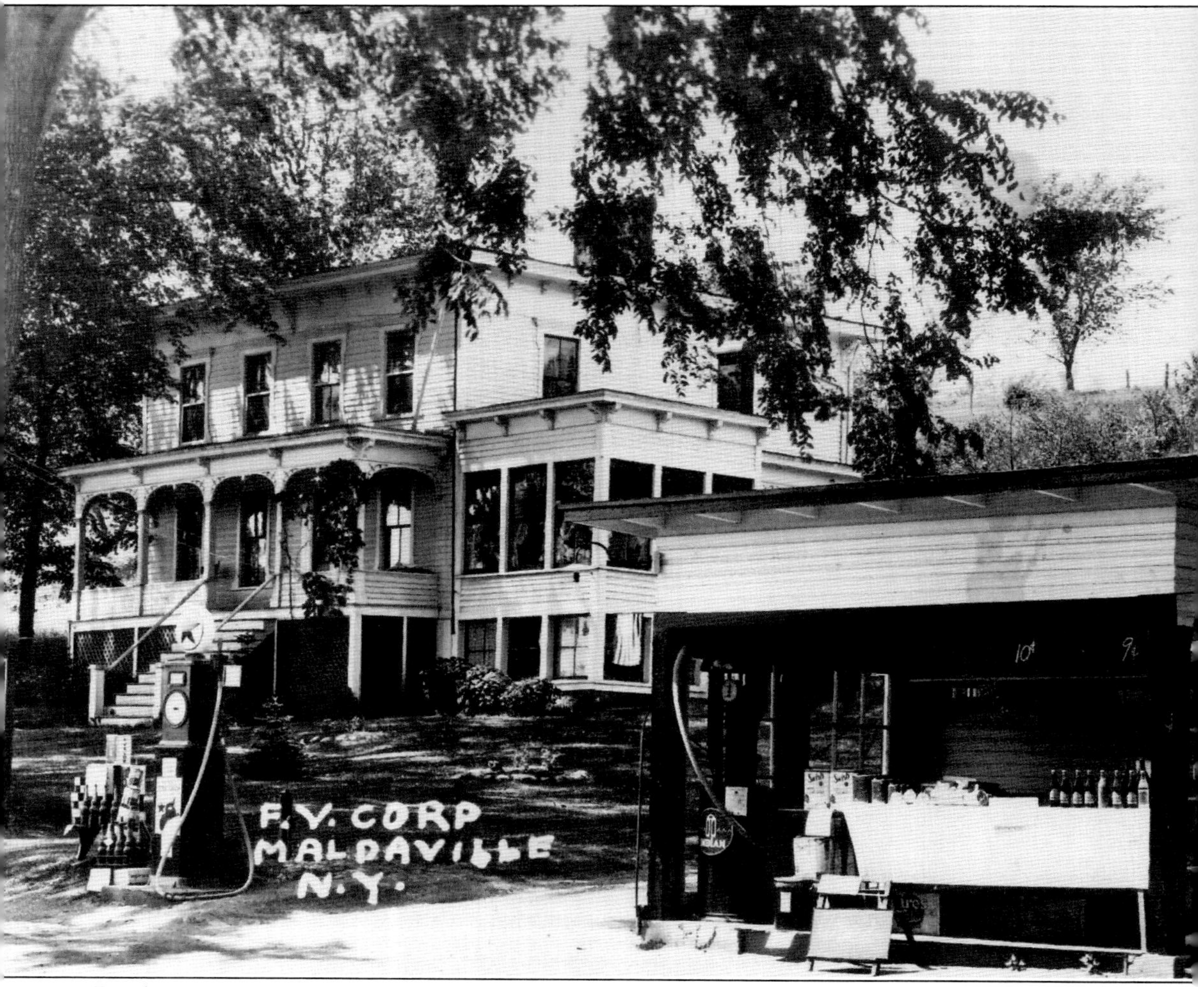

Frank V. Corp Home. Pictured here is the beautiful Victorian-style homestead of Frank V. Corp on Maltaville Road. This photograph was taken well after the advent of the motor car—note the Texaco sign at the far left. From the product stand two American flags at each end. It is probable that soda, ginger ale, and Hires Root Beer were sold here, and perhaps candy and ice cream, too. We are left to wonder what cost 10¢ or 9¢ as posted above the counter, as well as what was, as the sign at far right states, "Always Guaranteed Pure."

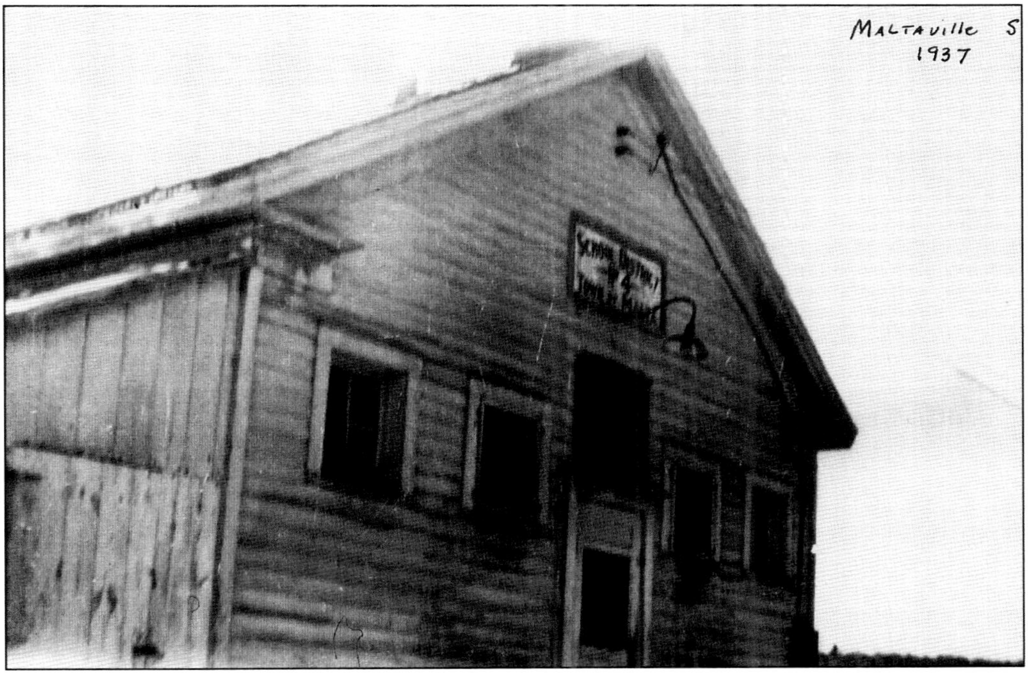

Maltaville Common School No. 4, old Route 67, 1937. Mr. Clarence Jones taught grades one through eight in this building with a wood stove but no running water. The custodian was generally one of the students. At a later time, May Pickett was also a teacher in this school. After completing their courses here, students went on to attend the Round Lake High School. Today the schoolhouse has been remodeled and is a private home.

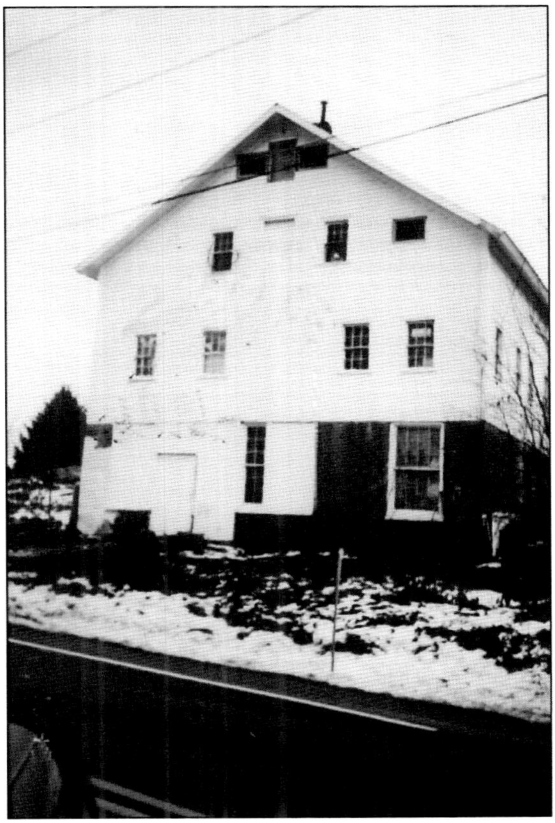

Malta Grange No. 1420, c. 1866. Although no longer active, the grange occupied this building on Route 67 for many years. This building was also the site of the carriage shop operated by Mr. John M. Simpson c. 1866. Mr. Charles Davis, a trunk maker, operated his business in Mr. Simpson's shop at the same time. Maltaville, the earliest settlement in the town, was a thriving community with over one hundred inhabitants, several businesses, a hotel, and a post office.

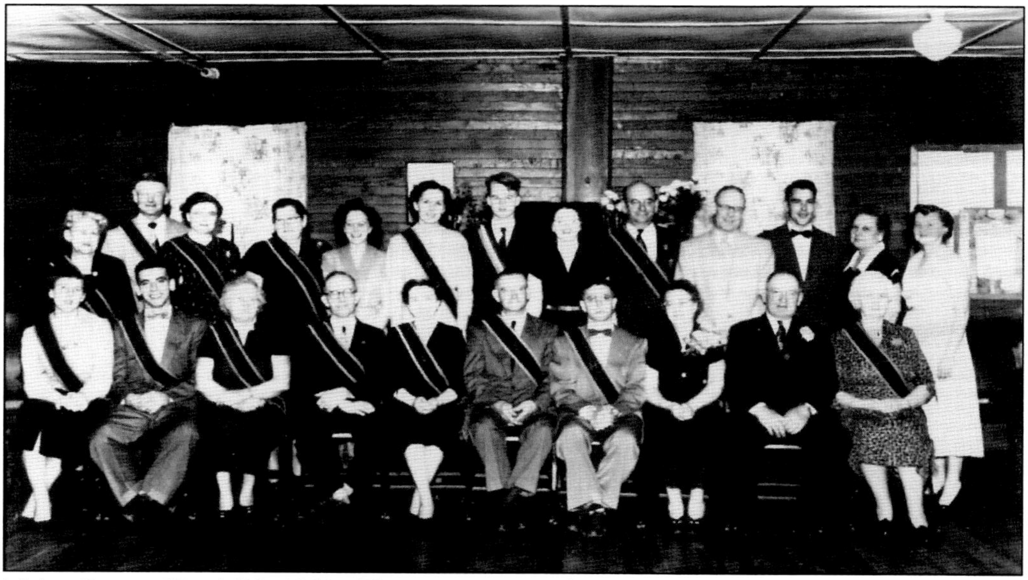

Malta Grange No. 1420, 1950s. This picture was taken upstairs in the official meeting room. Those pictured are as follows: (front row) Florence Cruz, Richard Rosenbrock, unidentified, Richard Gorsline, Marjorie Glasgow, Chauncey Gregg, Charles Cleveland, Elsie Martin, Ralph Williams, and Rosalie VanVechten; (back row) unidentified, Earl Edmonds, Sadie Edmonds, Emma Gorsline, Iris Civalier, Ruth Cleveland, Winand Von Perersdorf (an exchange student), Dorothy Gregg, Ernest Rosenbrock, and four guests.

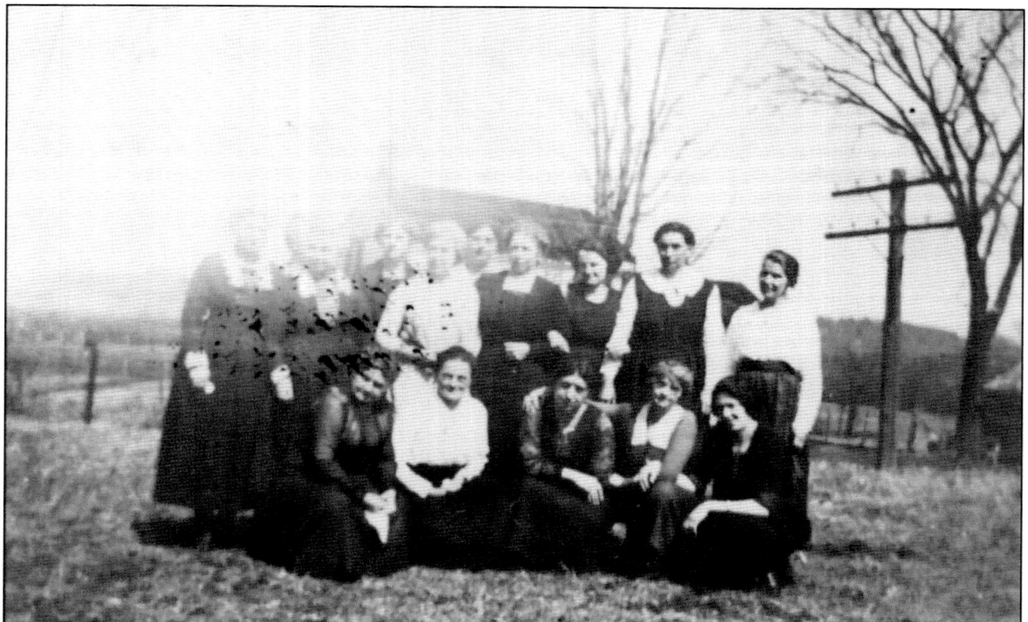

Grange hall ladies, 1922. The women are Lillah and Myrtle Bathrick, Marion and Lillian Fitch, Myrtle and Etta Knapp, Clara Olmstead, Agnes and Millie Barber, Hortense Turpit, Helen Collamer, Estelle Cooper, Mrs. John Wilmot, and Mrs. John Baker. We must assume that these ladies are grange or home bureau members.

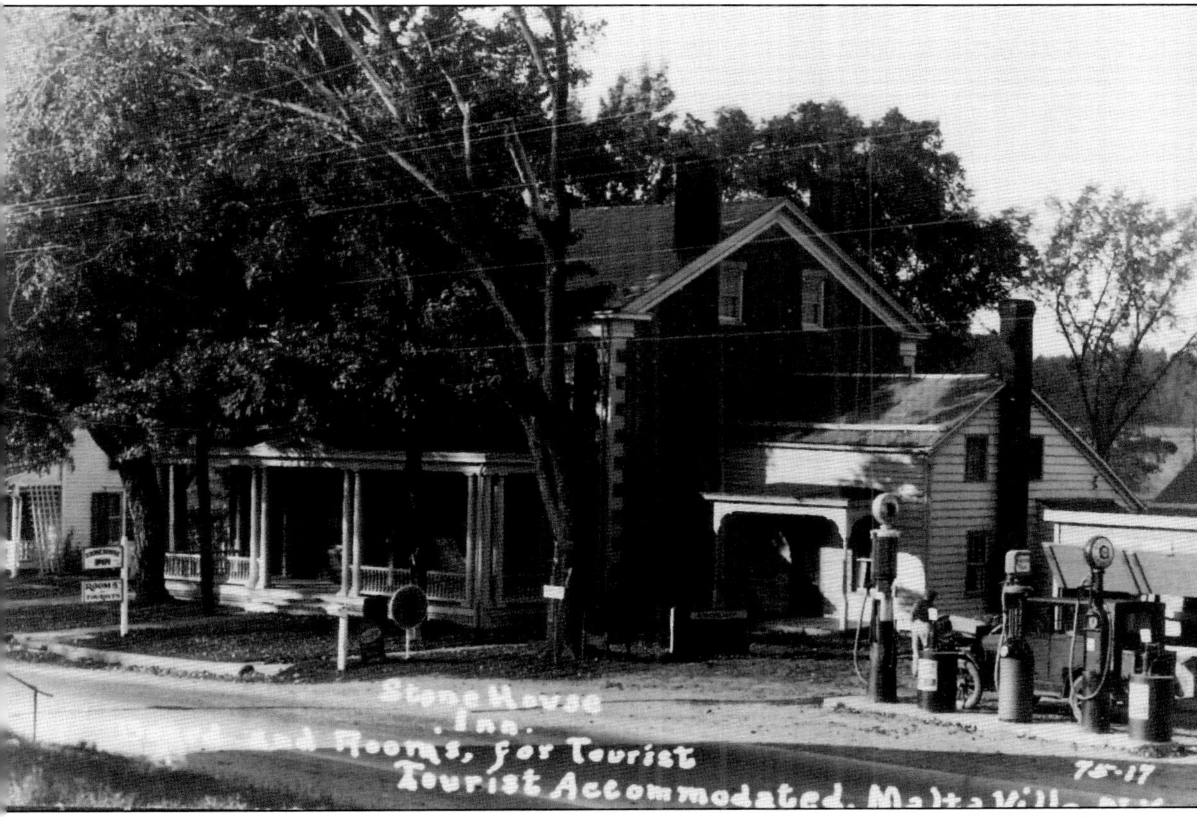

Stone House Inn, c. 1845. This photograph is of the cobblestone house at Maltaville, located at the intersection of Knapp Road and Route 67. This house was part of the Olmstead Homestead, which in early times covered most of Maltaville, including the Woolen Mill. Maltaville, a thriving community in the early 1800s, is considered to be the oldest community in the town of Malta. Through the years this lovely home has served as a residence as well as a restaurant, boarding house, and, presently, as a wonderful bed and breakfast. When the house was built c. 1845, or earlier, it is said that the fieldstones were put through a hole in a barrel. If the stone was too large to go through the hole, it was set aside and not used.

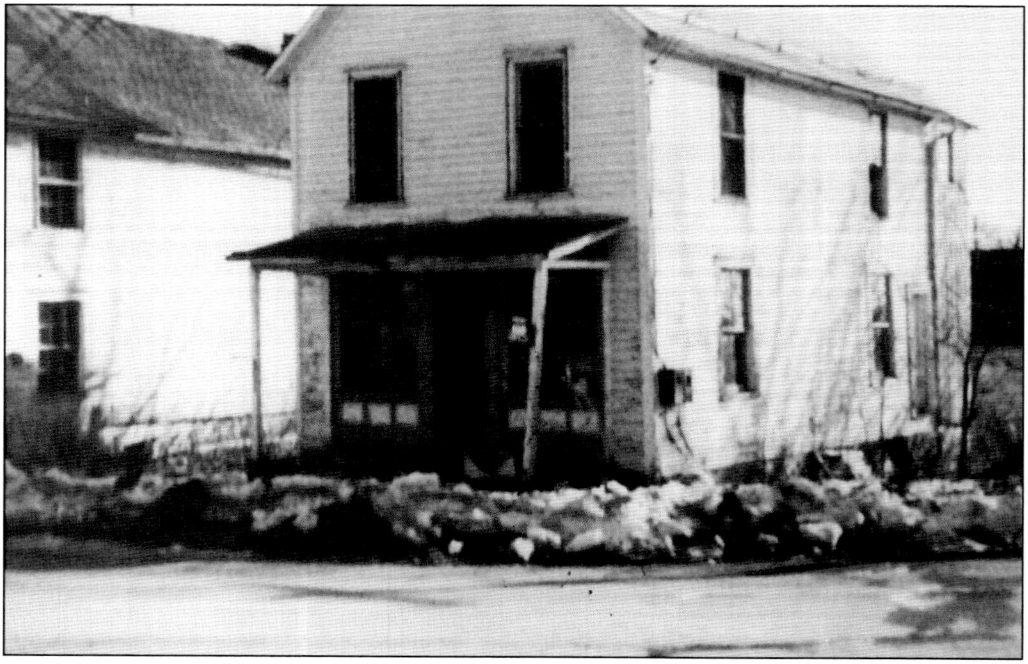

General store, 1977. This picture shows the structure that was once the general store at Maltaville at the intersection of Maltaville and Dugan Hill Roads. It stood on the south side of the road and was operated by Mr. Fred Corp. The building was demolished in the 1980s.

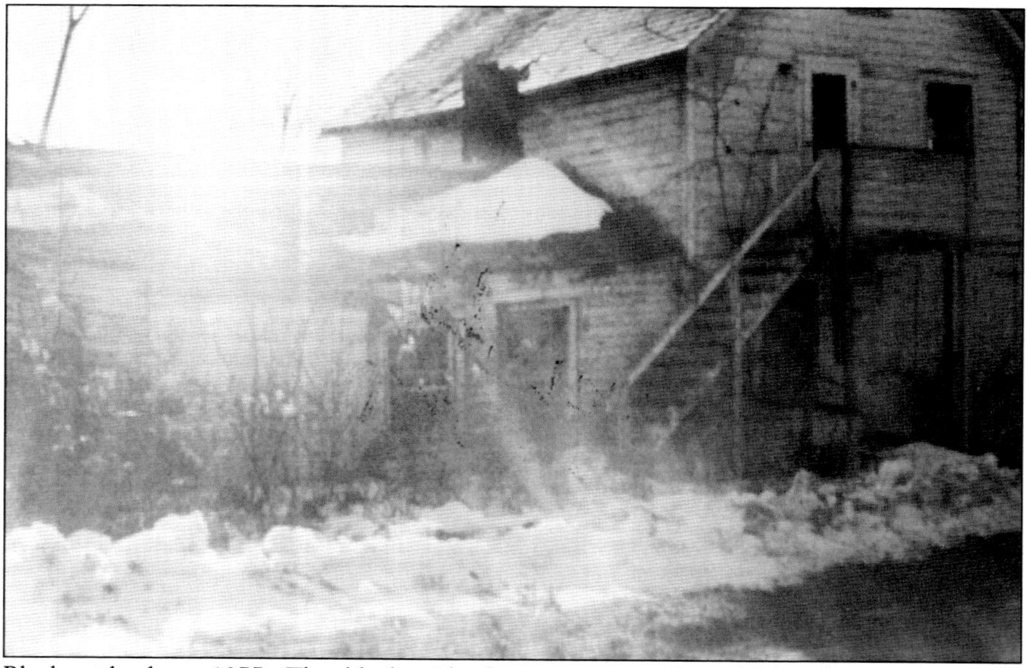

Blacksmith shop, 1977. The blacksmith shop was situated on Maltaville Road near its intersection with Dugan Hill Road, and just east of the general store in the previous picture. The owner-operator of this shop is not known.

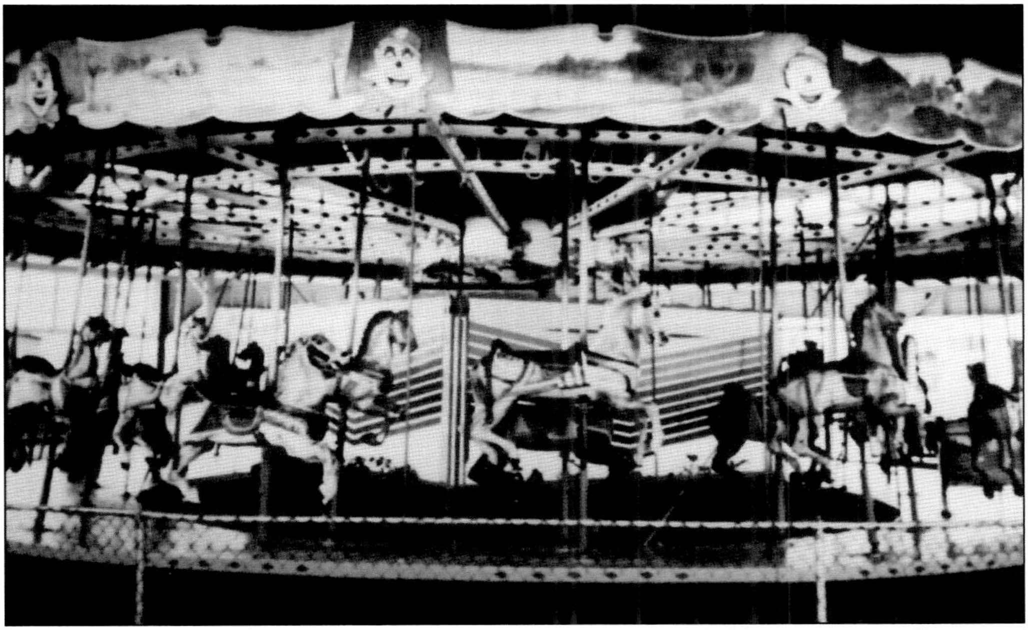

Carousel, *c.* 1904. In the late nineteenth century, amusement parks became very much a part of our way of life. The carousel, picnics, boating, strolling through the park, and all out-of-doors recreation were greatly enjoyed. This carousel was built *c.* 1904 by Marcus Illions, known in the carousel world as a master carver. The carousel at Maltaville arrived in 1931. It was first operated at a park in Clifton Park, and then moved to Forest Park at Ballston Lake where it remained until 1906. After leaving Maltaville in 1942, it moved to Kaydeross Park on Saratoga Lake, where it operated until the fall of 1987. It is now the property of the city of Saratoga Springs.

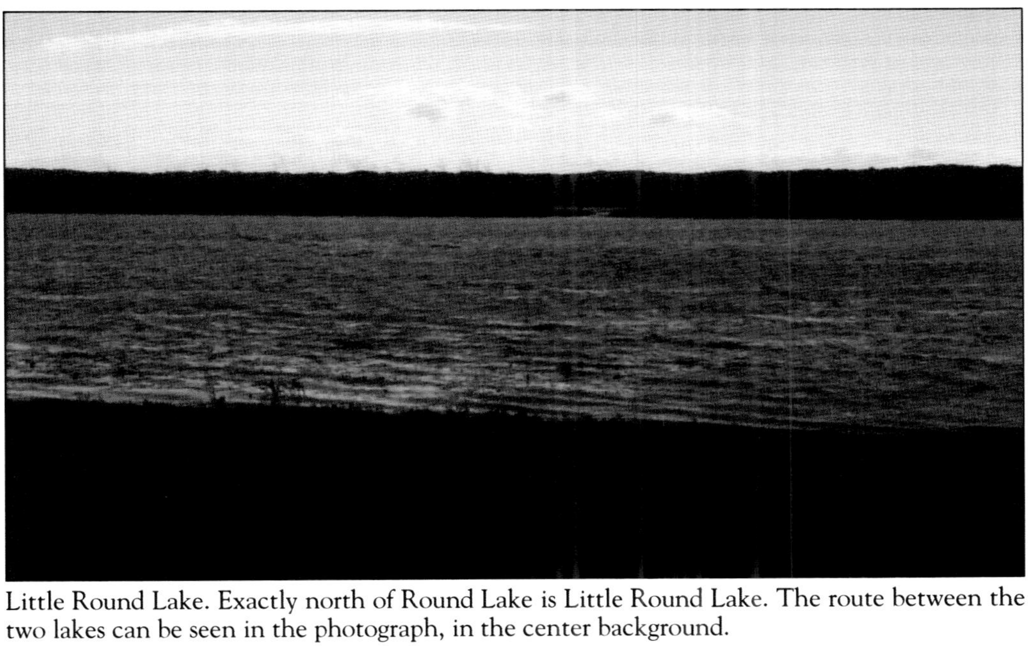

Little Round Lake. Exactly north of Round Lake is Little Round Lake. The route between the two lakes can be seen in the photograph, in the center background.

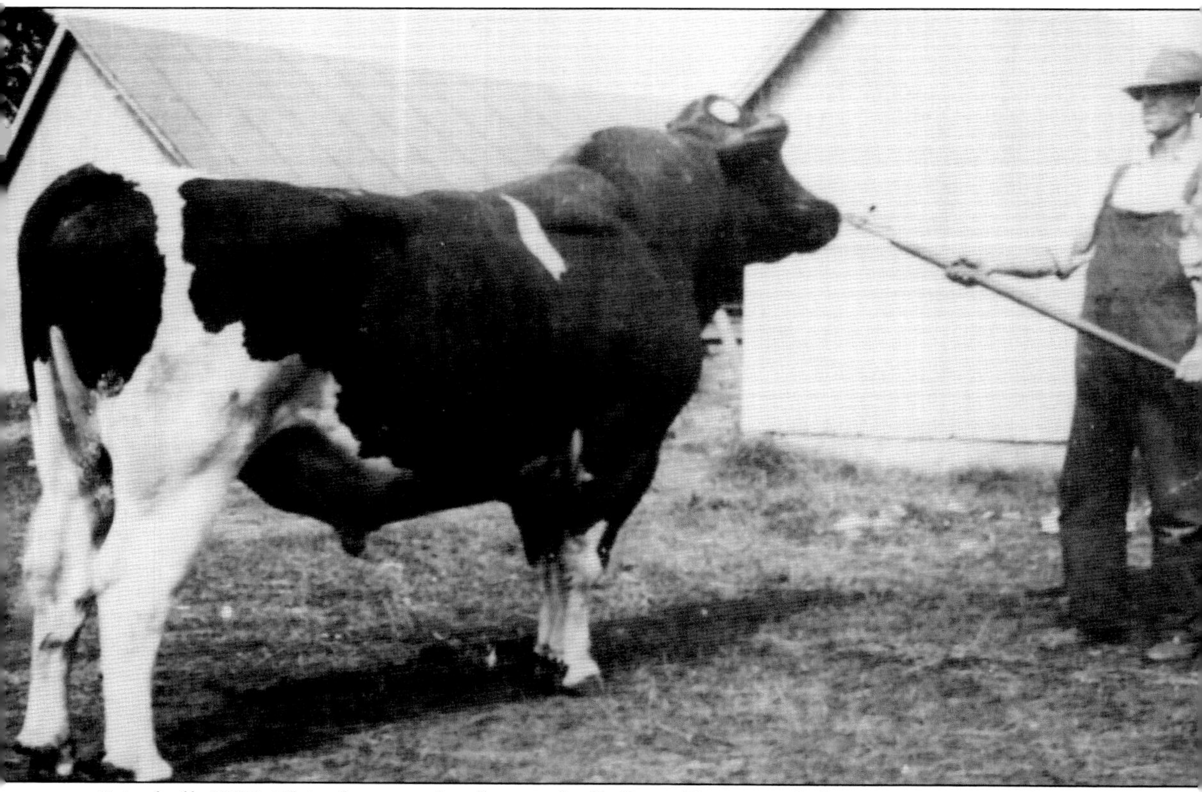

Prize bull, 1932. This photograph taken at the Ballston Fairgrounds features Mr. Howard Knapp, a prominent farmer of Malta, and the prize bull that he took to the Saratoga County Fair at Ballston Spa. In the background are the outbuildings that housed the animals at the fair.

Five

Round Lake

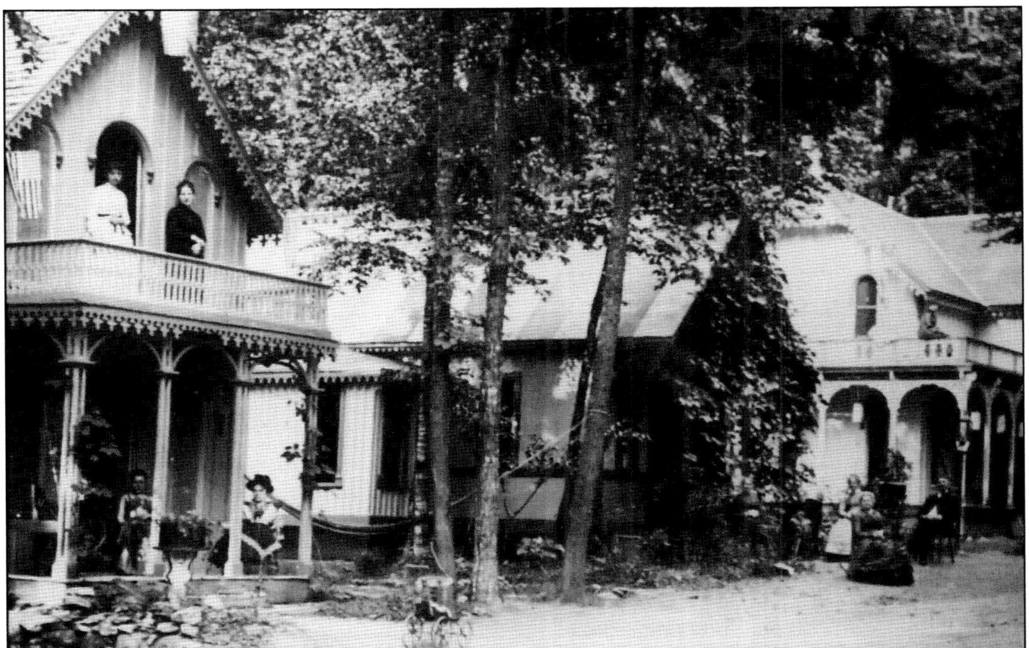

Village of Round Lake, *c.* 1910. A row of cottages formed the Round Lake Association. The view is of Covel Avenue looking east from Burlington Avenue.

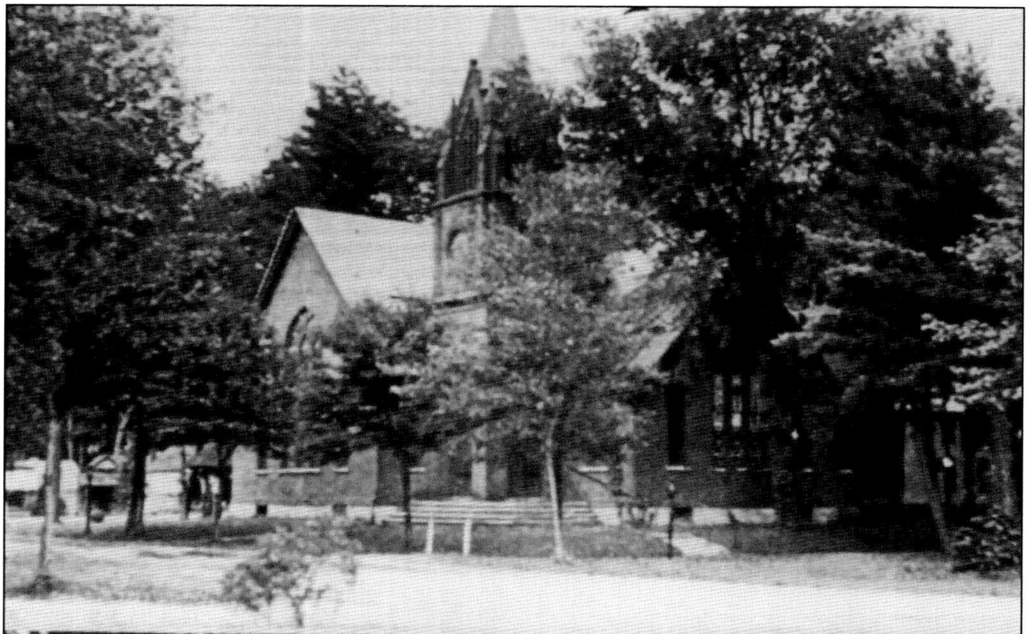

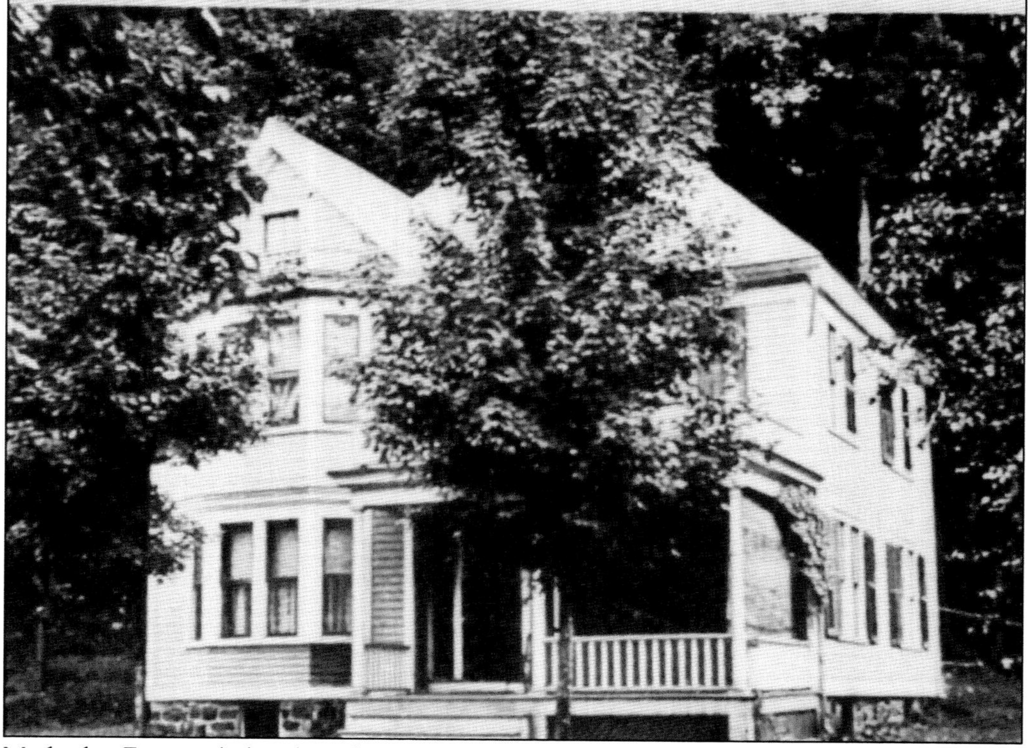

Methodist Episcopal church and parsonage. The site for the Methodist Episcopal church was chosen in 1889 in the village of Round Lake. Services were held in the Alumni Hall until the church was completed in 1894. The dedication of the church was held in July of 1895; the Reverend R.C. Heaxt was the first pastor.

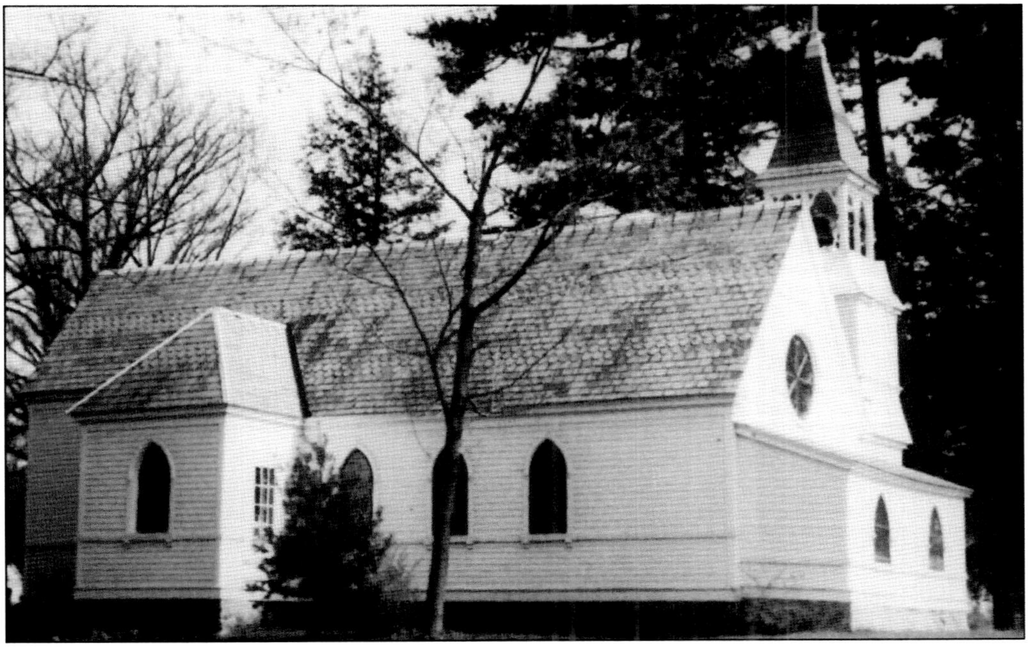

Round Lake All Saints Episcopal Church, built in 1892. Prior to 1892 the church services were held in private homes or in Guild Hall. The congregation, with the assistance of friends, raised the funds to make the building possible. Located among the tall pines of the area, the church remains active to this day.

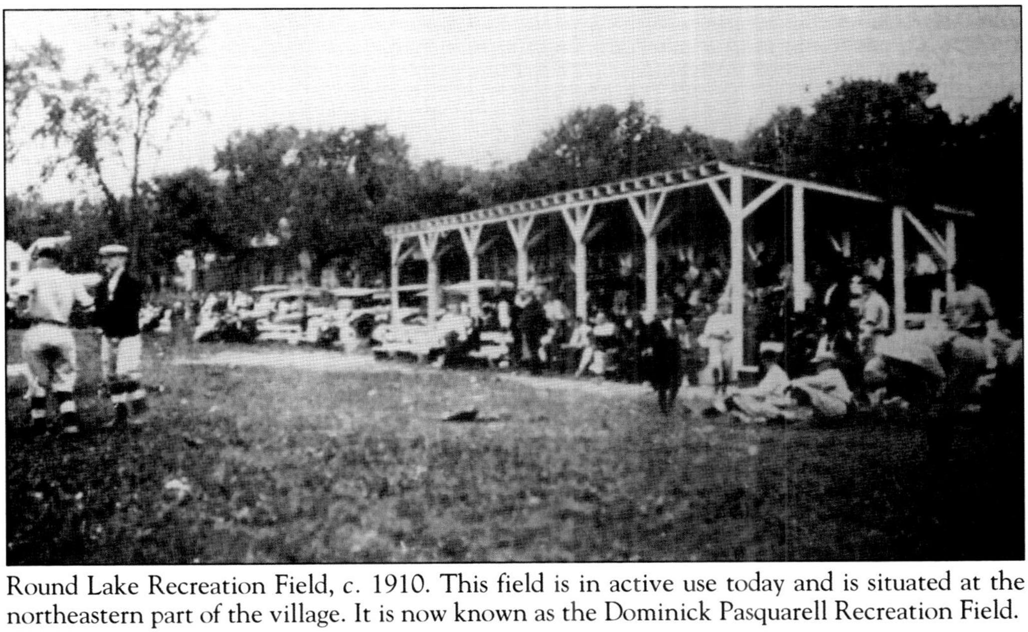

Round Lake Recreation Field, *c.* 1910. This field is in active use today and is situated at the northeastern part of the village. It is now known as the Dominick Pasquarell Recreation Field.

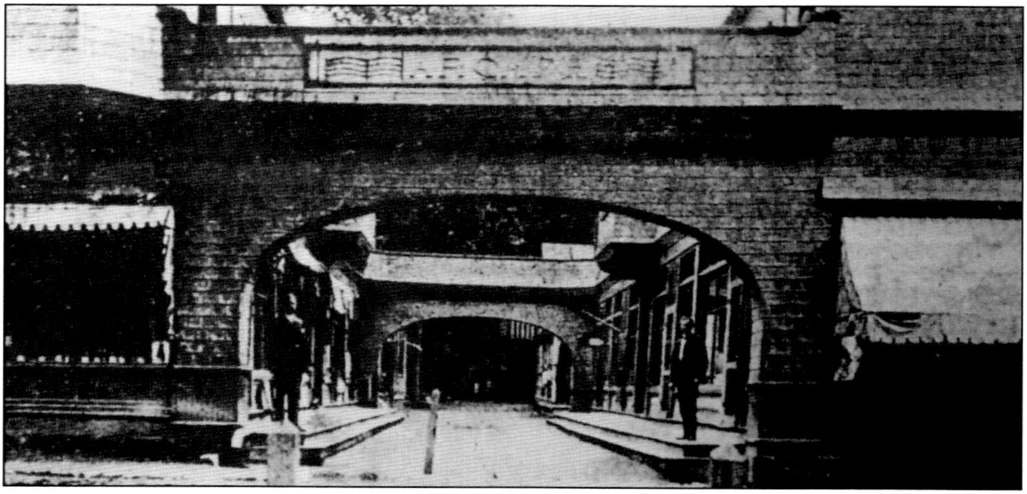

Arcade. The Arcade at Round Lake was built in 1885 through the efforts of William Griffin, president of the Round Lake Association. The Arcade was a large commercial building that housed several stores and offices, including a newsroom and a drugstore. Mr. Griffin's support encouraged further projects, which increased the success of the camp meetings. The Arcade could be considered a mini-mall before its time.

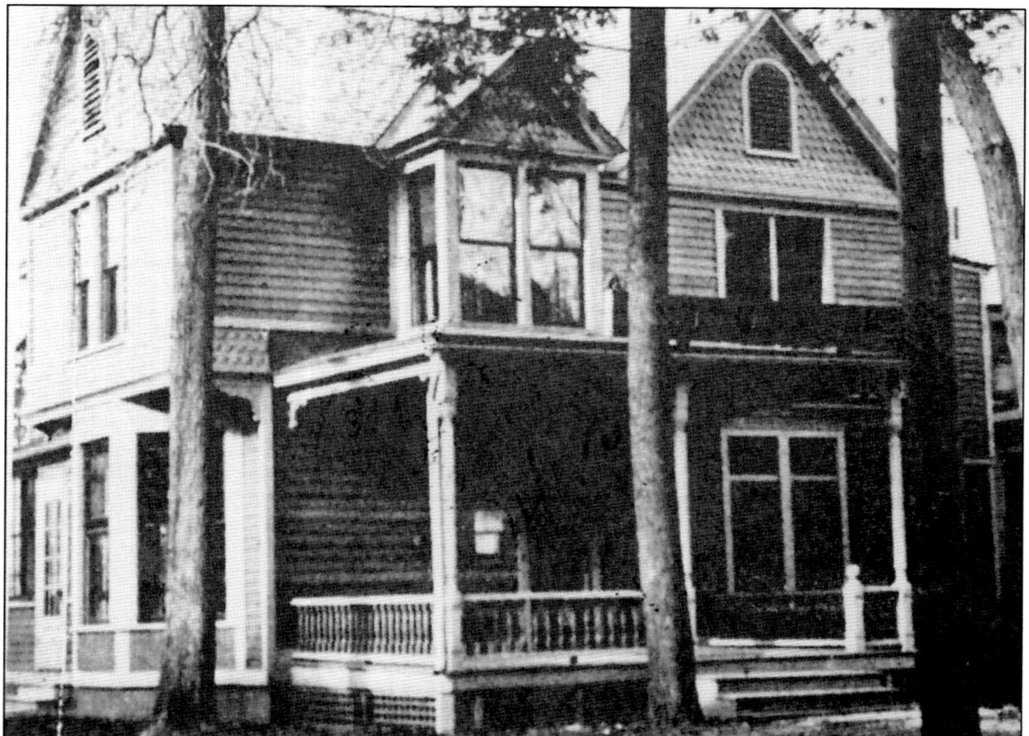

Round Lake Library. This photograph of the Round Lake Library was taken before the fire of 1921. The library opened its doors officially on July 6, 1897. It was the second library in Saratoga County, and the first to have its own building. In 1957, the Round Lake Library was the first to join the Southern Adirondack Library System.

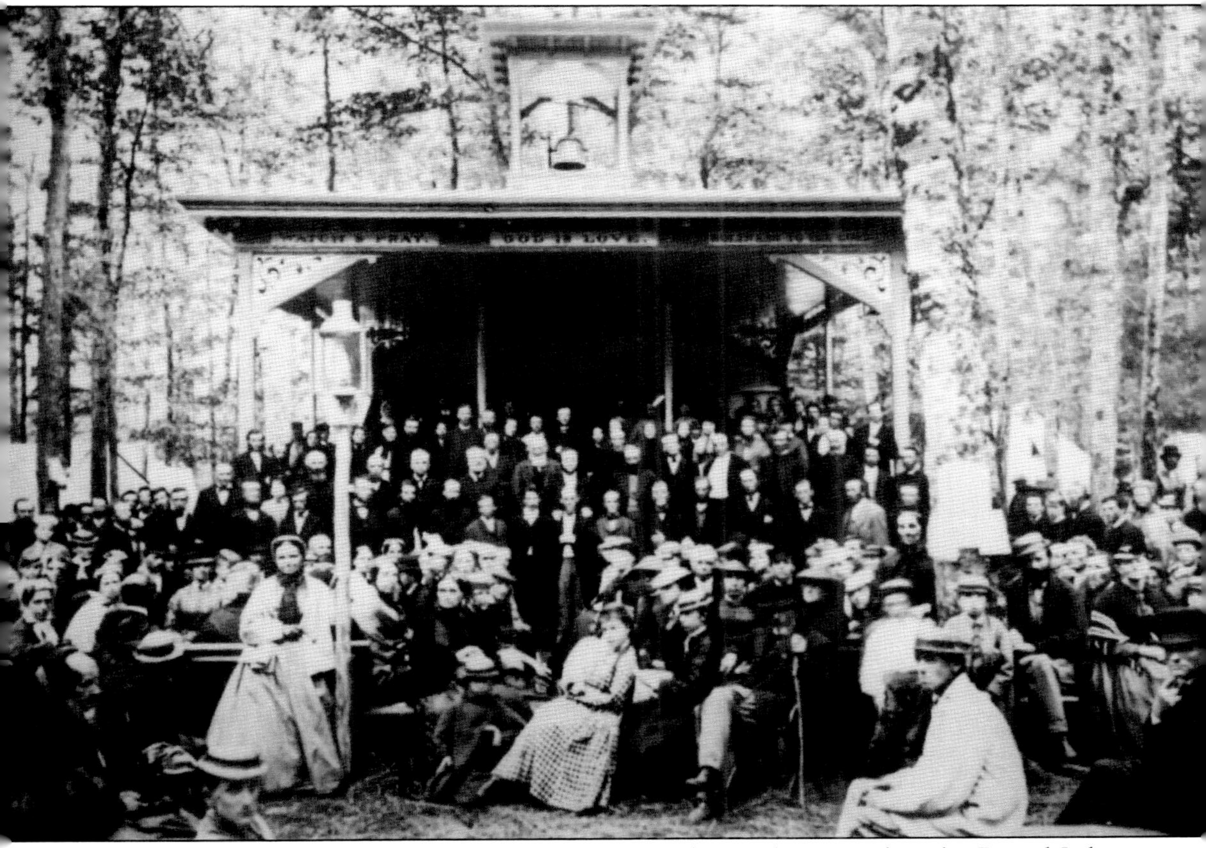

Earliest camp meetings, *c.* 1868–69. A gathering at the speakers' stand at the Round Lake Camp meeting grounds is depicted. The speakers' stand was built to shelter one hundred VIPs, while the audience sat on planks across the stumps of trees that had been cut to provide space. Take note of belfry on the roof of the stand, the wording across the top of the roof—"Watch and Pray," "God is Love," and "Holiness to the Lord"—and the tents in the background.

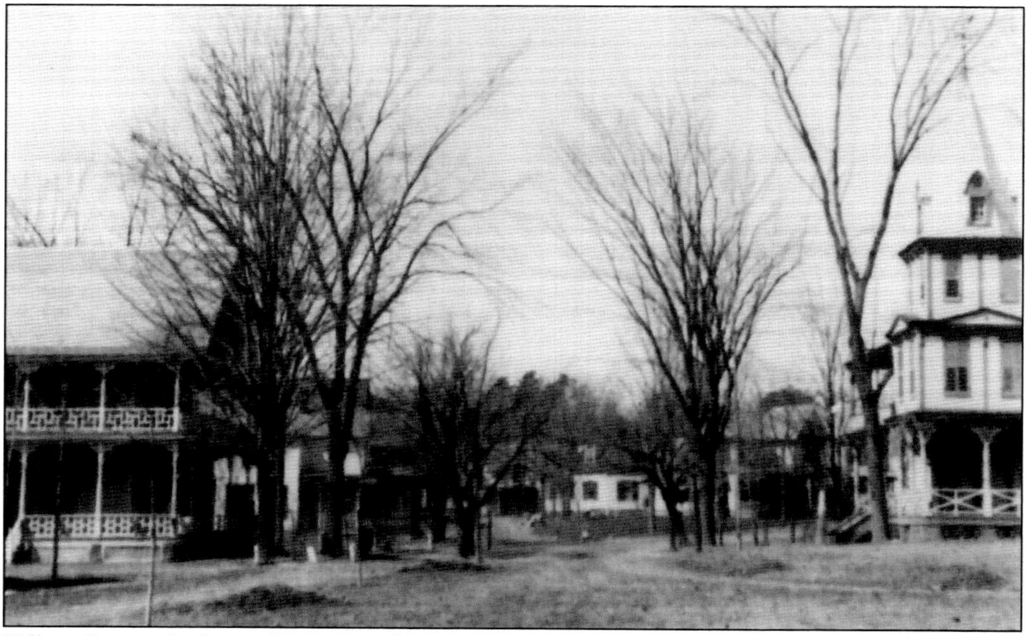

Village Street, Andrews Avenue, and Prospect Avenue. Looking west on Andrews Avenue from Prospect Avenue, on the left is the home of Robert and Jean Sweet. The "octagon house" in the center background is the home of Josette Snowden. The house on the right is no longer standing.

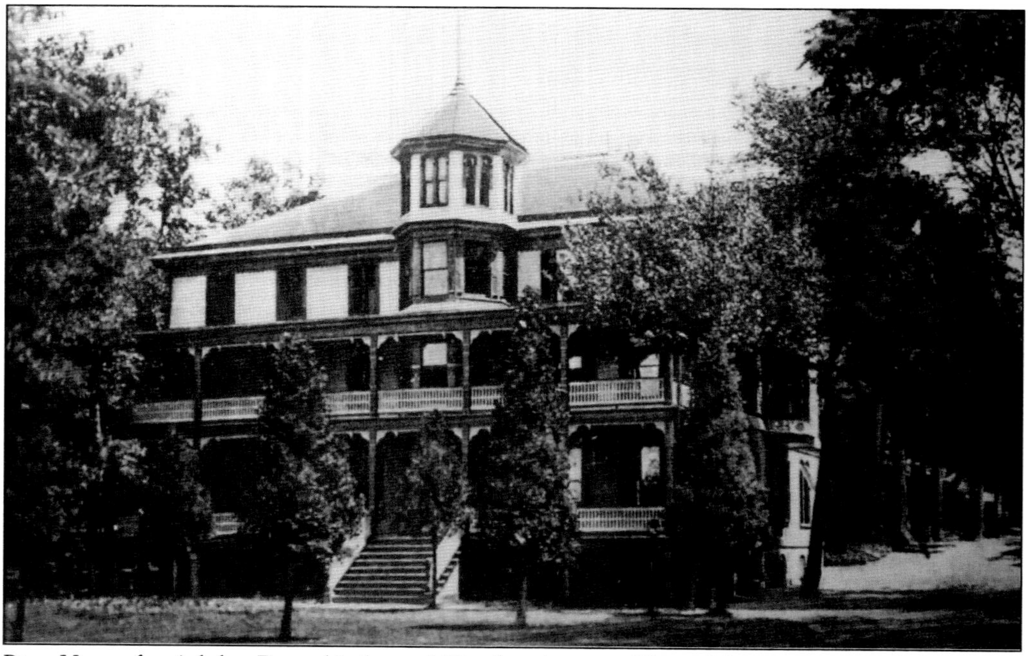

Pine Home for Adults, Round Lake and Kingley Avenue. This edifice was originally built as a hotel in 1886 and was then known as the Burnham House. Through the years it was also named the Lenox, and was called Manor Rest when it was used as a nursing home.

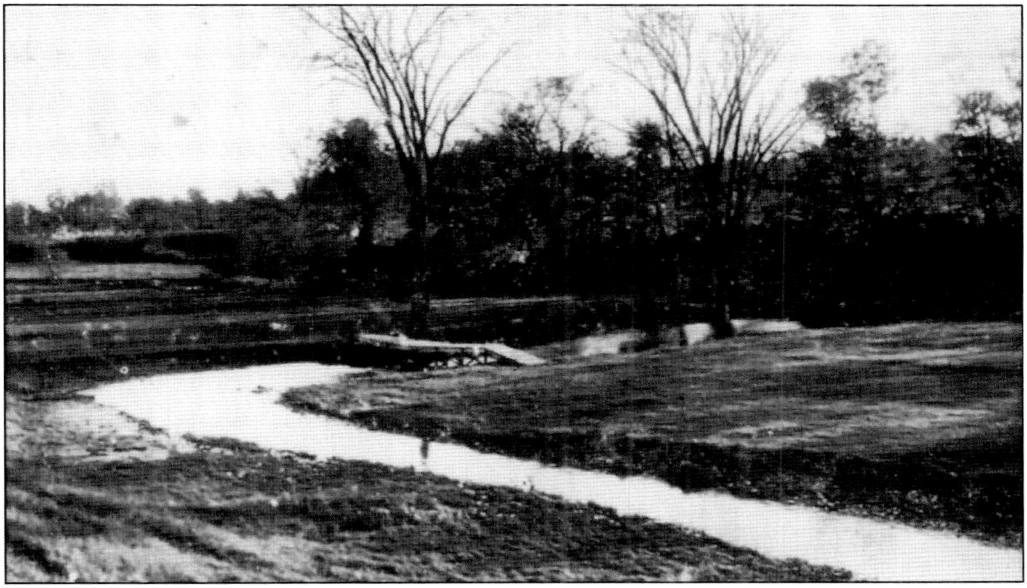

The golf links at Round Lake. The construction of U.S. Route 9 in the early 1900s brought about the end of the Round Lake golf course because the road cut the course completely in two.

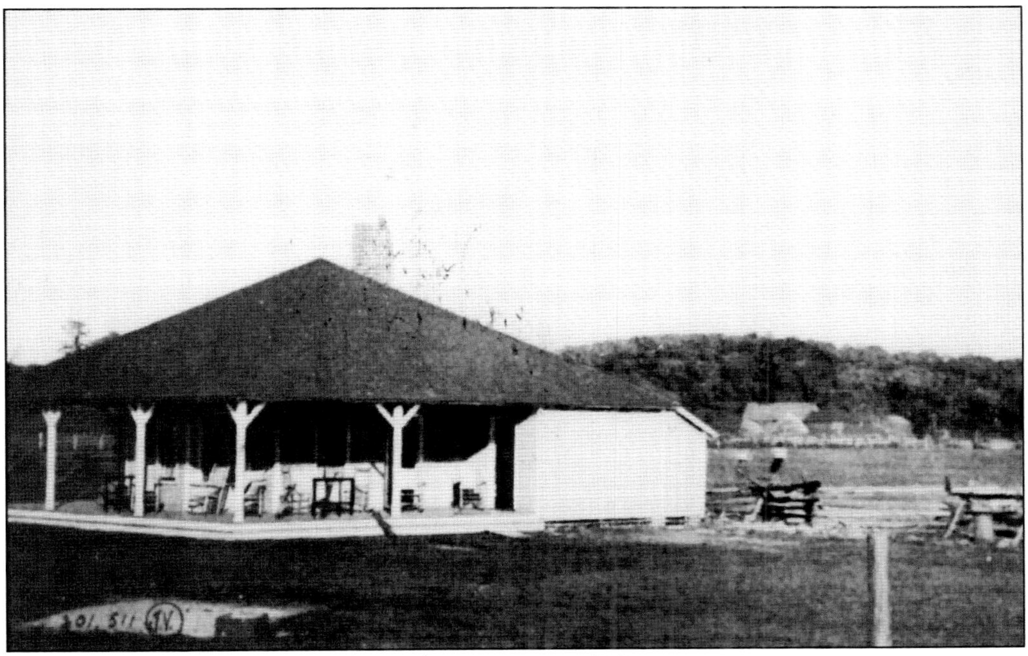

The golf clubhouse at Round Lake in the summer, *c.* 1917.

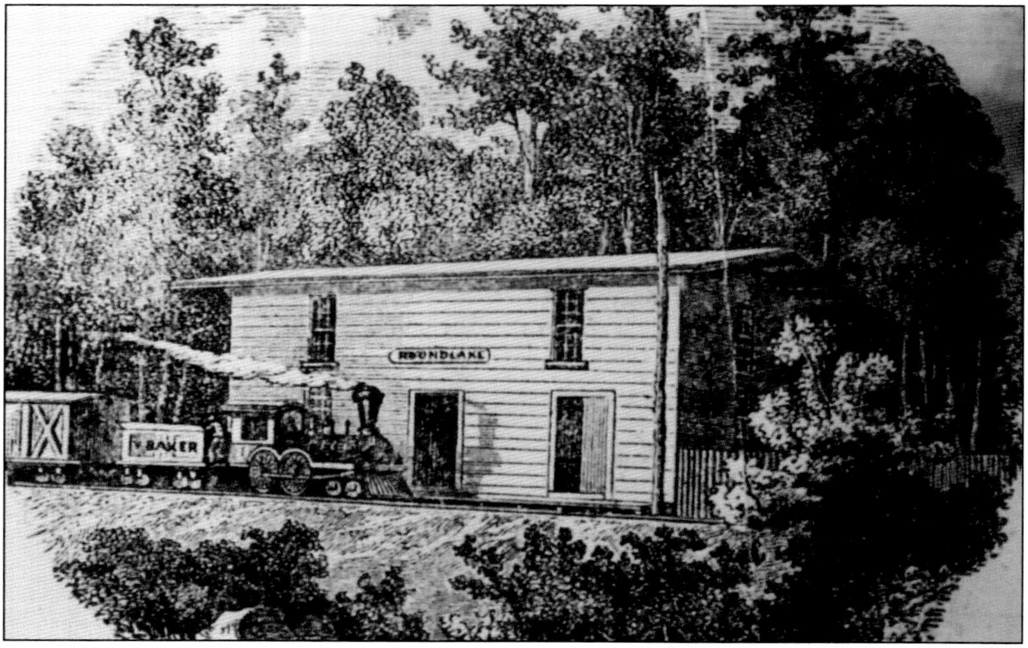

Old railway depot. This image depicts an early woodcut drawing of the Old Delaware and Hudson Railway Depot at Round Lake.

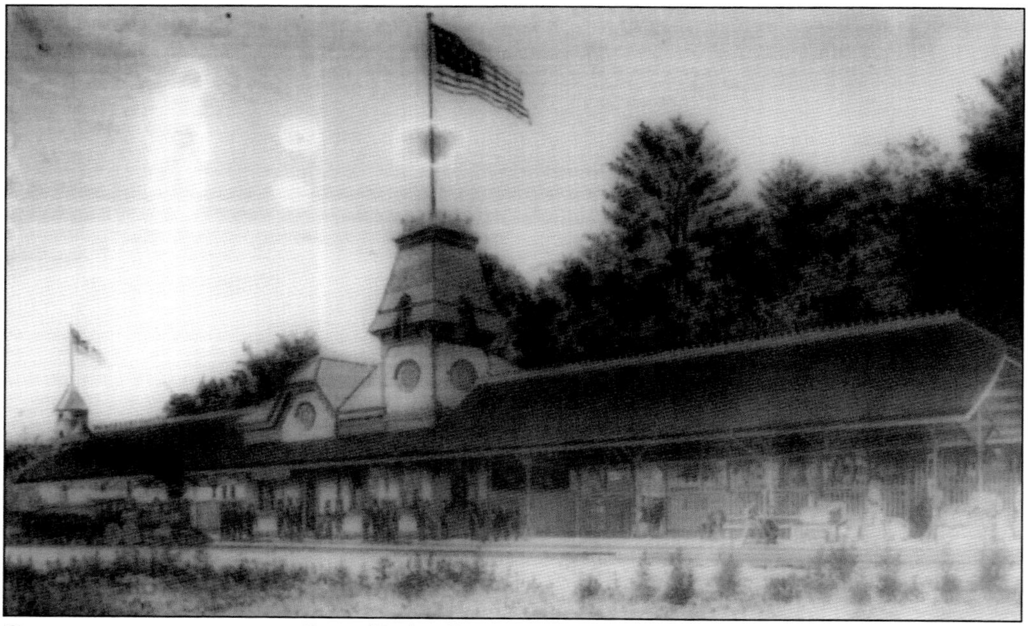

Ornate passenger station at Round Lake. During 1873–74, this station was built at Round Lake by the Delaware and Hudson Canal Co. It was constructed using corrugated, galvanized iron. There were wings on each end of the main building that housed the ticket office, baggage section, and waiting room. It is said that as many as thirteen trains daily brought people to Round Lake during the summer sessions of the Round Lake Epworth League Institute. The station was slowly dismantled between the years 1930 and 1940.

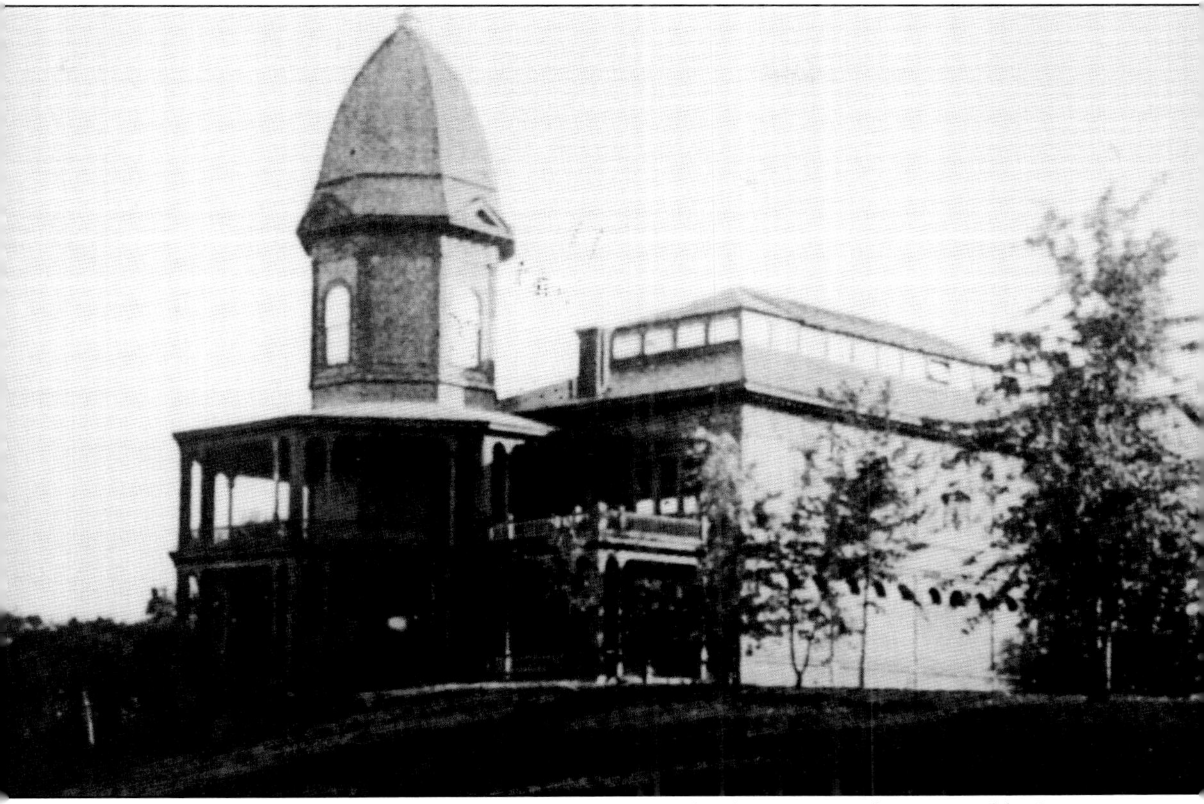

George West Museum of Art and Archeology in Round Lake. In 1887 the Honorable George West of Ballston Spa, a wealthy industrialist and inventor, gave the George West Museum of Art and Archeology (1887–1965) to the community. West was the inventor of the square-bottom paper bag that we use today. The museum housed many notable exhibits of geological mineralogical specimens, paintings and art of many kinds, Native American artifacts, bird collections, antiques, and many other articles of interest. Early in the twentieth century it was converted to the Round Lake High School.

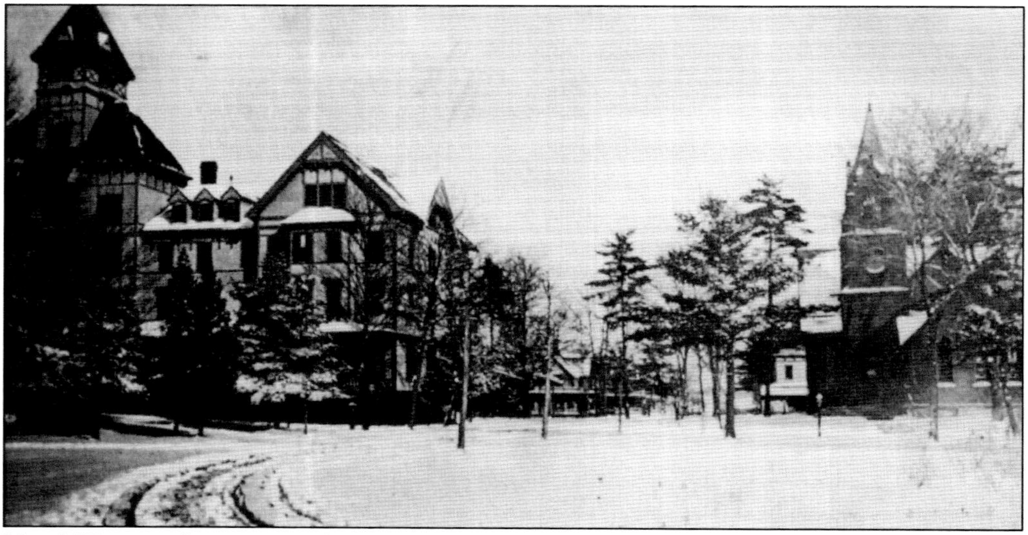

Hotel Wentworth, *c.* 1906. This winter scene pictures the Hotel Wentworth, which was built in 1878. It was situated just opposite the Methodist church. This hotel was privately operated and contained sixty rooms. Weekly dances were held, and in 1906 fire prevention equipment in the form of ropes and hooks was installed. In later years, this old hotel was renamed The Gotham Hotel. It was destroyed by fire in 1933.

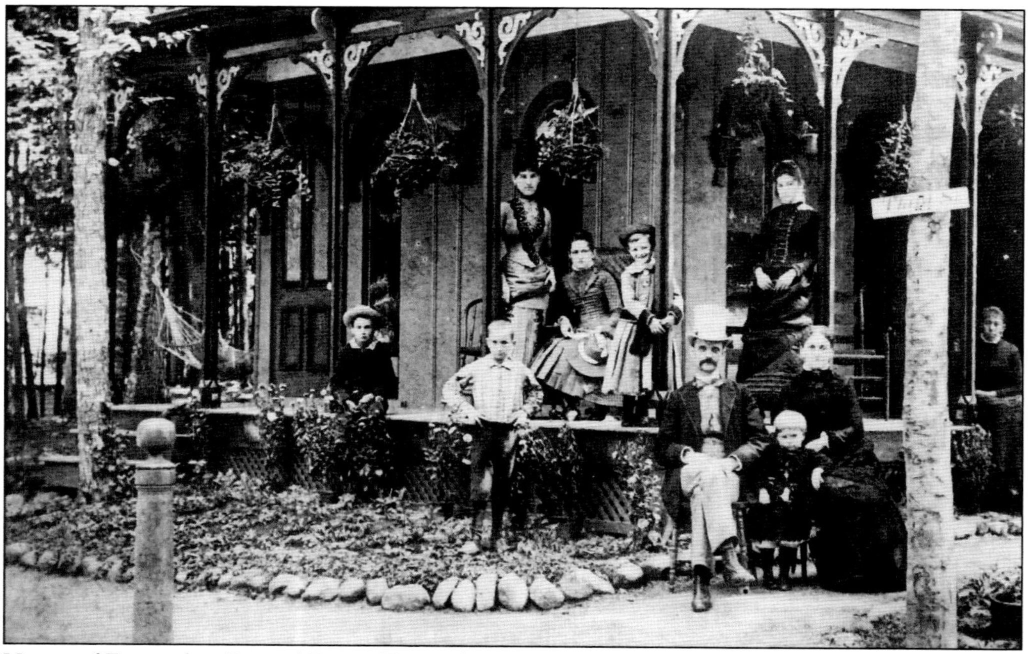

Home of Evangelist Samuel Jones. Evangelist Samuel Jones and his family are in front of their home on the corner of Third Street and Covel Avenue, Round Lake. Upon careful examination, you can find the name "Jones" spelled out in the flowers in the front of the porch.

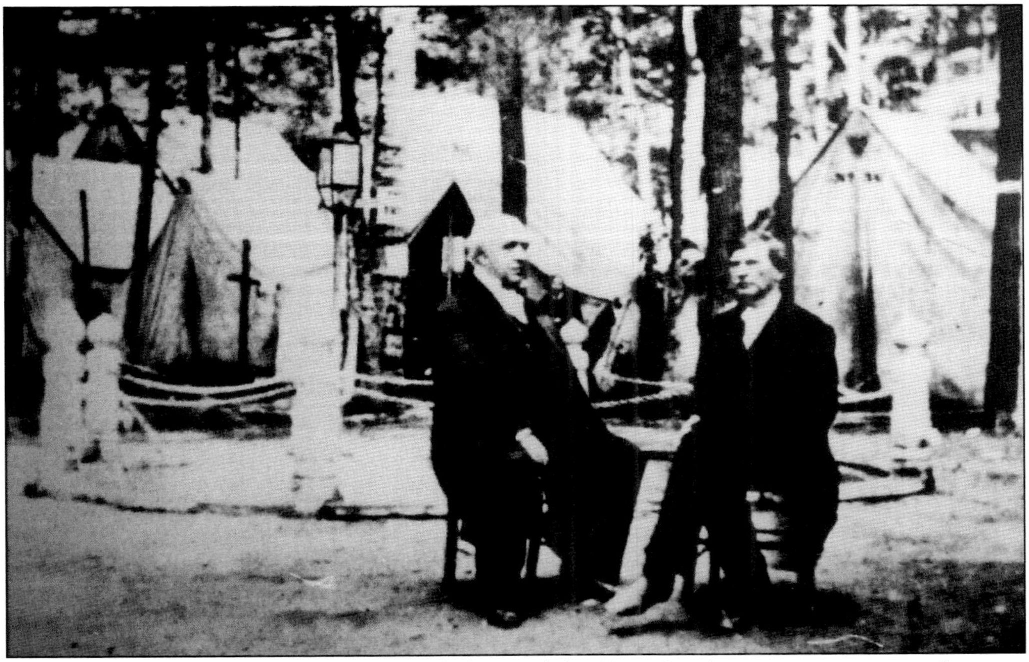

Bishop Peck and Bishop Simpson. Two bishops of the Troy Conference were in attendance at the campgrounds at Round Lake. Bishop Peck is seated to the left and Bishop Simpson is seated on the right. In the background is a row of tents used in the early years for guest quarters. In the extreme background, a few glimpses of the auditorium can be seen through the trees.

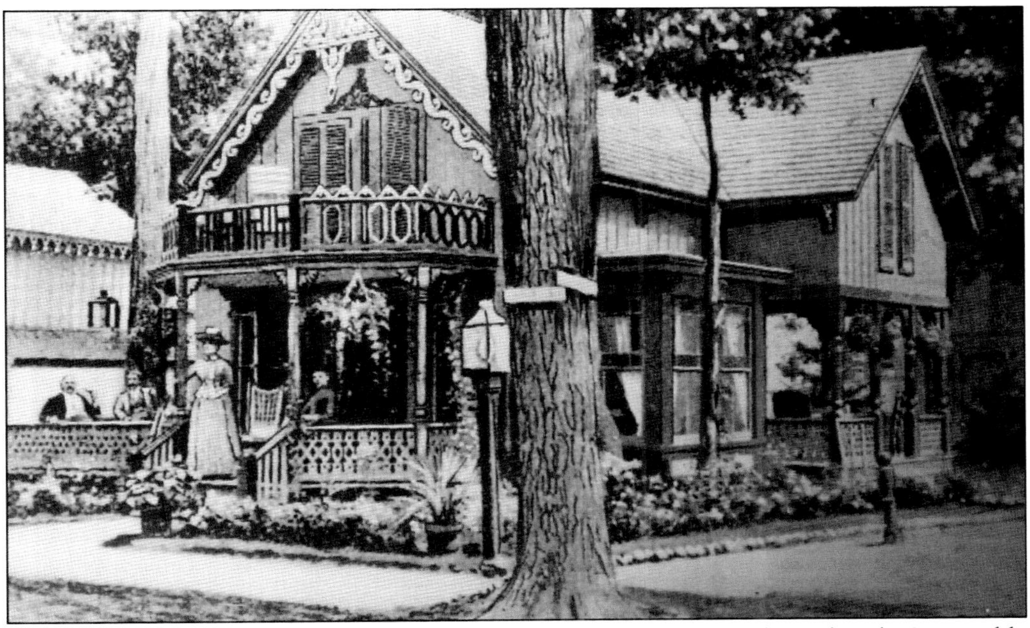

Hitts cottage, *c.* 1880. This is an illustrated view of the cottage that belonged to the Honorable Galen R. Hitts at the Round Lake Campgrounds. This residence is typical of the "cottages" that were to be found on the site.

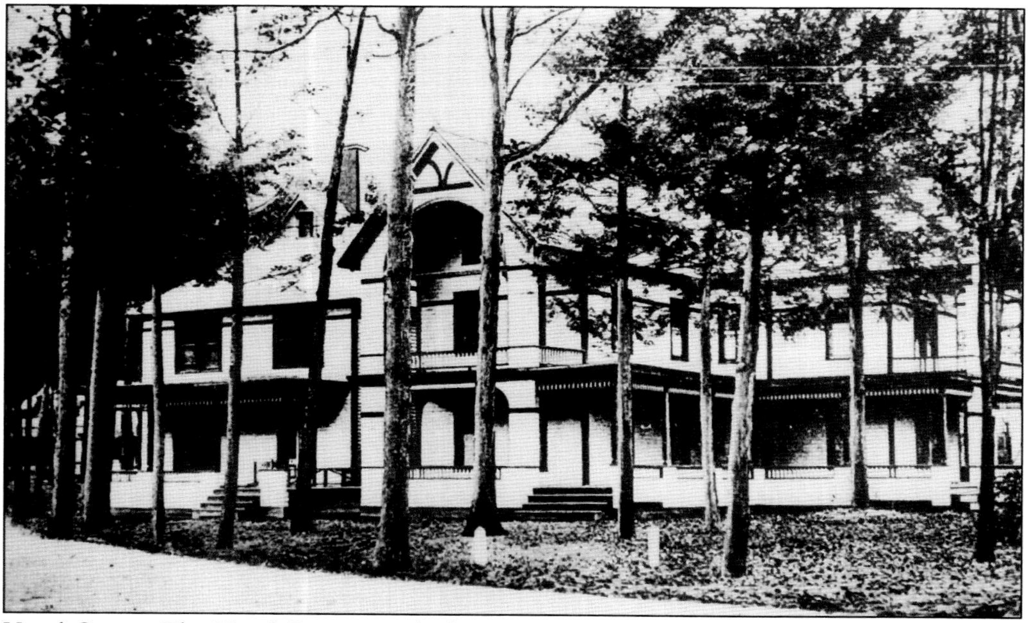

Hotel Orient. The Hotel Orient was built in 1880. It contained seventy rooms and was used as a hotel for nearly ten years. It was originally intended as a place of rest and recreation for missionaries returning from abroad. It also served as the Round Lake Summer School of Theology, the Round Lake Epworth League Institute, and the Women's Christian Temperance Organization. The building survived until 1956.

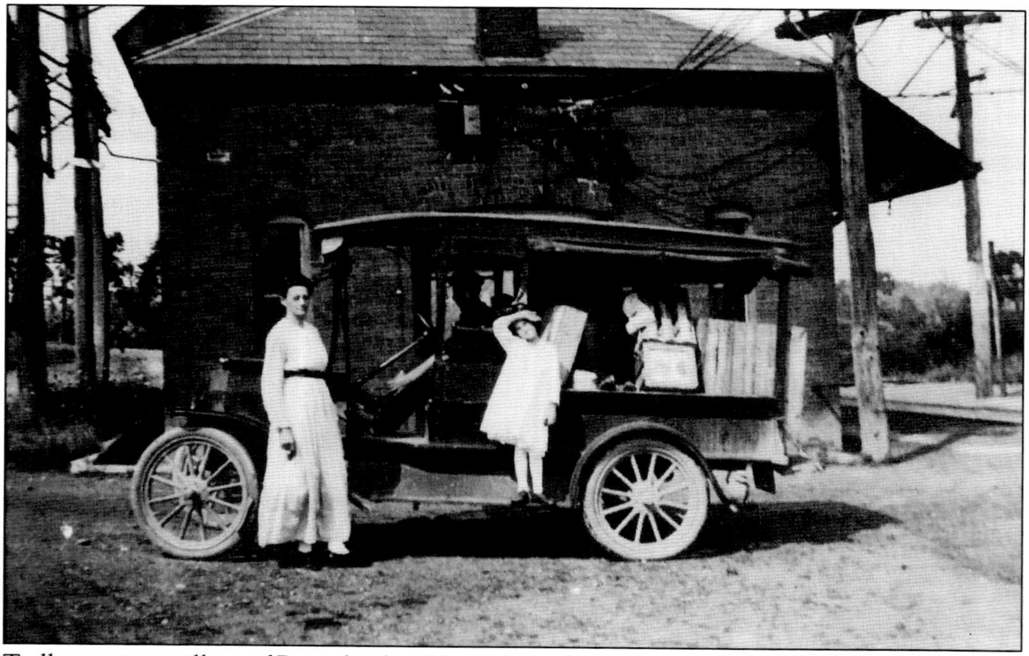

Trolley station, village of Round Lake. The Wilmot family waits at the trolley station at Round Lake to pick up a delivery from the 3 pm express. The trolley station stood between present-day Route 9 and the shore of Round Lake.

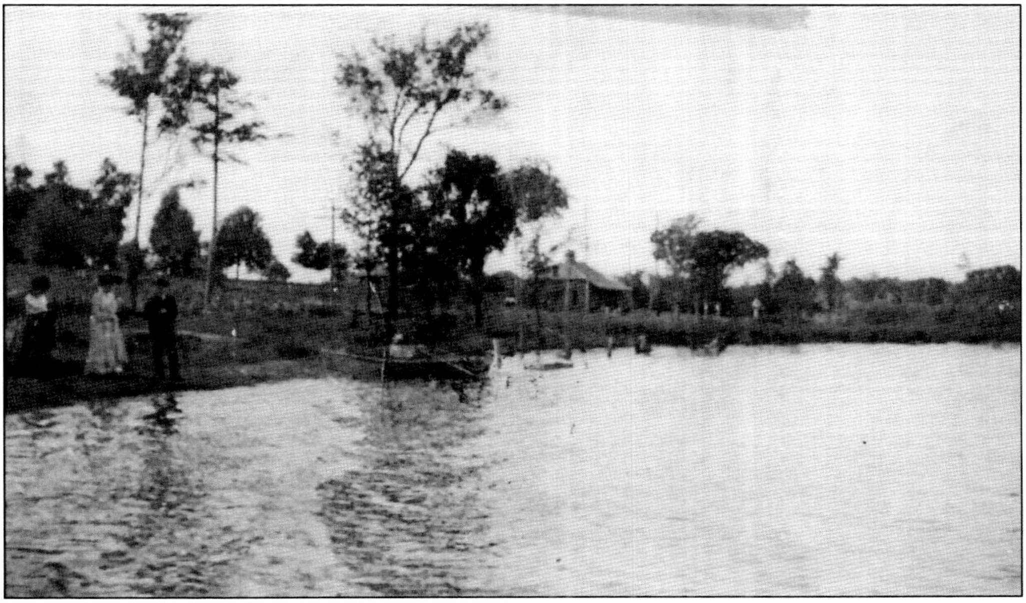

View of Round Lake with trolley station.

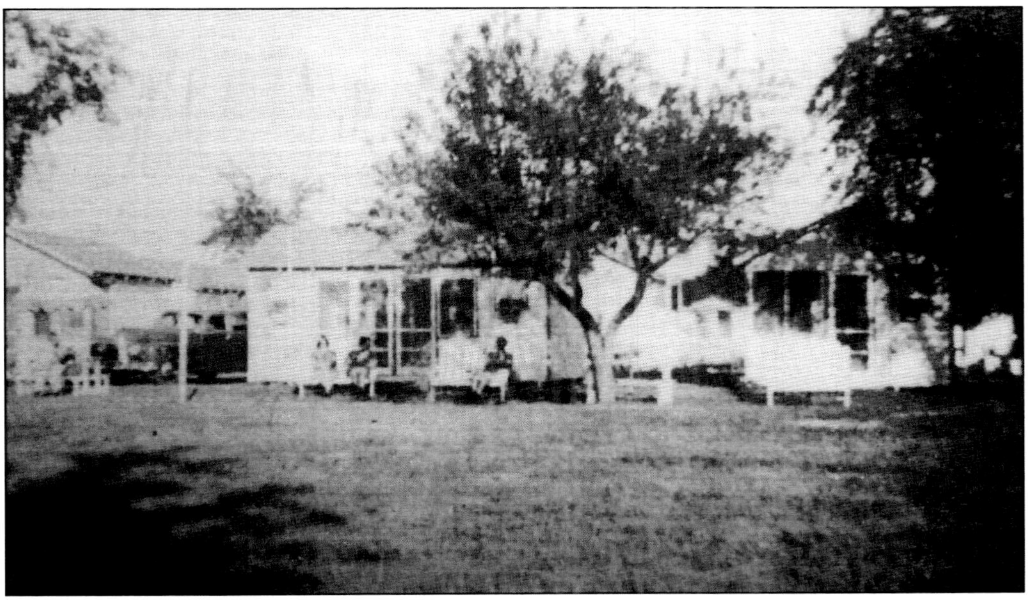

Lakeside Park, c. 1930s. Lakeside Park, situated on the north end of the lake on U.S. Route 9, was a modern cabin and trailer camp. Before present-day motels and recreational vehicles existed, little cabins like these were used by travelers for overnight stays along the highway as they traveled to their destinations.

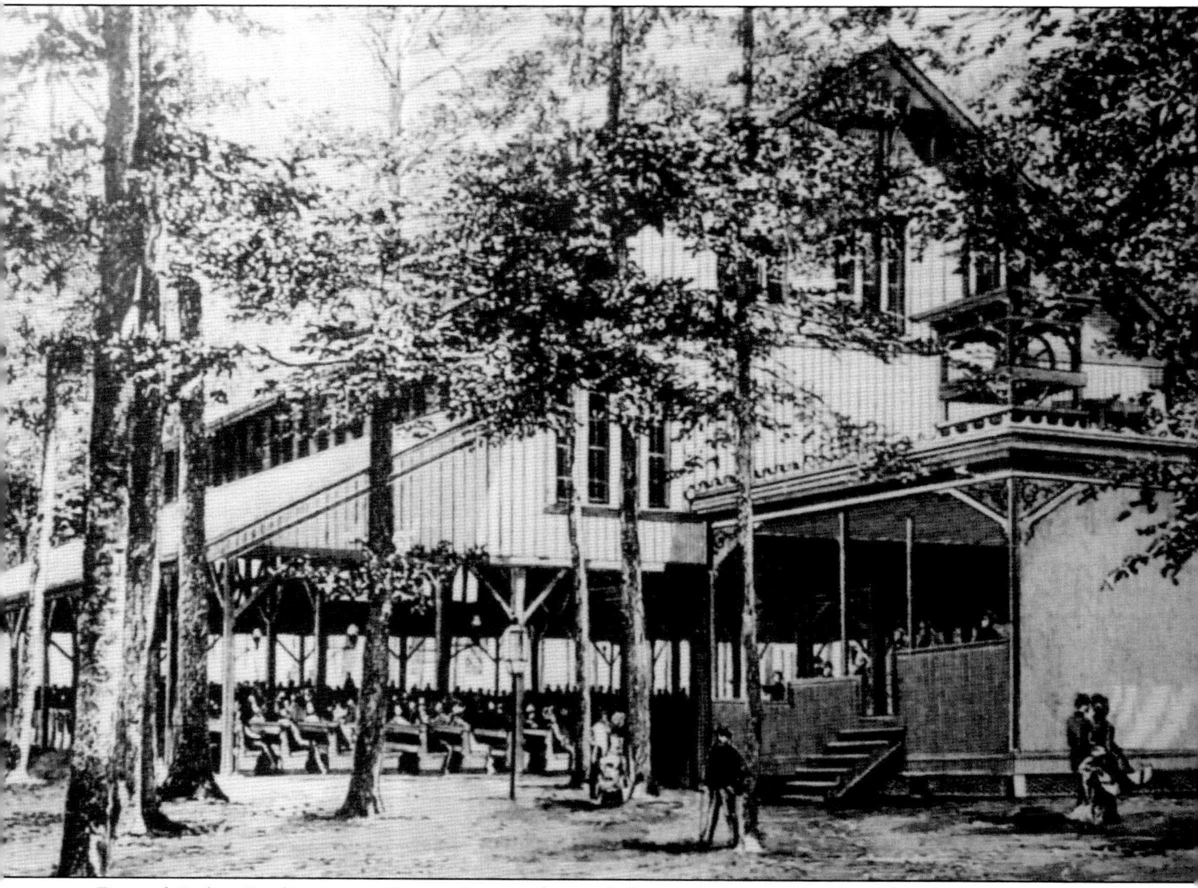

Round Lake Auditorium. An early woodcut of the auditorium at Round Lake Campgrounds shows the speaker' platform on the right. A canvas canopy was erected on framework in 1876 at the location where the auditorium would later stand. In 1884, an 80-by-140-foot building was erected which seated two thousand people. The dedication was held on July 19, 1885, with the Reverend J.P. Newman, DD, officiating. In 1888 the building was enlarged to make room for the famous Terris Tracker organ built in 1847. By 1912, the auditorium was completely closed in and permanent seating was installed.

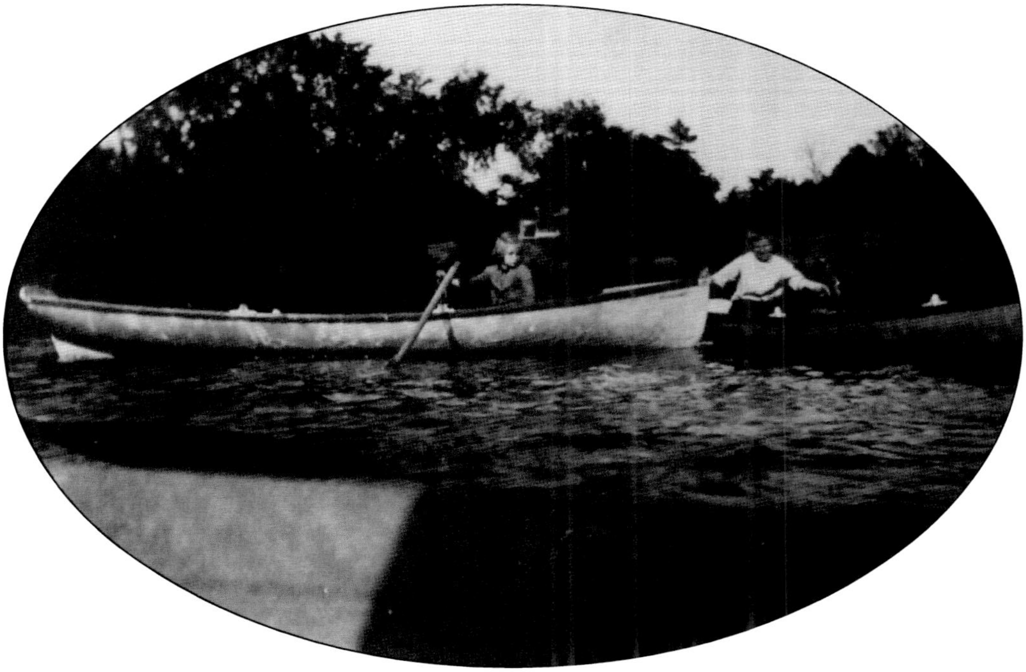

On the Lake. Two youngsters enjoy Round Lake on a summer's day. It would appear that there is a small problem with rowing the boats ashore.

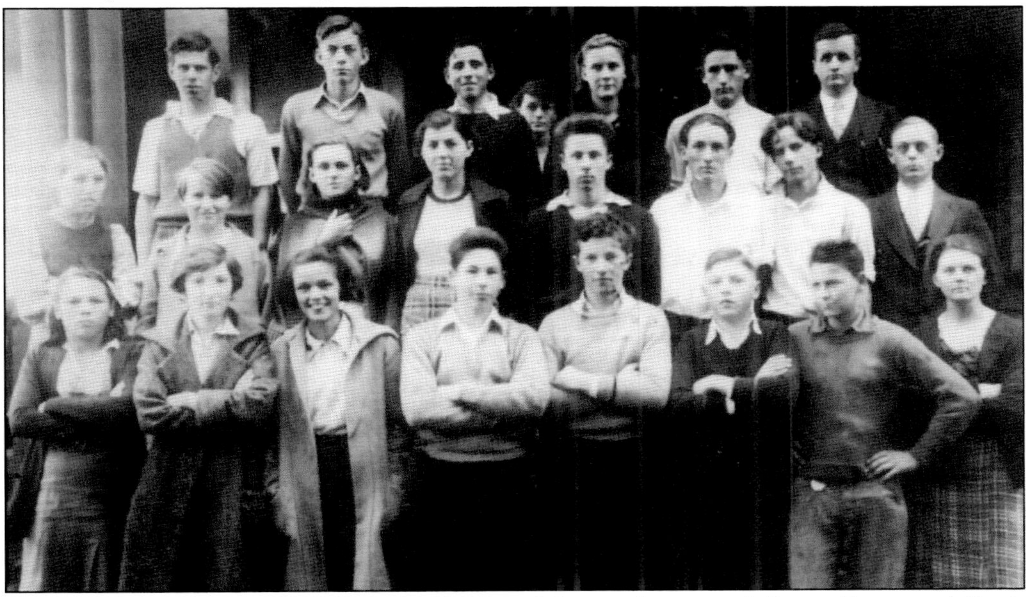

Round Lake High School students, 1935. From left to right are as follows: (front row) Doris Barber, Joyce Hill, Betty Foster, Robert Hitchcock, Robert Northrup, Ray Fuller, David Tritt, and Mildred Ruhle; (middle row) Annabelle Evans, Betty Urban, Betty Williams, Mildred Corp, Norman Hitchcock, Bernie Herrington, Allen Herrington, and Mr. Sprague; (back row) Harold Osborne, Clifford Corp, Harold O'Brien, Miss Watts, Stella Williams, George Clements, and Dr. Goldsmith.

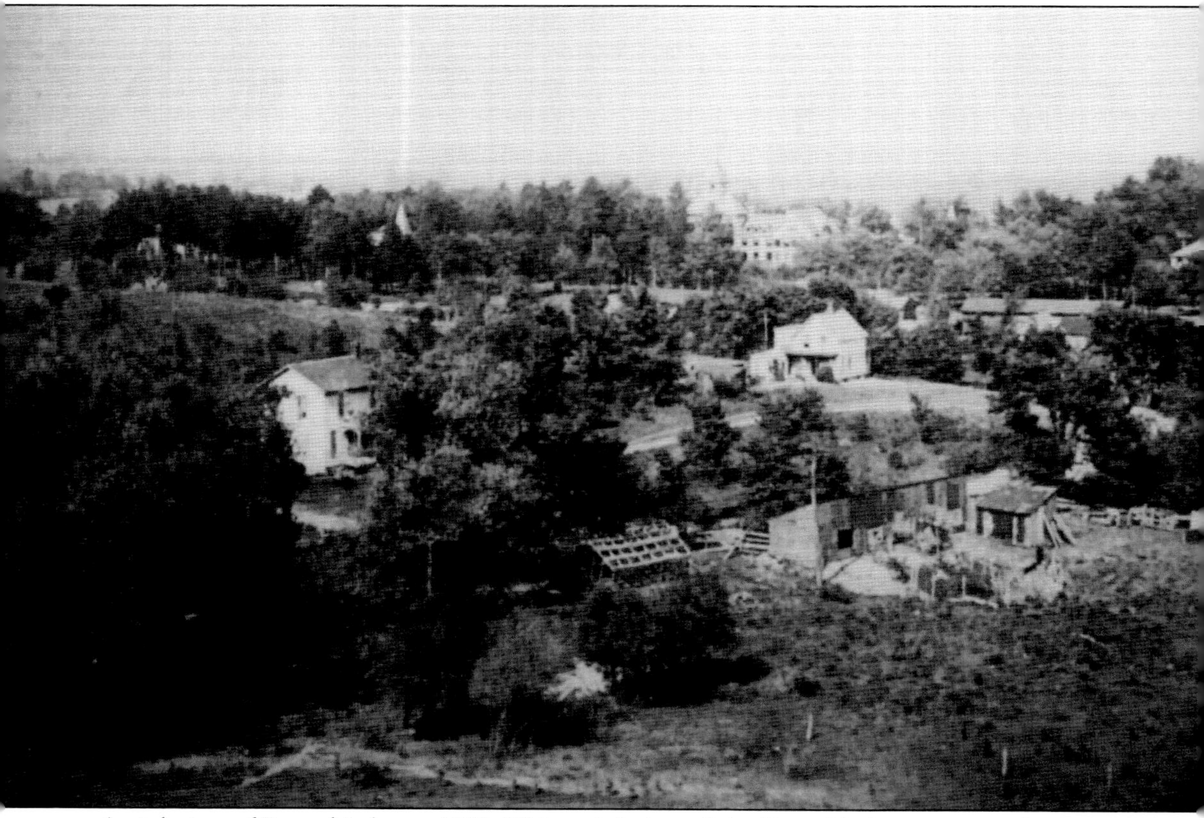

Aerial view of Round Lake, c. 1900. This aerial view of the Round Lake area was taken near today's exit eleven on the Northway. The large hotel in the background is the Wentworth, which eventually burned down. The lake is in the extreme rear of the picture behind the trees. The Burnham House (The Pines) is located at the extreme right of the picture. The homes of the Brenn and Simkins families and Tim O'Brien can be seen in the center of the photograph.

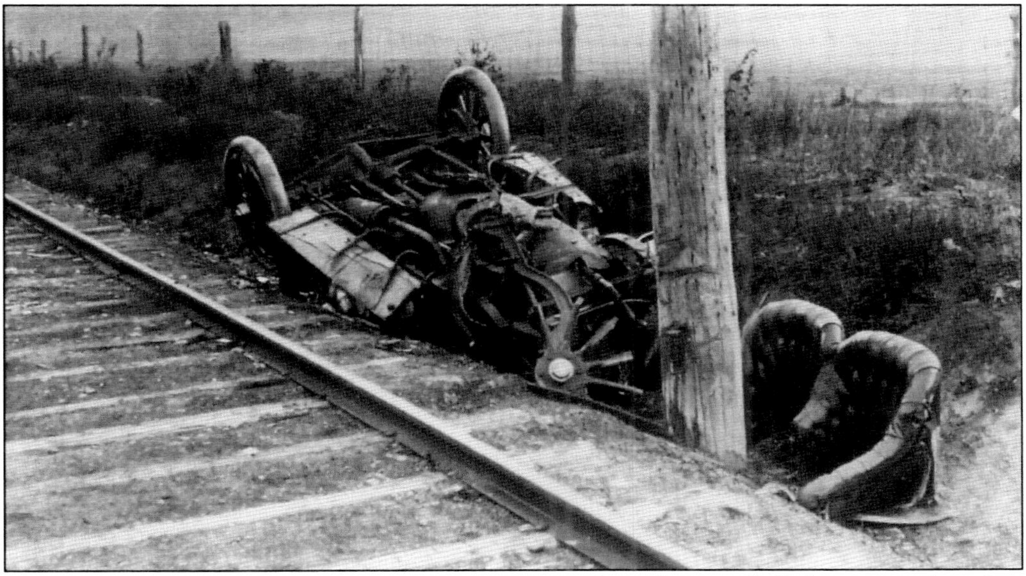

Automobile accident, 1909. Dr. Pierson C. Curtis, age forty-five, was killed in an accident that occurred on Labor Day, September 6, 1909, at the Golf Links Crossing on Goldfoot Road in Round Lake. Dr. Pierson C. Curtis was a well-known physician in Round Lake, where he had practiced for nearly twenty-five years. He was a graduate of Albany Medical College in the class of 1884. The collision occurred when the Hudson Valley Railway Car No. 125 traveling northbound from Round Lake hit the automobile broadside at the Golf Links Crossing on Goldfoot Road.

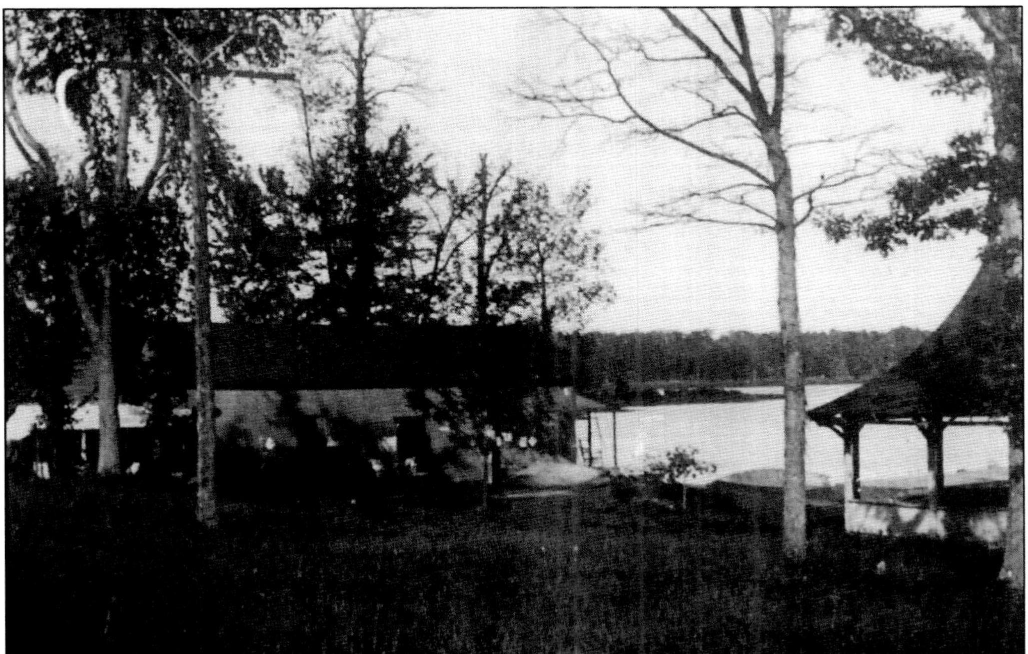

Boathouse, *c.* 1910. On the western shore of Round Lake are the boathouse and rental service owned and operated by Henry Corp. The bandstand is on the extreme right.

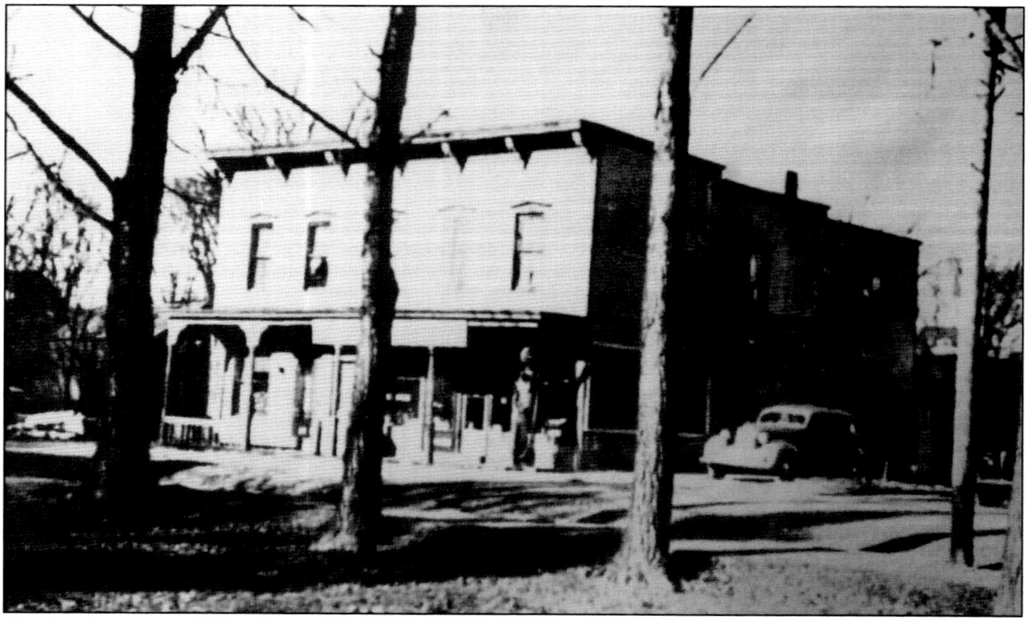

Shafts Store, c. 1937. For many years Shafts was an important business in the community, serving the needs of the people of Round Lake and the surrounding area. It is located at the foot of Round Lake Hill, just east of Exit 11 on the Adirondack Northway 87. Now owned by Sue Shull and Karyl Hopp, it is known as Bear Blossoms Flowers and Gifts.

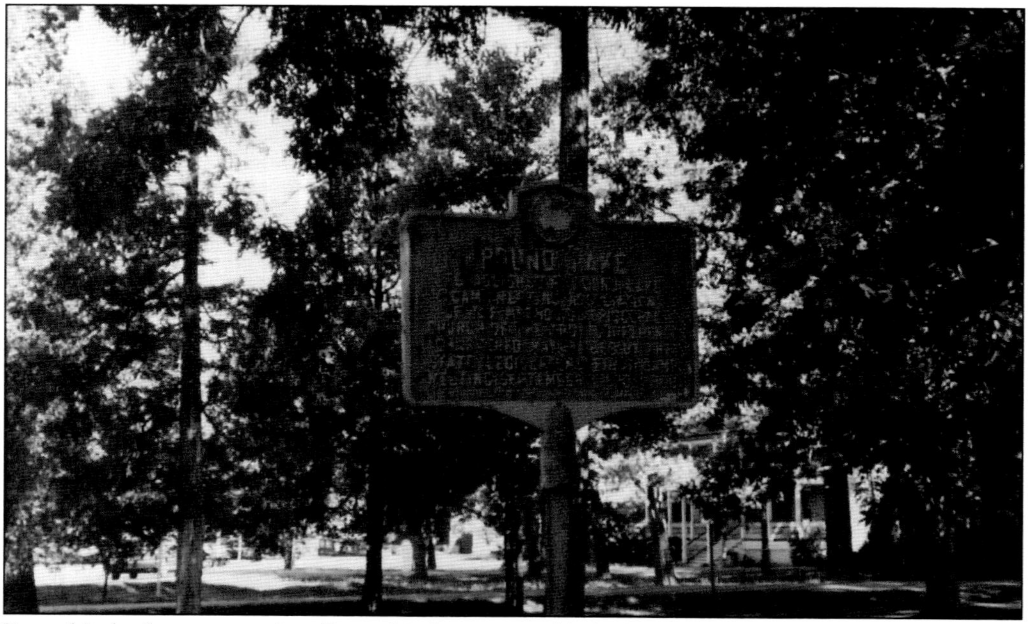

Round Lake historic marker. Round Lake was established by the Round Lake Camp Meeting Association of the Methodist Episcopal church of the Troy Conference and chartered May 5, 1868, by the state legislature. The first camp meeting was held September 1–10, 1868. This designated landmark marker was erected by the Town of Malta in 1968, one hundred years after the first camp meeting.

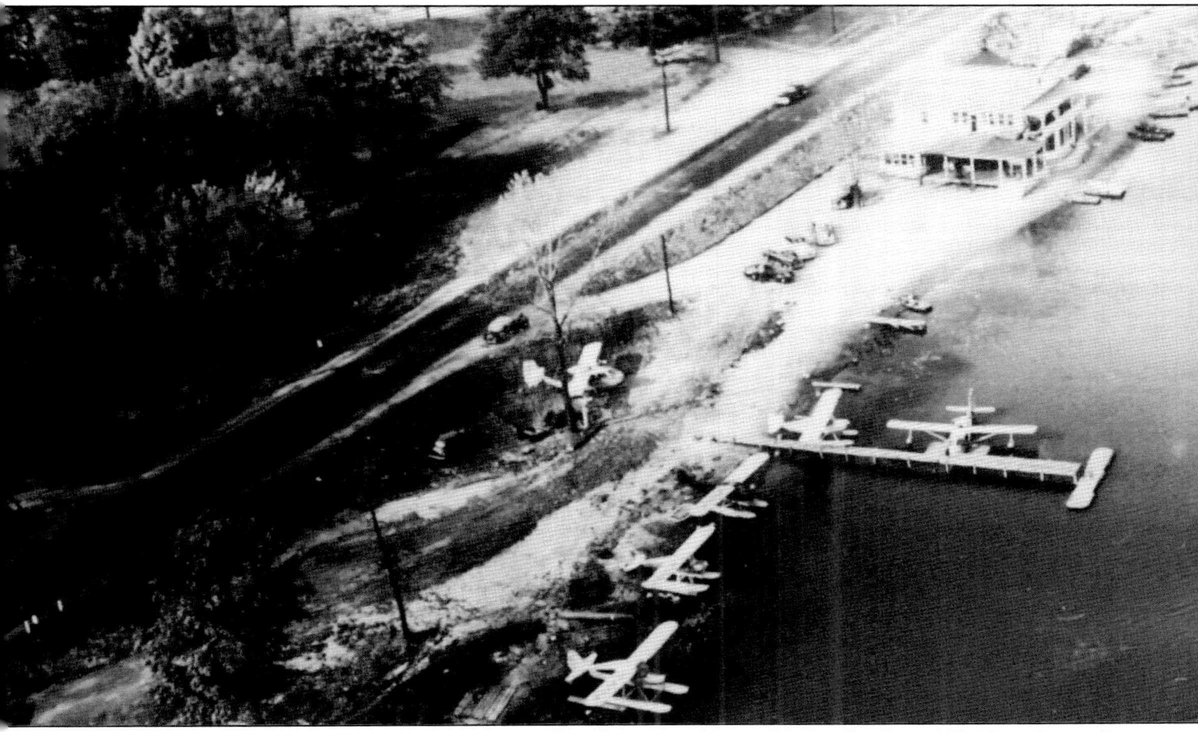

Aerial view of Round Lake boathouse. The boathouse on Round Lake, built in 1926 by Howard Lenox, was the site of Lavery's Seaplane Service from 1938 to 1954. World War II created a demand for licensed pilots, and the Army Air Corps accepted over two thousand pilots trained at Lavery's flight school. The boathouse and seaplane base were landmarks along U.S. Route 9 as well as favorite stopping places for residents and travelers alike. This 1947 photograph shows the beach that "Lew" and "Mike" created from swampland. The boathouse foundation is still visible today.

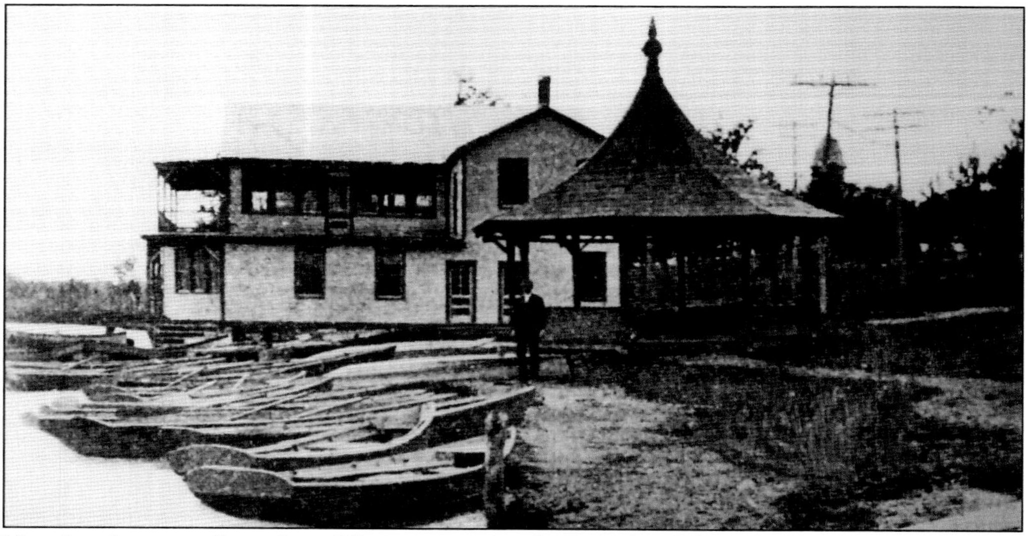

New boathouse and pavilion. This is an early photograph of the casino and bandstand that stood on the western shore of Round Lake near U.S. Route 9. In the early years, the casino was operated by Howard Lenox. Between the years 1936 and 1954, the Casino Restaurant and Boat Rentals was operated by Margaret Lavery, the wife of Lewis F. Lavery (who operated Lavery's Seaplane Service). In 1954, the business moved to the east side of Round Lake, and the old casino was demolished.

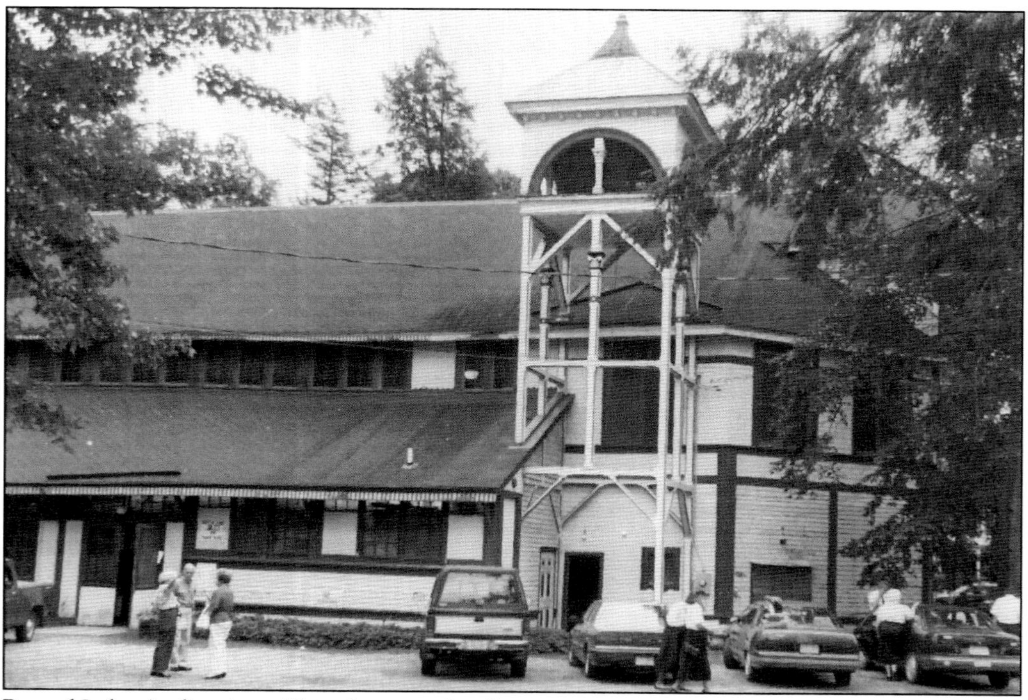

Round Lake Auditorium. This photograph offers a more recent view of the auditorium.

Six

Saratoga Lake

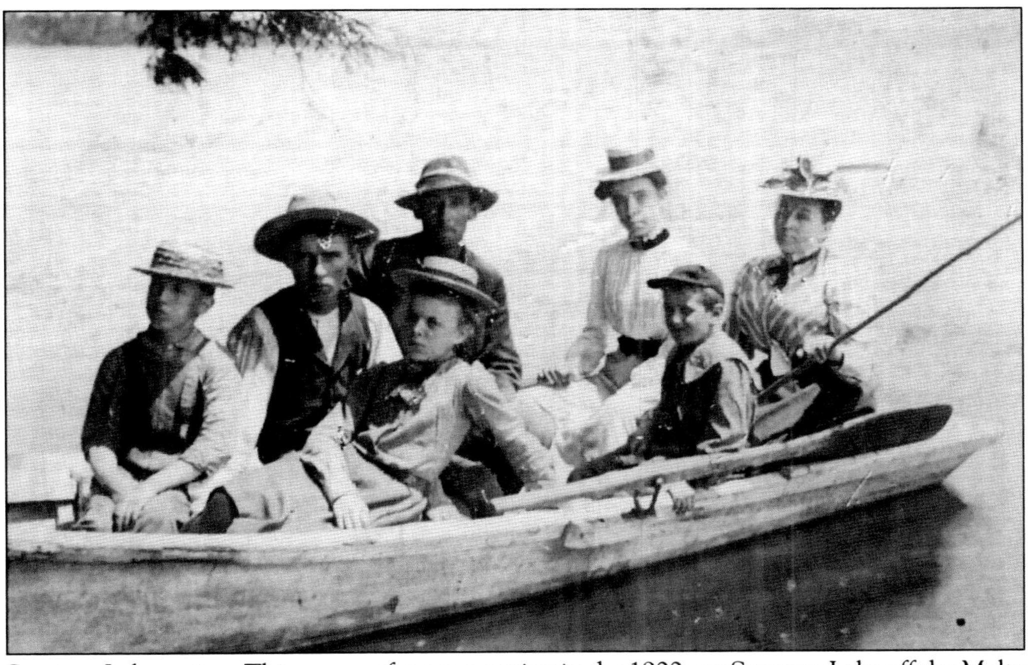

Saratoga Lake outing. This was an afternoon outing in the 1900s on Saratoga Lake off the Malta shore. Pictured from left to right are Charles Gueperoux, John Ramsdill, Grace Gueperoux, Simeon Morehouse, Mary Ramsdill, Armand Gueperoux, and Ida Firth Gueperoux.

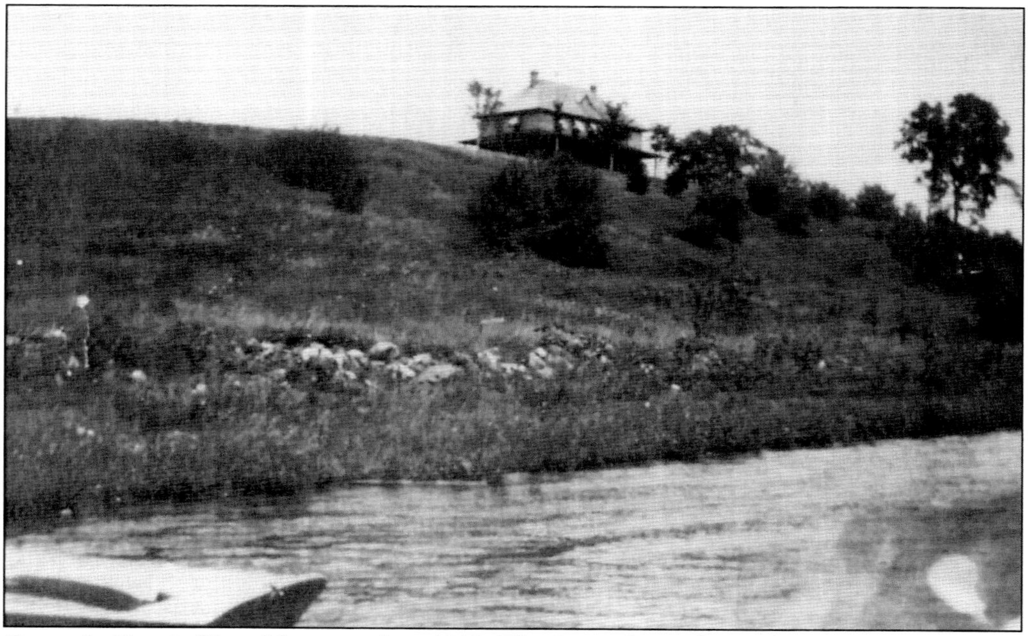

Ostrander/Austin/Kunz Homestead, *c.* 1910. The home located at Riley's Cove on Saratoga Lake was built in the 1900s. Mr. Austin, president of the Pullman Car Company and second owner of this home, installed lavatories in each bedroom exactly like the ones found on the Pullman cars.

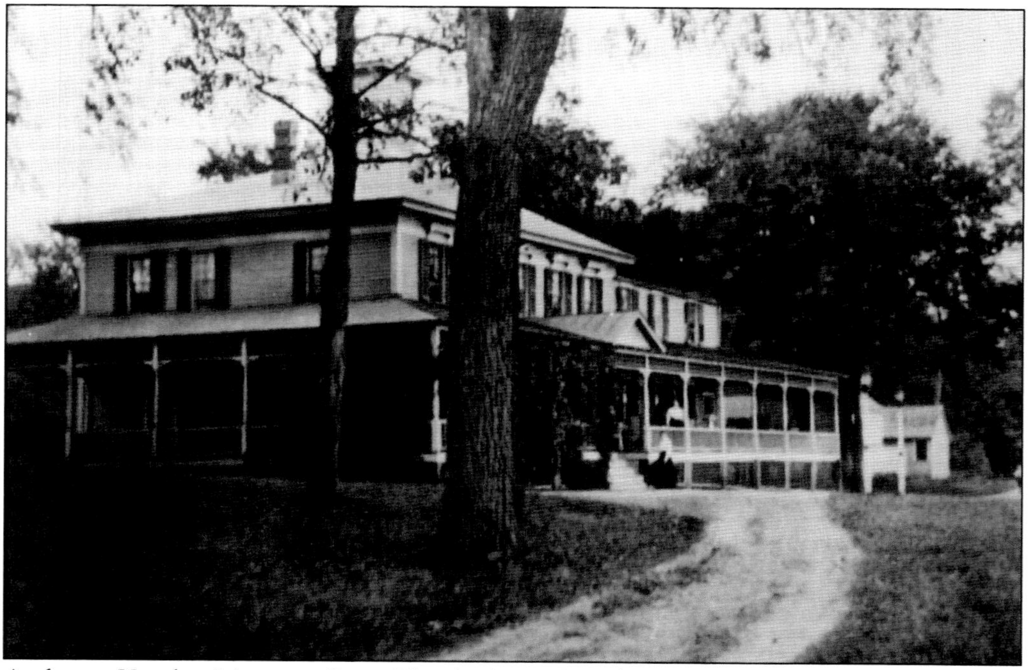

Anderson Hotel at Manning Cove. The Anderson Hotel at Manning Cove on Saratoga Lake stood on the corner of Edgewater Park and Manning Road. It burned down many years ago.

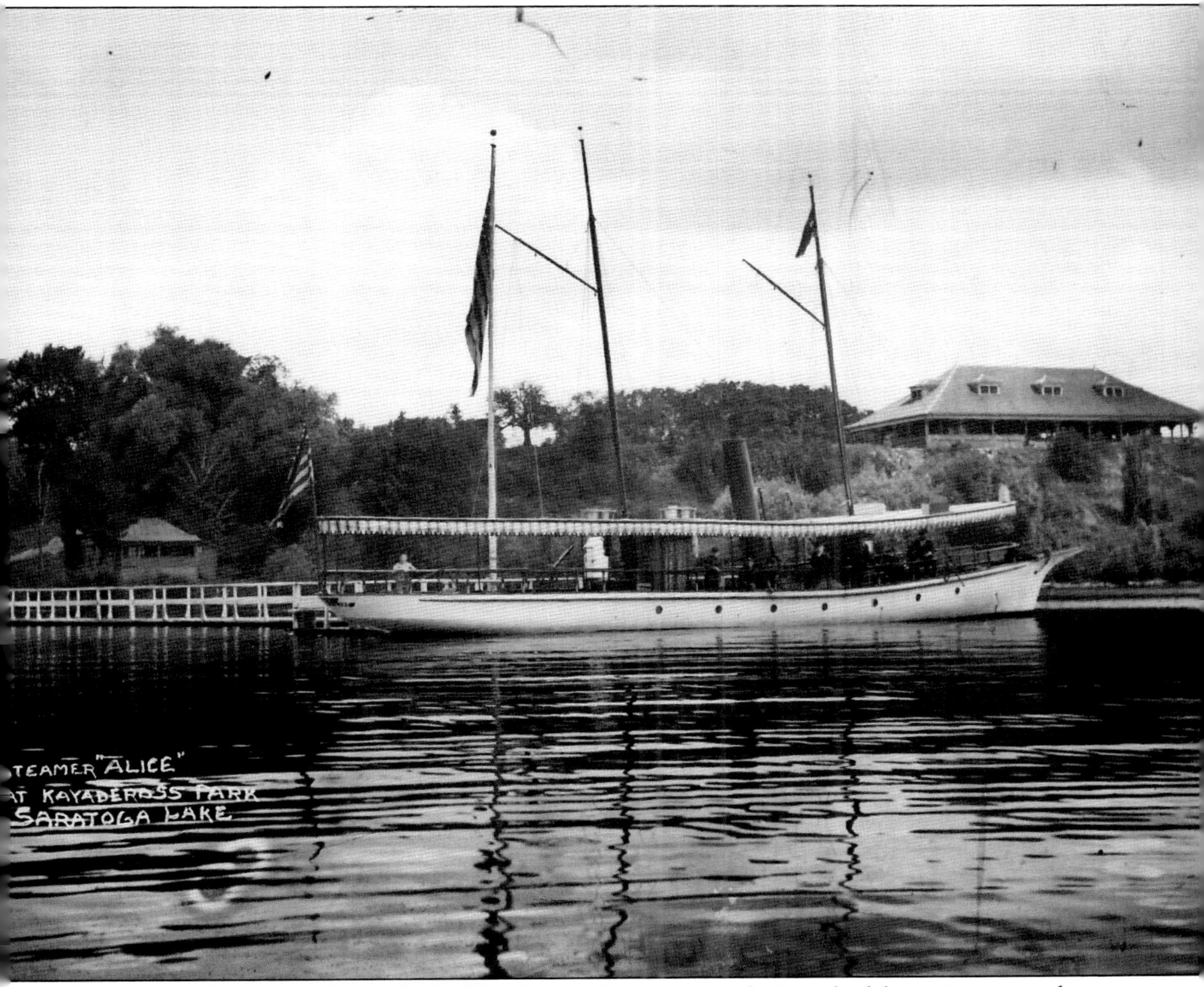

Steamer *Alice* at Kaydeross Park. The beautiful steamer with its colorful awnings must have been a lovely sight on Saratoga Lake. Also shown here are the long pier and the pavilion of Kaydeross Park (in the background on the hill to the far right). Although Kaydeross Park was located geographically in Saratoga Springs, the *Alice* and the park were favorite recreational spots for Malta residents. The *Alice* was named after the wife its owner, Thomas C. Luther, a resident of Malta and owner of the White Sulphur Springs Hotel. Captain Arnold piloted the steamer *Alice* and lived in Wayville, NY.

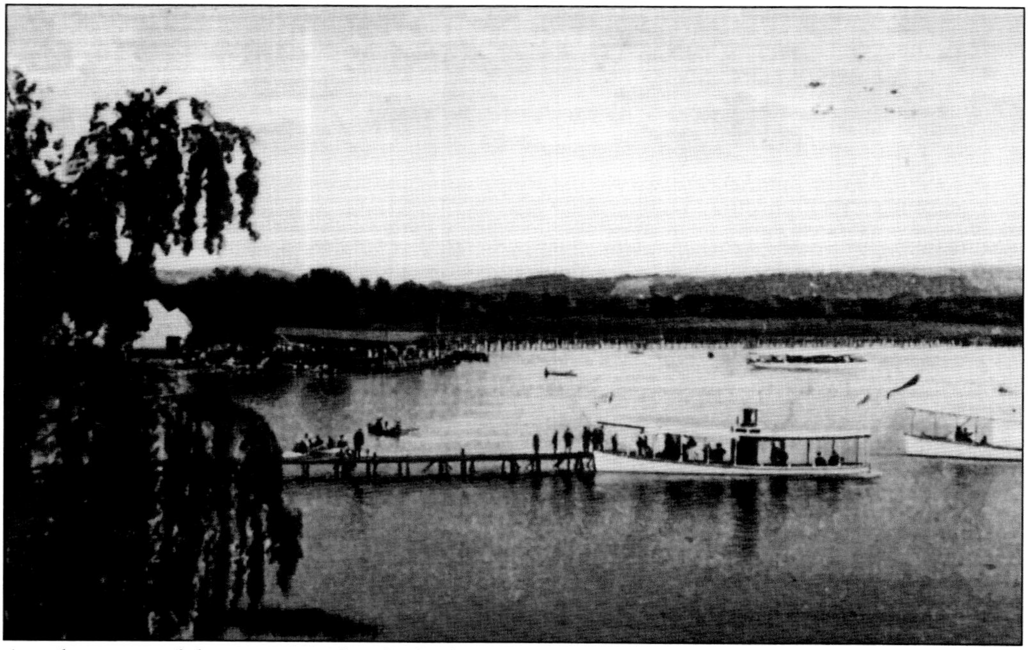

Another view of the steamer *Alice* docked at Kaydeross Park.

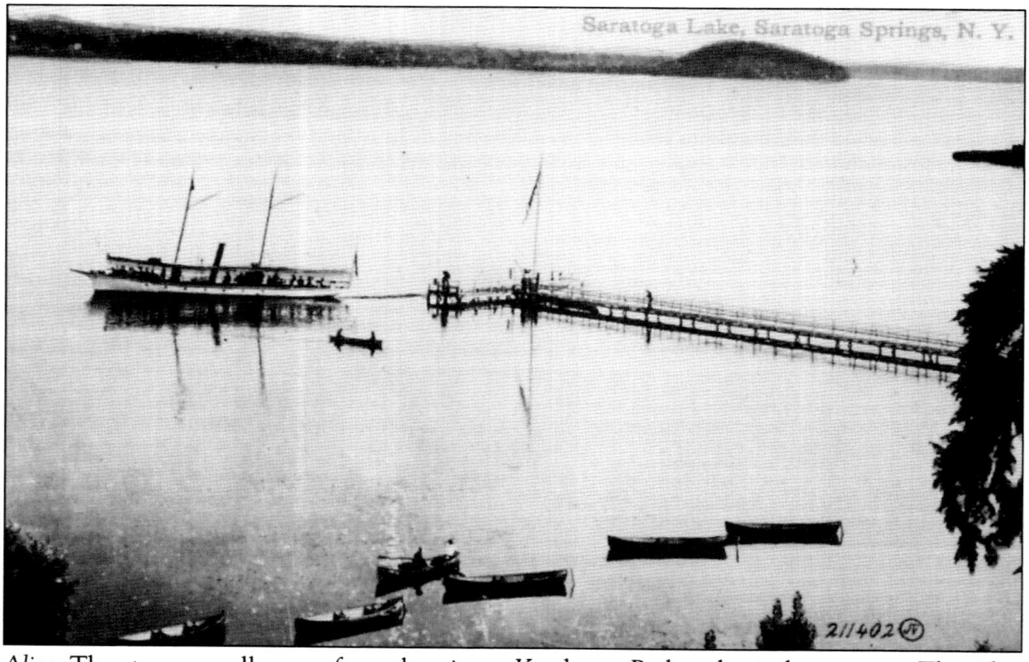

Alice. The steamer pulls away from the pier at Kaydeross Park to begin her voyage. The *Alice* will turn toward the southern shore and make her way toward the White Sulphur Springs Hotel in full sight of the Malta shores.

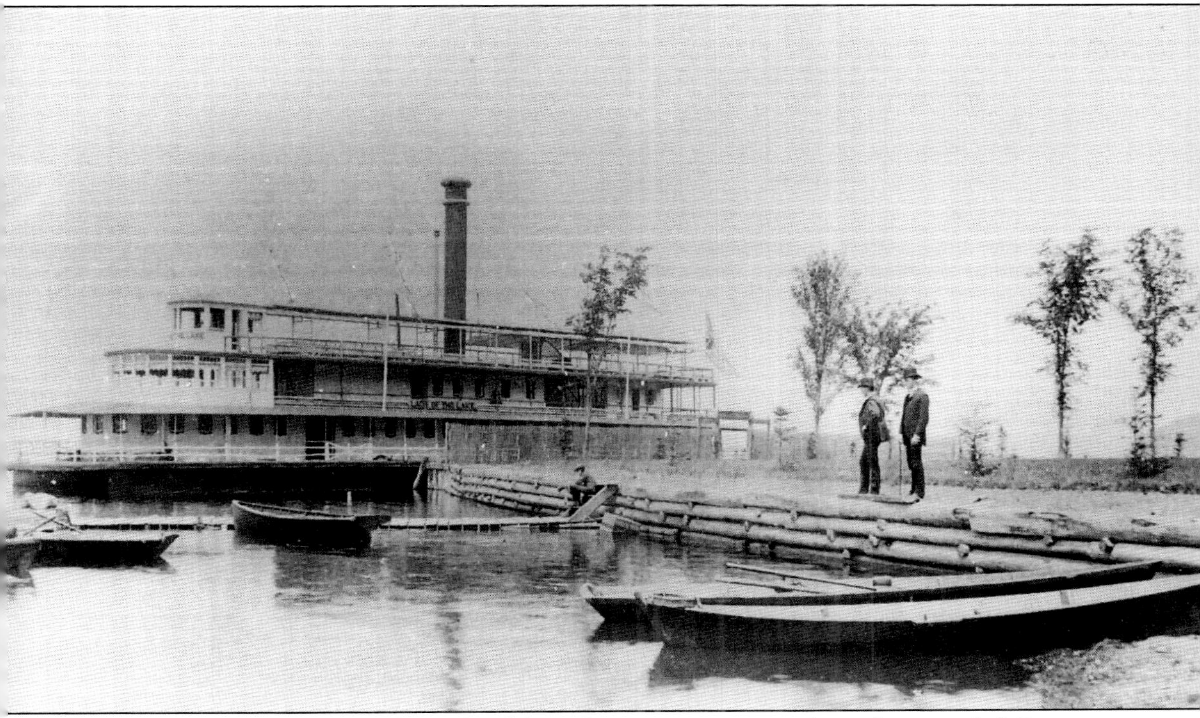

Lady of the Lake, c. 1880. The *Lady of the Lake* was an excursion boat that traveled Saratoga Lake daily. While the exact location of this mooring spot is undetermined, it is extremely likely that it is at or near the White Sulphur Springs Hotel. This was a favorite recreation spot for Malta families.

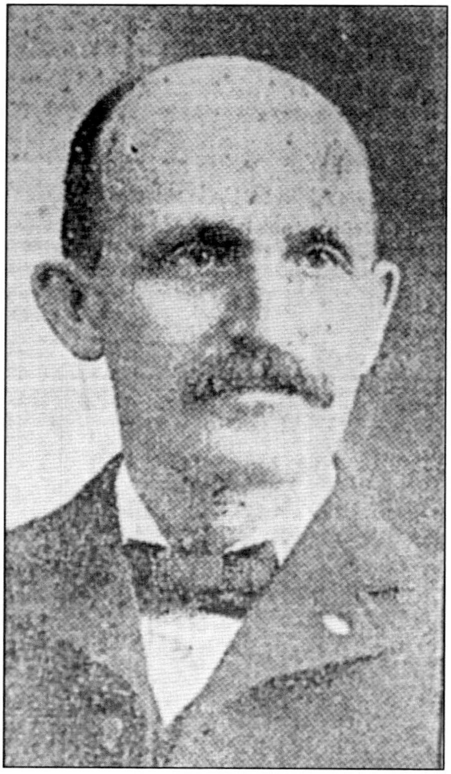

Fancher J. Riley (1861–1926). The son of Benjamin Riley was born in the old Riley Hotel, which stood on the shores of Saratoga Lake at Riley's Cove. Mr. Riley developed the west shore of the lake and gradually erected many camps and cottages there; the area became known as "Chinatown." At the time of his death in 1926, he owned virtually all the lands upon which these cottages had been built. Mr. Riley also served as supervisor to the town of Malta for two successive terms (1917–18 and 1919–20) and as the organist in his church, the First Methodist Episcopal Church of Malta Ridge.

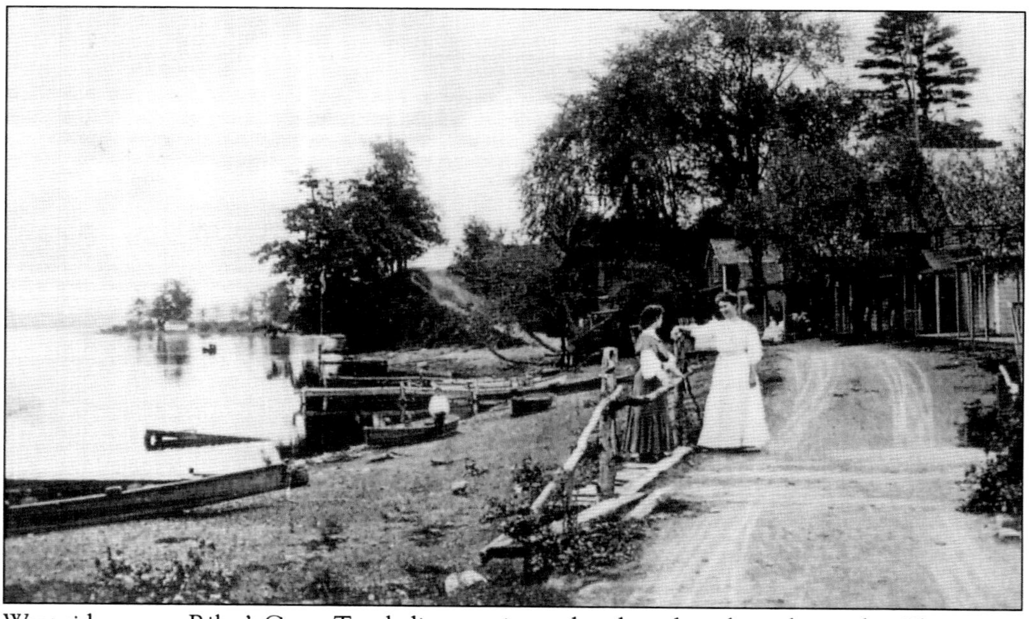

West side camps, Riley's Cove. Two ladies are pictured as they chat along the road at Chinatown on Saratoga Lake. We can observe that the road climbs up and over a hill; Stony Point can be seen in the far background.

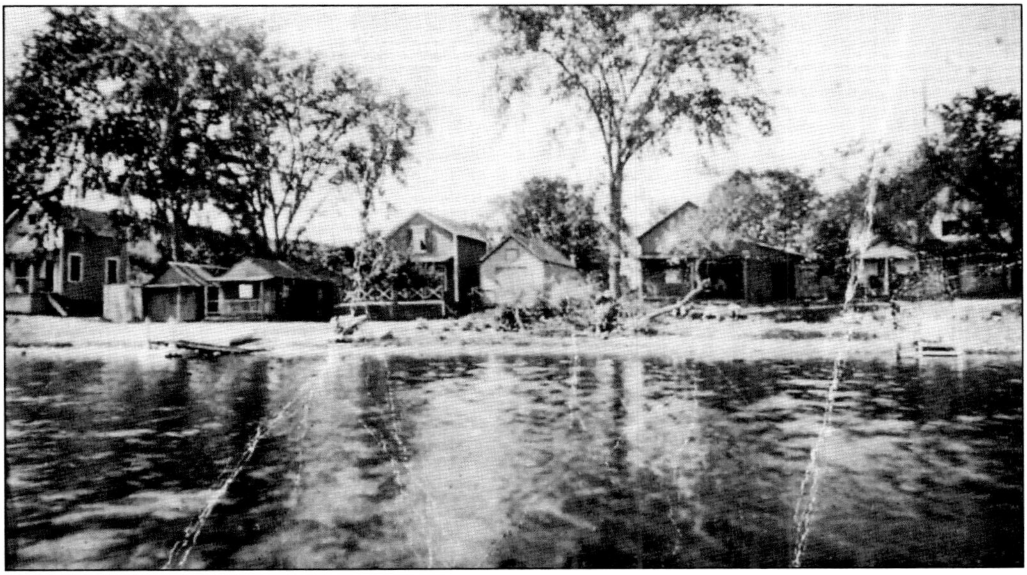

Riley's Cove, Saratoga Lake. This picture clearly shows the architecture of the area once called Chinatown.

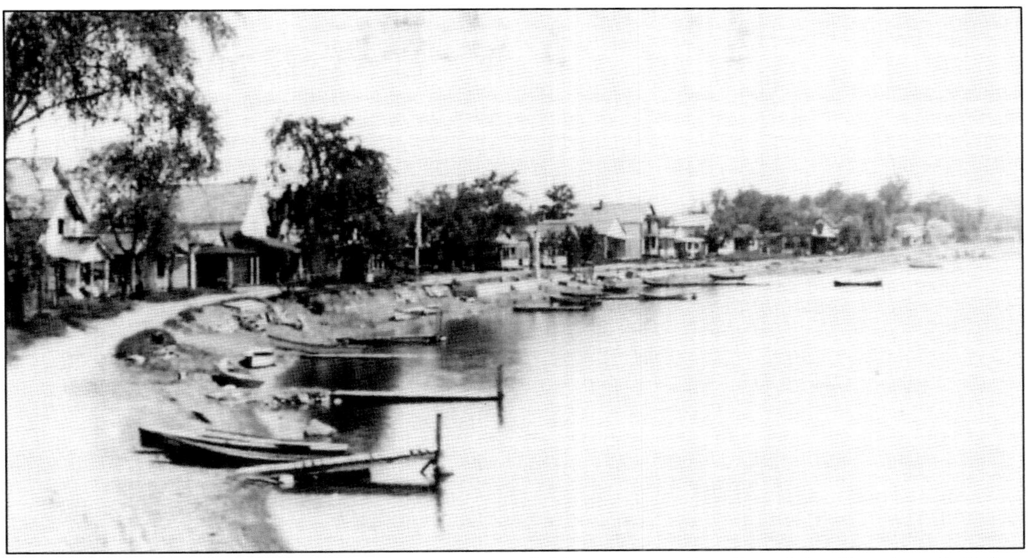

West side of Saratoga Lake. The community of Chinatown, developed by Fancher J. Riley, acquired its name from the paper oriental lanterns hung on the buildings in the evenings by the residents of the area. It was lovely to see the lantern lights projected out onto the water. In addition, the architecture and character of the cottages themselves contributed to the name given to this area.

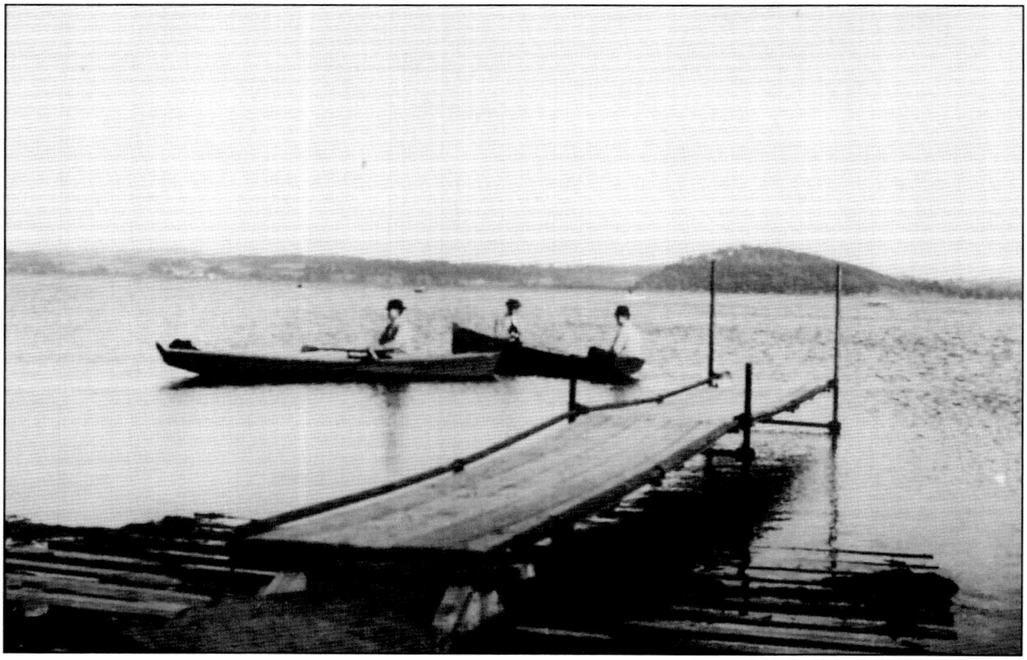

Saratoga Lake view. Boaters are seen on Saratoga Lake from a dock at Riley's Cove, Chinatown. Snake Hill can be seen in the distance across Saratoga Lake.

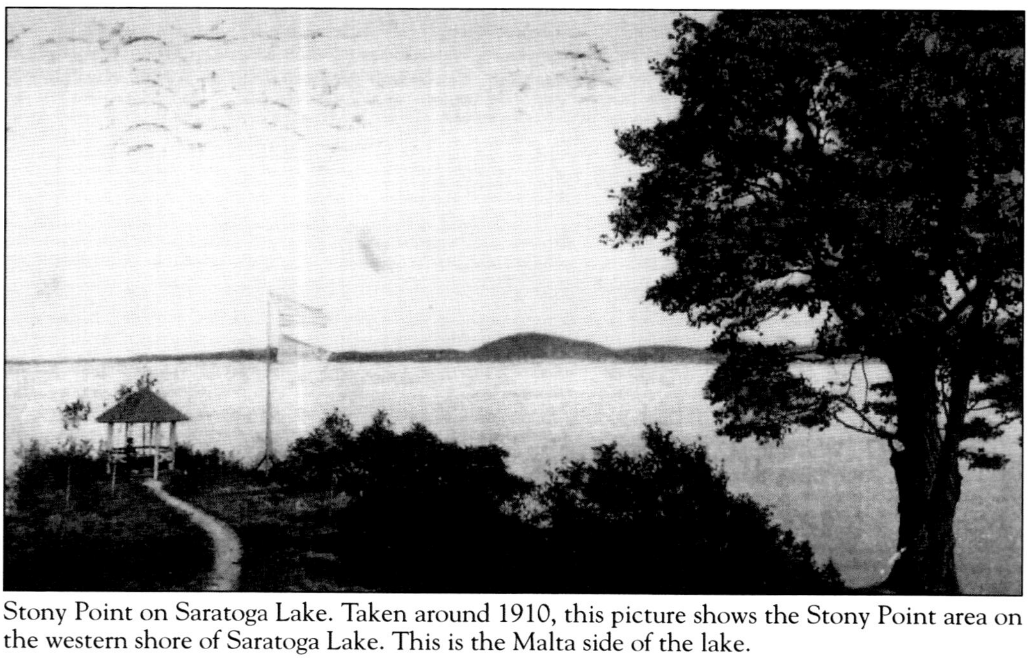

Stony Point on Saratoga Lake. Taken around 1910, this picture shows the Stony Point area on the western shore of Saratoga Lake. This is the Malta side of the lake.

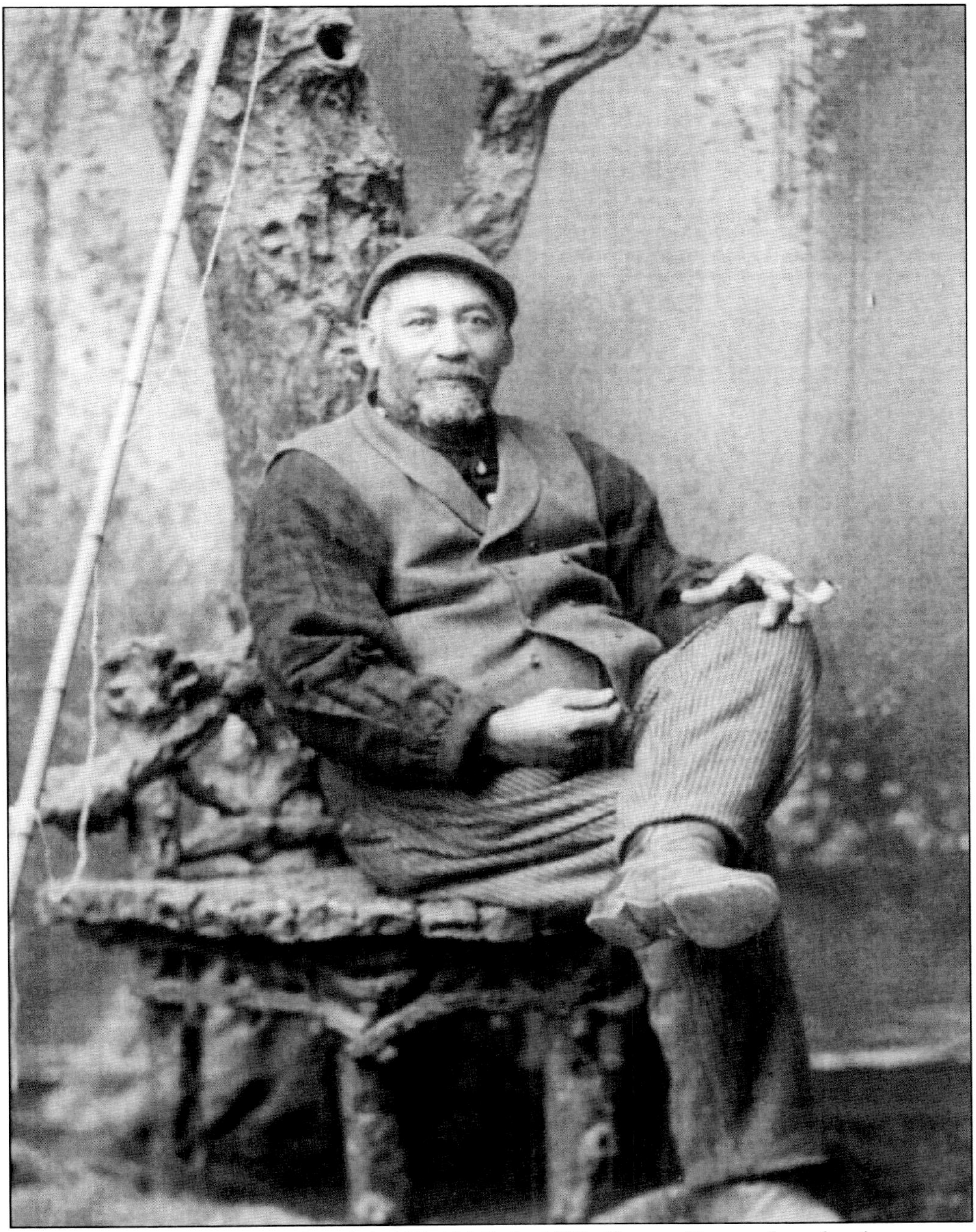

George Crum, a.k.a. George Speck (1825–1914). In 1882, George Crum, whose legal name was George Speck, opened a restaurant called Crums Place in Malta on the west side of Saratoga Lake near Riley's Cove. Soon it was well known for his famous preparation of excellent fish and wild game dishes. He and his sister-in-law, Aunt Kate Weeks, are also credited with the invention of the Saratoga Chip, known commonly today as the potato chip. George Crum was born in Saratoga Springs in 1825. He lived for many years in the Malta area, and he died in 1914.

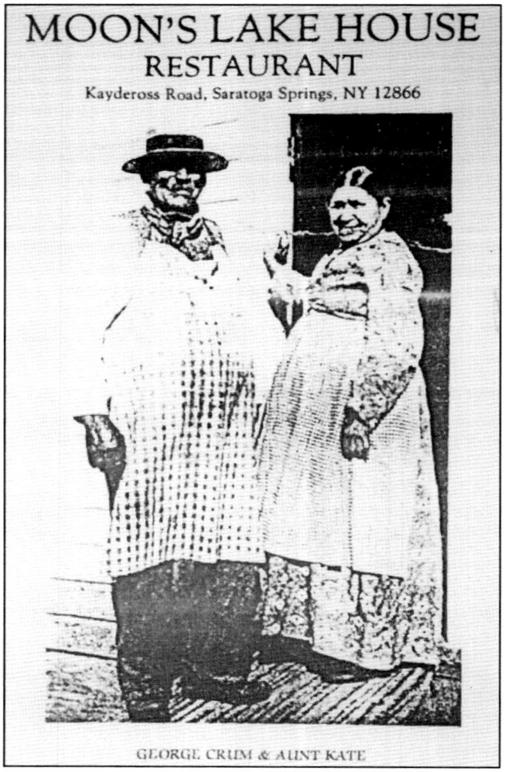

George Crum and Aunt Kate. George and Aunt Kate were in charge of the kitchen at Moon's Lake House on Saratoga Lake, which opened in 1853. In the second year of Moon's operation, a patron sent his french fries to the kitchen claiming that they were soggy. Viewing this problem with some hostility, George sliced potatoes extremely thin and cooked them in a kettle of boiling grease. When the potatoes were finished cooking, he salted them and sent them to the guest. The potatoes, called Saratoga Chips, were a huge success. When asked why he chose the name Crum, George replied that a crum(b) was larger than a speck, which was his given name.

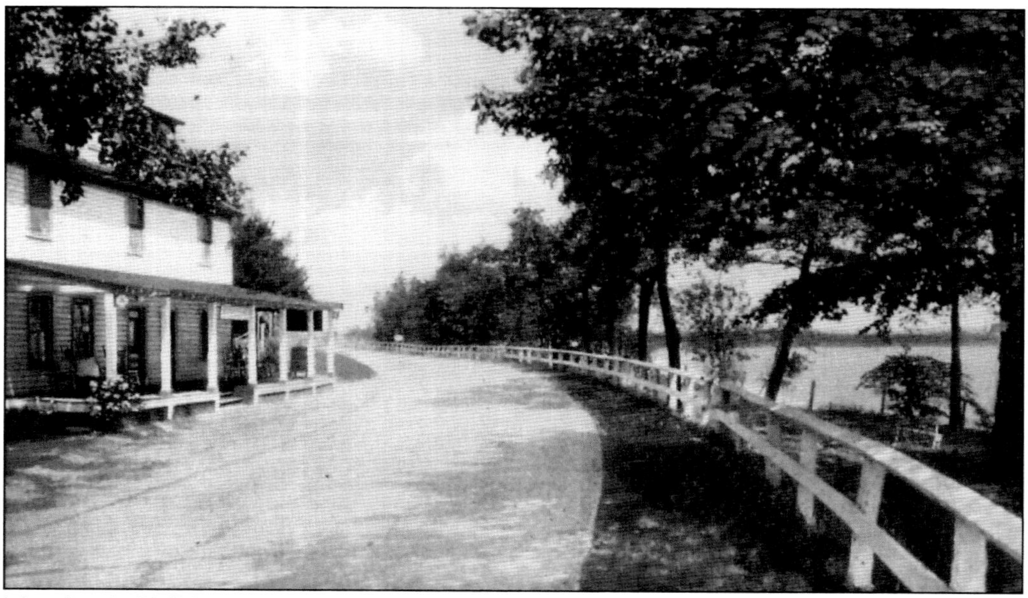

Monahan's Cliff House on Saratoga Lake. During the 1930s, Monahan's was a popular local tavern. It was located in a beautiful spot at the southern tip of Saratoga Lake. When the road was eventually widened, the building was torn down.

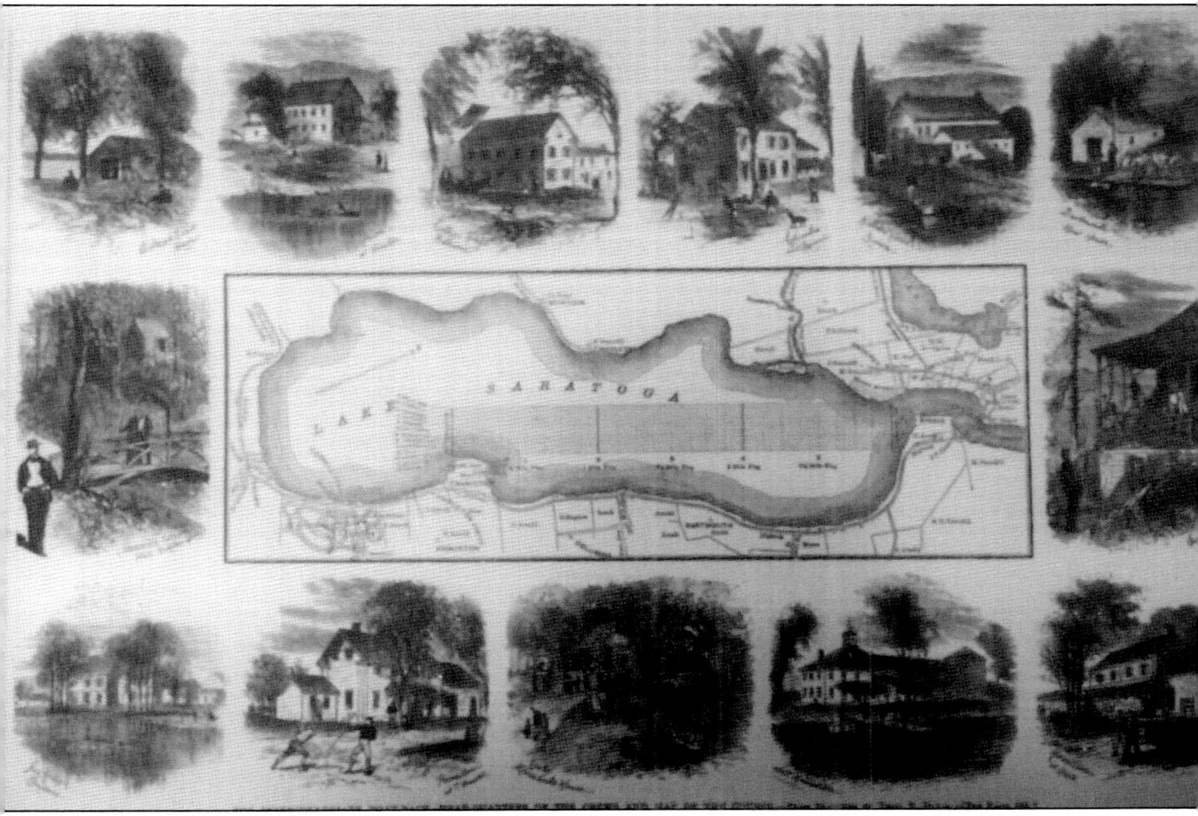

Intercollegiate boat races, 1875. The intercollegiate boat races held at Saratoga Lake were conducted on a course running from the Snake Hill area to the outlet of the lake at Fish Creek. The headquarters of the various crews participating in the race are visible in this picture. Participating universities were Williams, Cornell, Amherst, Bowdoin, Brown, Columbia, Wesleyan, Princeton, Dartmouth, Yale, Hamilton, Harvard, and Union. This picture was taken from a print in *Harpers Weekly* dated July 24, 1875. Cornell University made its headquarters in Malta.

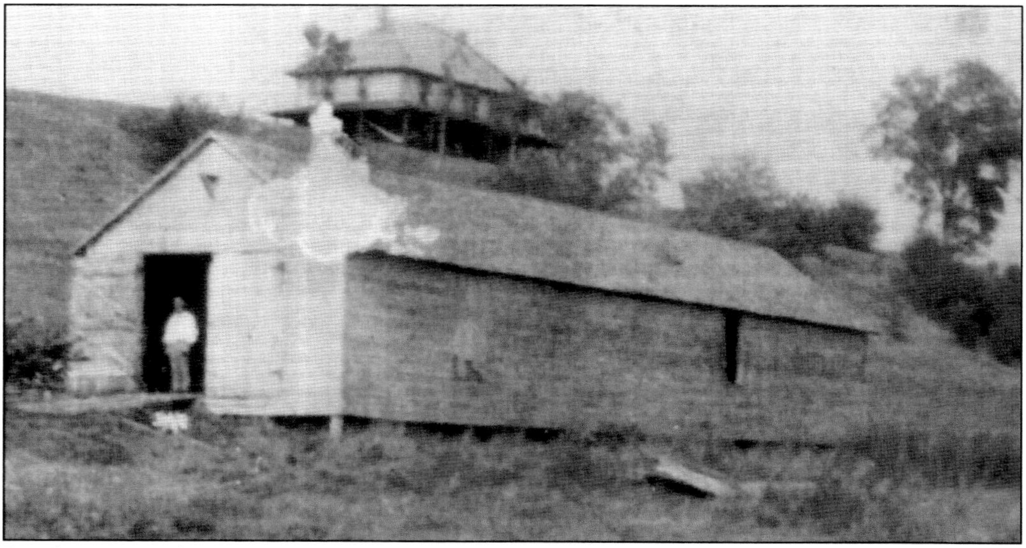

Boathouse at Riley's Cove, *c.* 1904. This structure today belongs to Ernest and Marion Kunz, and their home can be seen in the background. The boathouse was once used by the Cornell University rowing team. In the summer of 1890, Robert Fitzsimmons, a famous Australian boxer, trained in the Ostrander Boat House and stayed at the Hotel Piscatory near Manning Cove. In 1897, Fitzsimmons defeated Jim Corbet to become the heavyweight boxing champion.

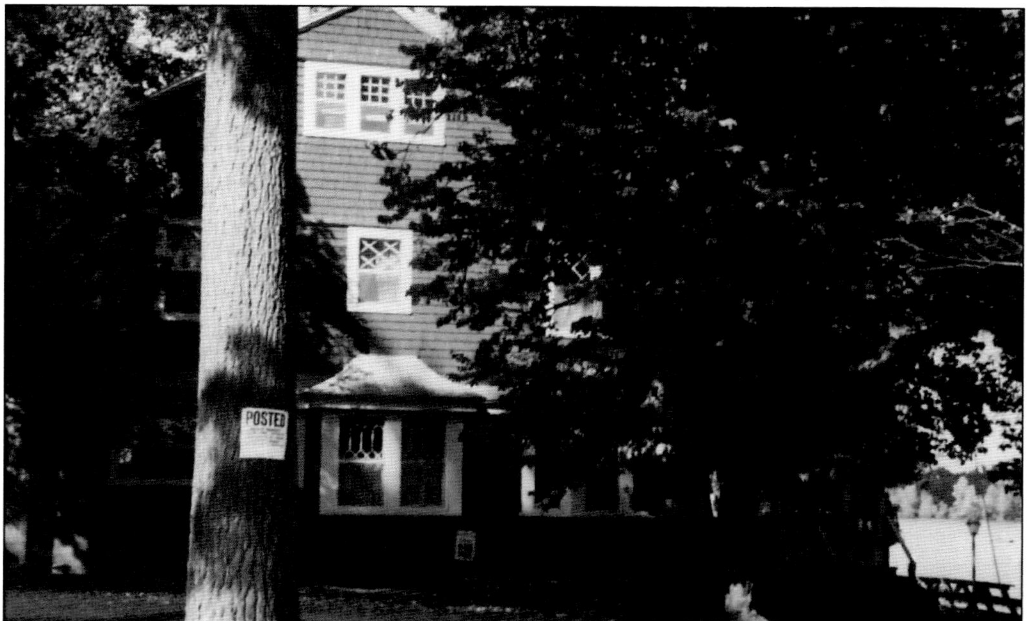

Manning/Melander residence. This same location on Saratoga Lake once raised top-quality, award-winning leghorn chickens and was known as Turtle Point Farm of Saratoga Springs. In 1914, Turtle Point Farm was owned by Mr. W.H. Manning and managed by Mr. W.M. Anderson. In later years, this residence became the home of Raymond Melander and his family. The Manning/Melander residence on Saratoga Lake is now the home of the Saratoga Lake Sailing Club.

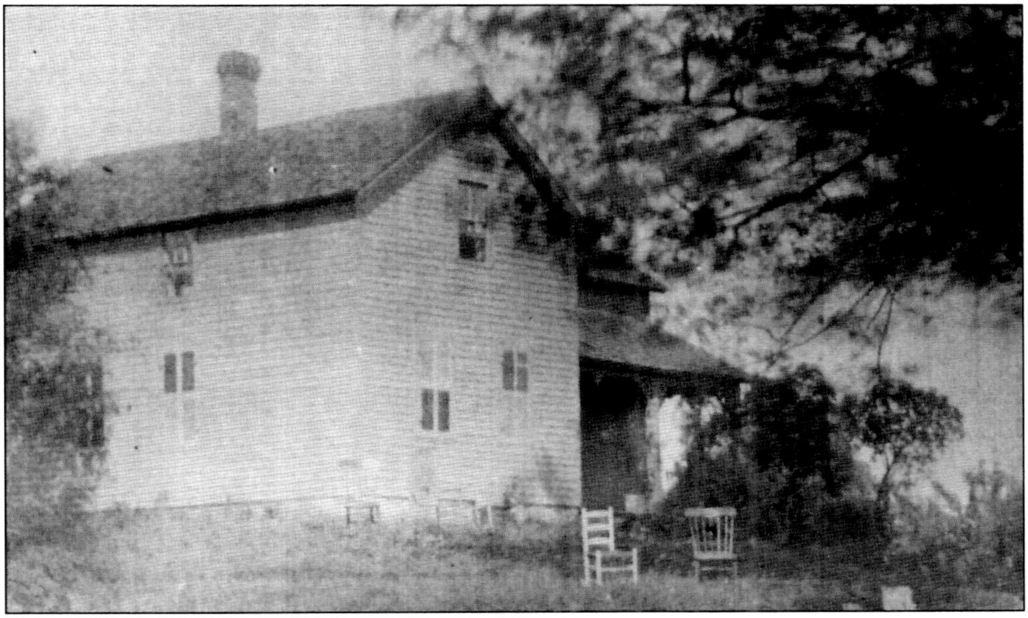

Gates Homestead. The homestead located on Silver Beach Road near Saratoga Lake is pictured as it appeared about the turn of the century. It is now the home of Mr. George R. Devore.

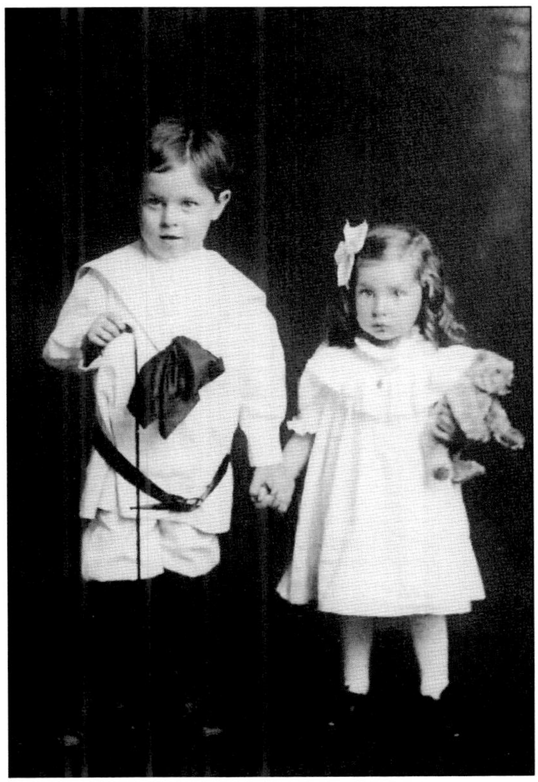

Earl F. Gates and his sister, Margaret. The children of Frank and Mary Ramsdill Gates, Earl and Margaret were photographed at ages five and three, respectively, around 1908. Both Earl and Margaret were lifelong residents of Malta, as were their parents. Earl wrote a history of the town of Malta entitled *History of Malta, Developed by People*. It was published after his death in 1991. Margaret married Clarence Melander.

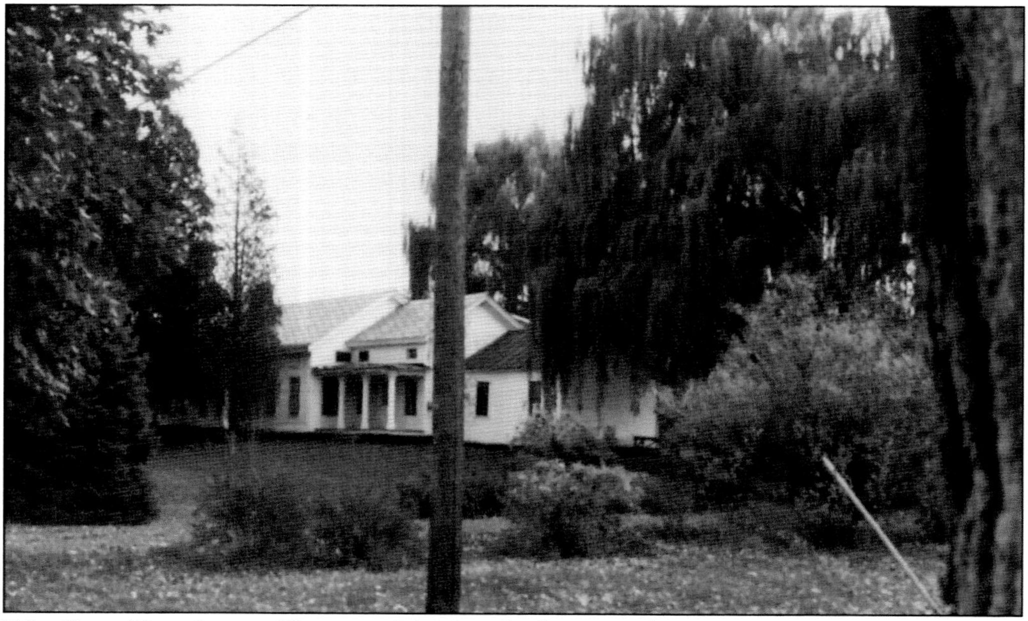

Riley/Reno/Cornthwaite Homestead. Today the homestead at 768 Malta Avenue Extension is the residence of Schuyler and Helen Cornthwaite and their son, Miles J. Cornthwaite. Mr. Clarence Molloy, who was the mailman in the days when horses were a common means of transportation, told Miles J. Cornthwaite that the Reno family made a practice of leaving their barn door unlatched during a snowstorm. The unlatched door allowed Mr. Molloy and his horse to get out of the bad weather and warm themselves.

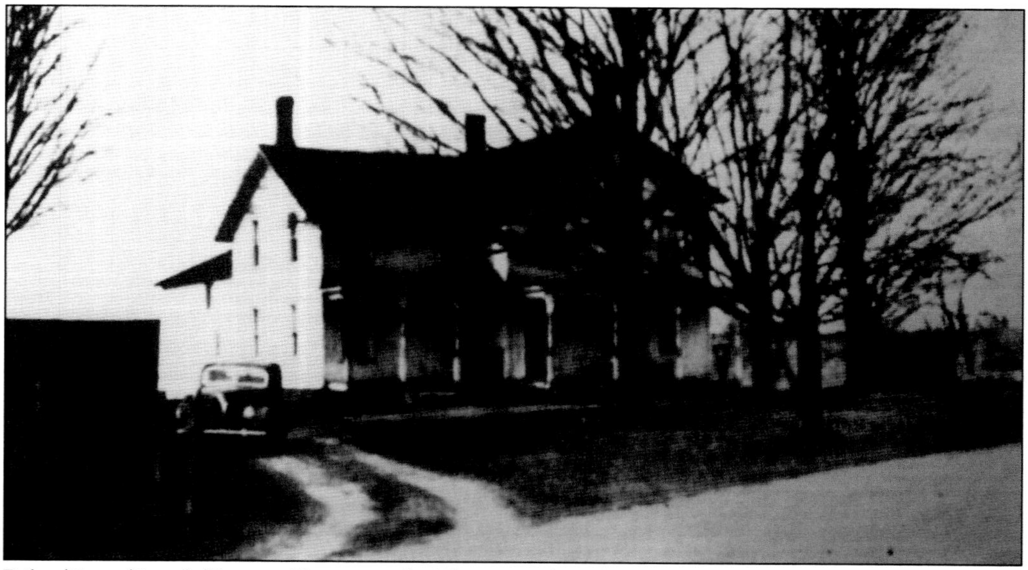

Riley/Zonn/Beach/Dixon Homestead. This stately old farmhouse at 786 Malta Avenue Extension is surrounded by many large, old maple trees and was listed in the Beers atlas of 1866 as the home of George Riley. In later years it became known as the Zonn Farm, and in 1941 it was sold to Ernest V. Beach Sr. and family. The present owners, William and Nancy Dixon, purchased the home in 1961.

Seven

Around the Town

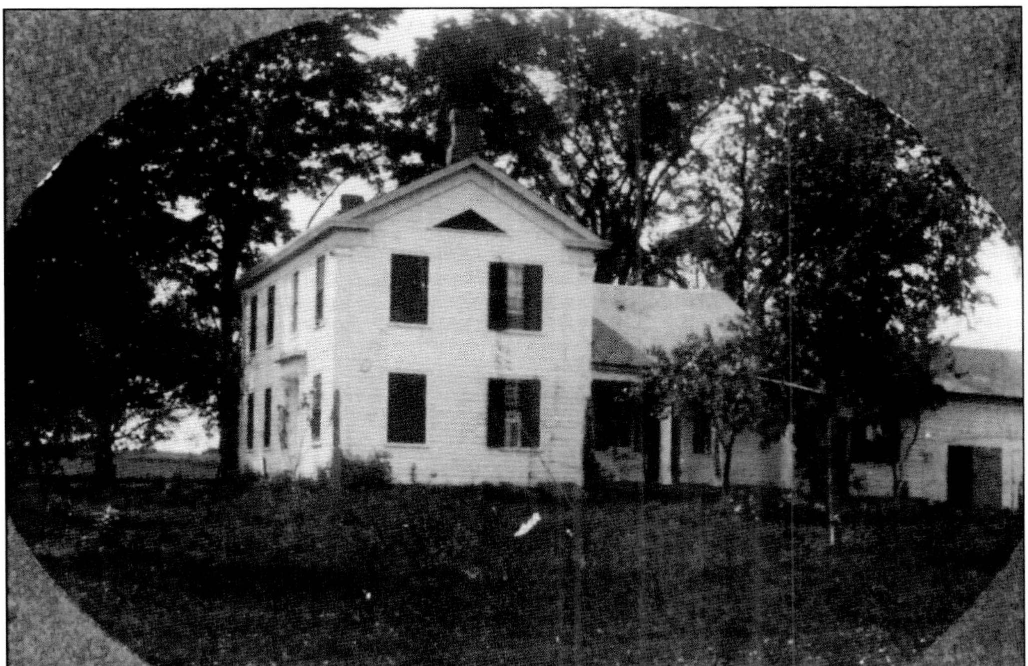

Homestead of the Rice Hall family, c. 1825. At one time, Mr. Hall was one of the largest landholders in Saratoga County. It has been said that the land on which the village of Round Lake stands was owned by this family. This property remained in the Hall family for well over one hundred years until 1927, when it was sold to Robert and Emma Kopp. The house is remembered for its beautiful rock garden located in the front yard, its magnificent flower gardens, and the lovely open stairway in the wide front hall. It was destroyed by fire in the early 1970s. Today the Round Lake Insurance Company occupies its location.

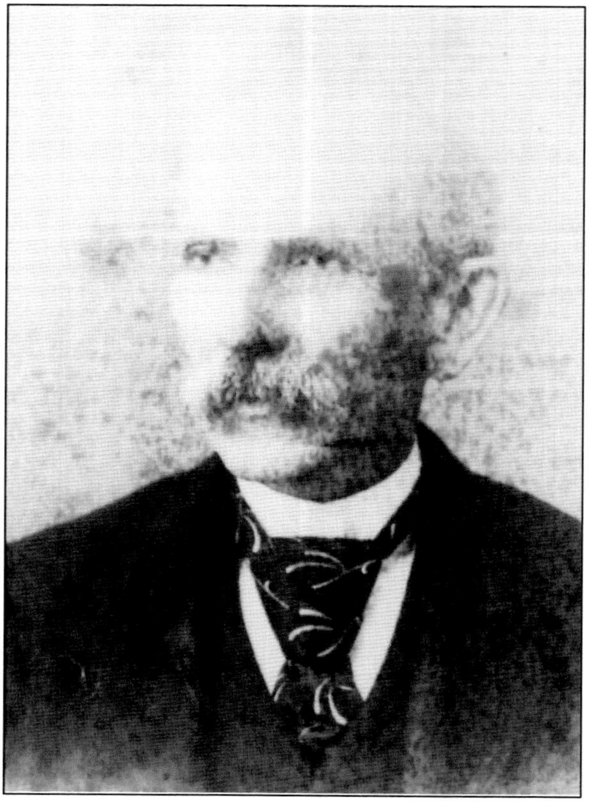

Mr. Philip Riley, the owner and possible builder of the Riley/Allen Cobblestone Home on Malta Avenue.

Homestead of the Philip Riley family, *c.* 1845. The homestead of Philip Riley and his heirs, built *c.* 1845 by Joseph Lockrow, was most likely a tenant farmhouse on a larger estate. The cobblestone construction of this home on Malta Avenue is quite rare in this area. The Riley family lived on what was once a large, 135-acre farm from 1857 until 1971. Since 1974, the property has been the home of Robert and Melinda Allen. It was designated as a historic landmark by the Town of Malta in 1993, and as such has an historical marker identifying it as the Riley-Allen Cobblestone House. Mr. Allen presently serves on the town board of the town of Malta as a councilman.

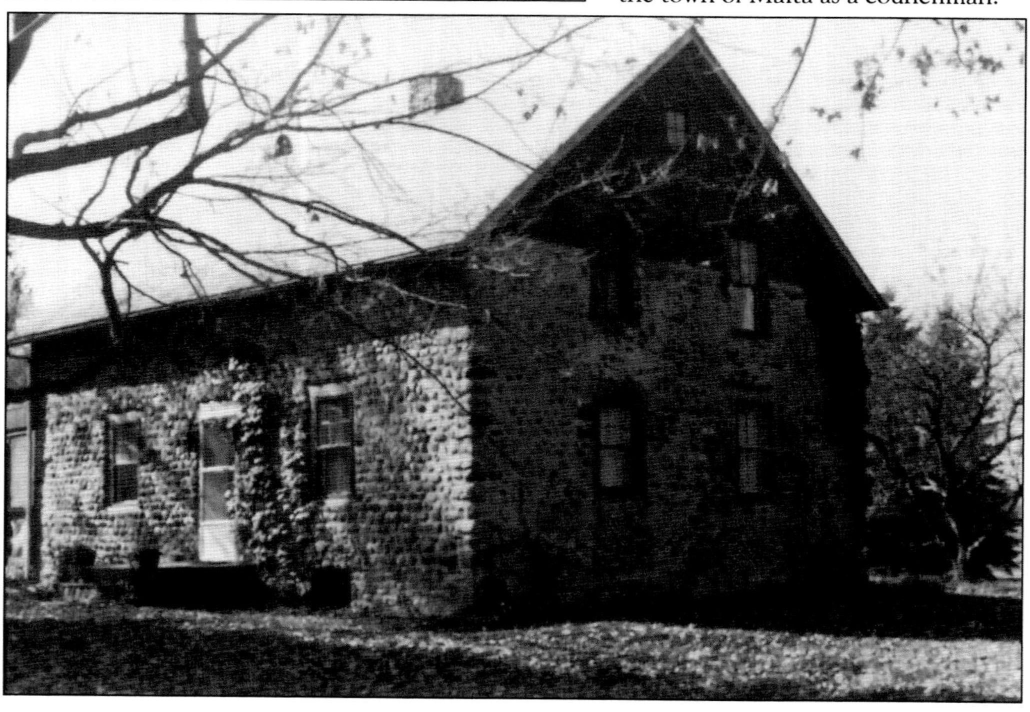

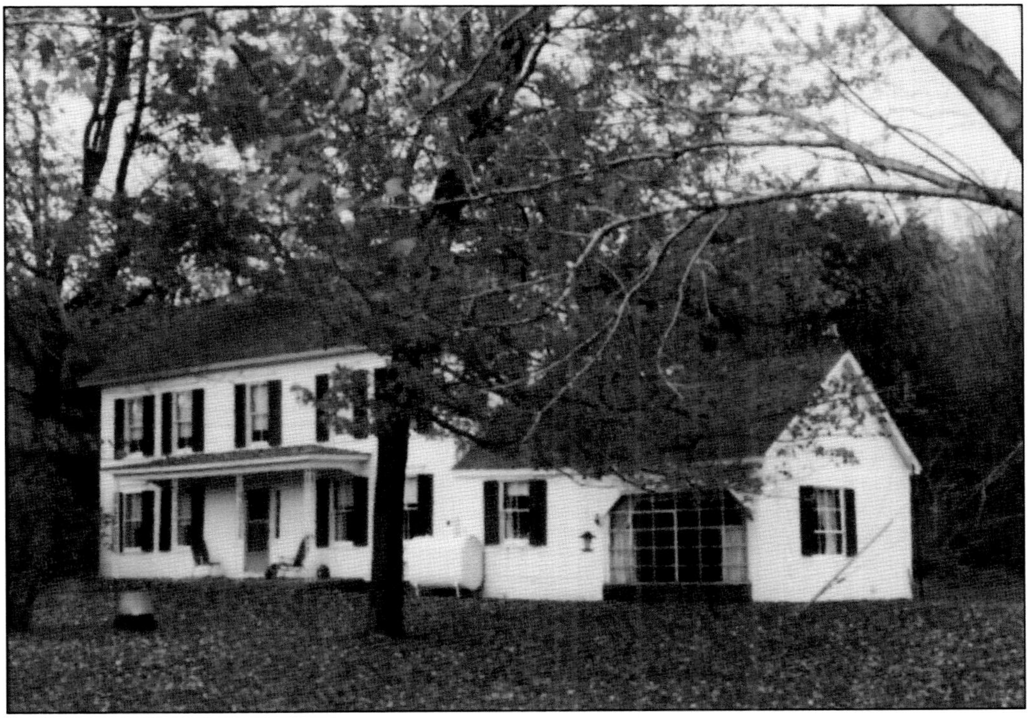

Vincent/Van Hyning/Cramer Homestead, c. 1830. This home, situated on the corner of 145 Cramer Road in Malta, is a late Federal-style farmhouse built c. 1830. Merritt R. Vincent was an early owner. In 1868 it was purchased by Daniel Van Hyning and it stayed in his family for seventy-six years. In 1944, Frank and Edith Cramer purchased the home and moved in with their nine children. It has remained in the Cramer family to the present time.

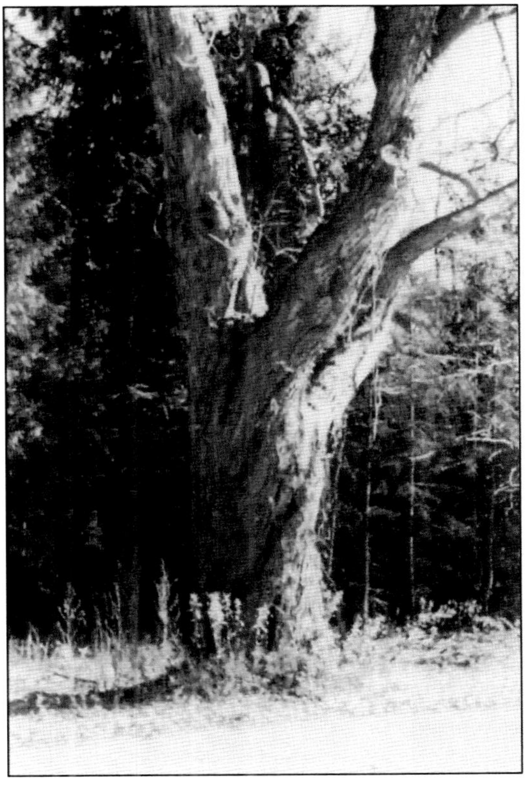

The Twisted Tree Mystery. For over two hundred years this great red maple stood on Van Aernem Road near its intersection with Atkins Road. The tree had to be removed because it became in danger of collapsing. When it was cut down, over one hundred fifty rings were counted, and some others were so twisted that they could not be tallied. Dr. Valentine Baker, an amateur naturalist, speculated that the tree was deliberately twisted by Indians while it was still a young sapling to mark the trail. The tree was cut down in the spring of 1978.

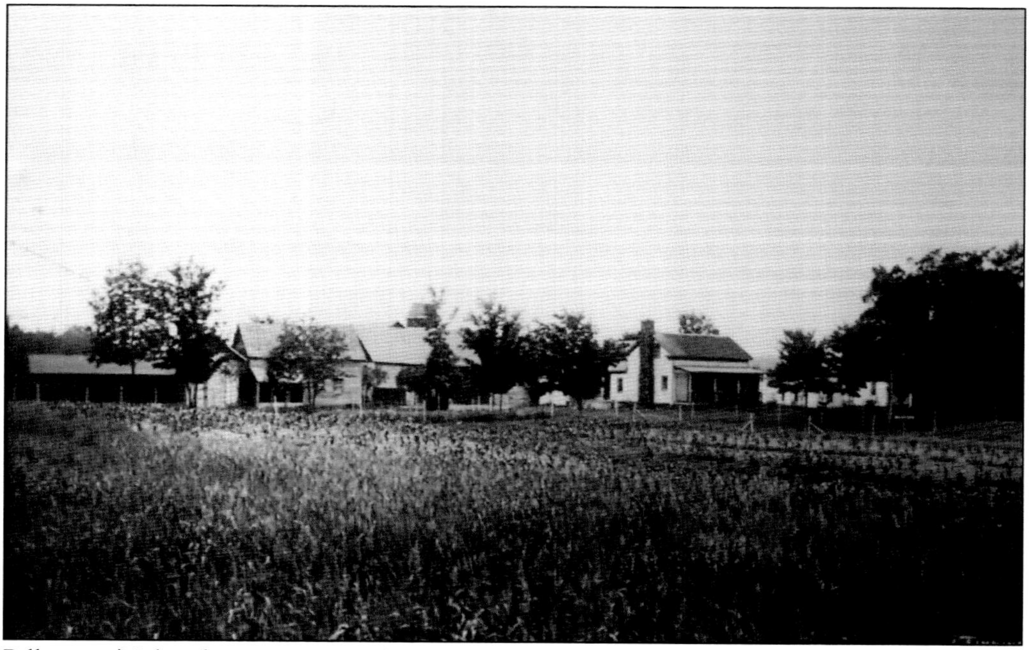

Billington/Nolan farm, *c.* 1900. This farm on East High Street was situated just east of the Mourningkill Creek on the same site that the Spa Brauhaus Restaurant occupies today. At one time the farm was large and productive; it extended to both sides of the road. The 1866 Beers atlas map indicates that this property was then the home of F. Billington, about whom nothing further is known.

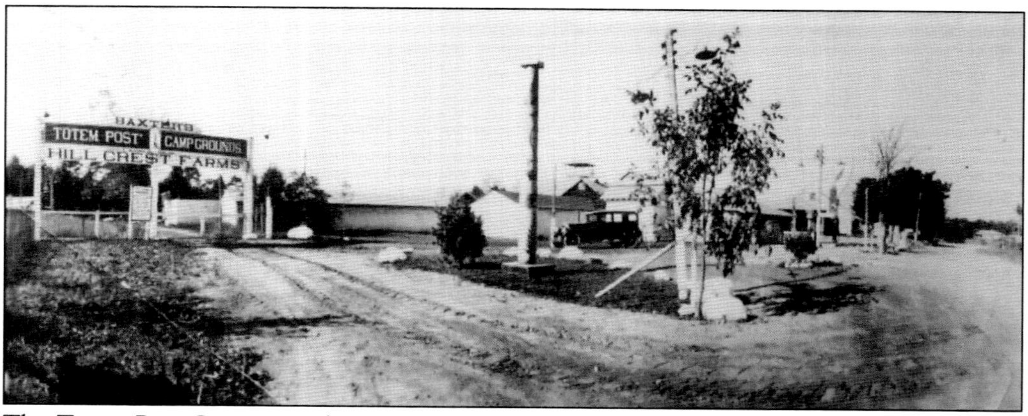

The Totem Post Campgrounds on rural East High Street, next door to today's Spa Brauhaus Restaurant. In the 1920s and 1930s this was a popular vacation spot. Its creator and owner, Alex G. Baxter, served in the New York State Senate for two terms. He purchased the old Nolan farm and built the campgrounds and the Wampum Club, a popular restaurant. It is interesting to note that the front steps of the Wampum Club descended directly down to the road, and that the tall chimney of the Nolan homestead is the same as the chimney of the Spa Brauhaus today.

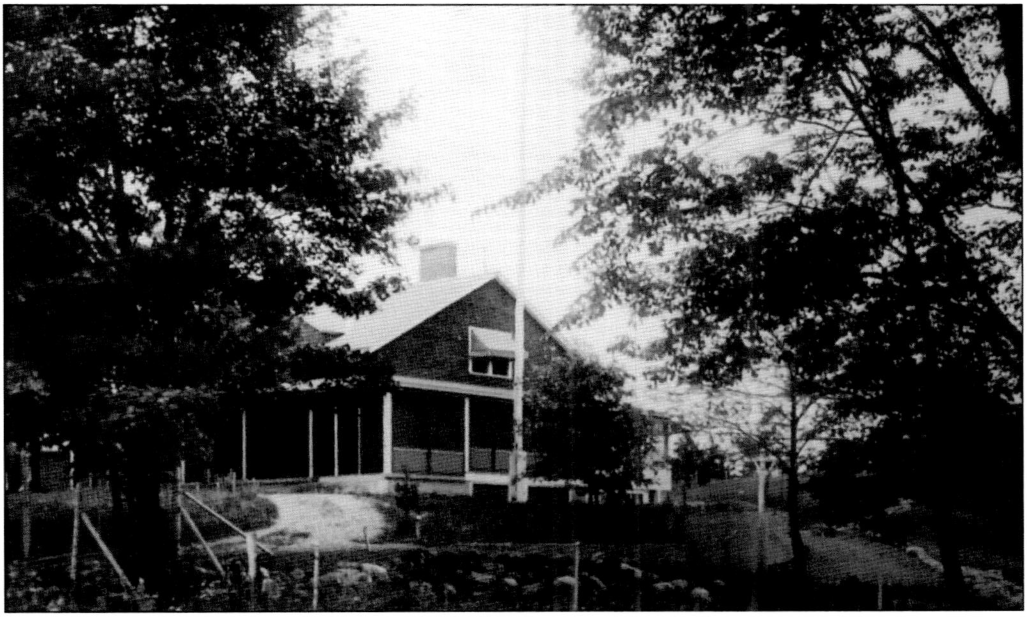

The Wampum Club. This restaurant, owned by Senator Alex G. Baxter, was a popular eatery of the 1920s and 1930s. Today this is the site of the Spa Brauhaus Restaurant.

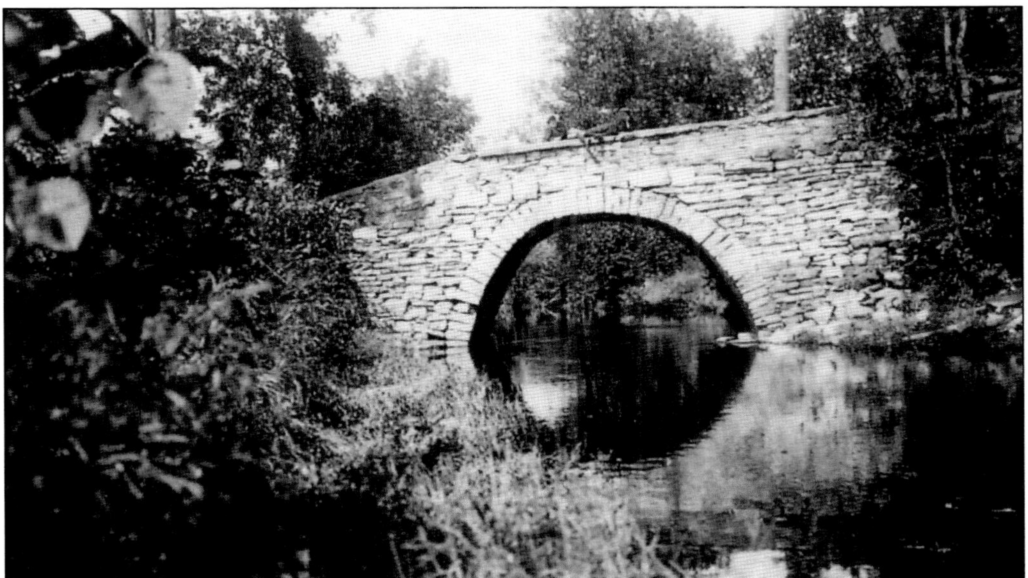

Mourningkill Bridge. The Mourningkill Bridge is located on East High Street just west of the Spa Brauhaus Restaurant at the extreme west boundary of the town of Malta. The Mourningkill Creek empties into the Kayaderosseras Creek, which travels to Saratoga Lake. Legend tells of a terrible battle between the Iroquois and the Algonquins that occurred here. Early settlers named the area Mourningkill because of a custom kept as late as 1770 by local Native Americans. It is said that they assembled at the site of the battle to celebrate mourning rites for those who had fallen in the battle. Another legend tells us that the actual site of the battle was in the town of Charlton.

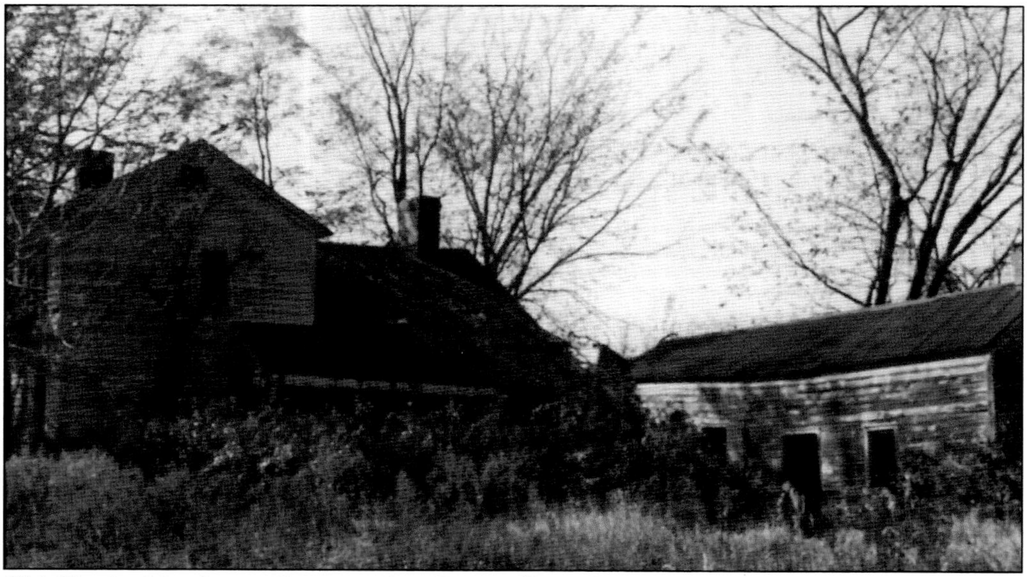

Old Charles Morehouse Homestead on Brownell Road, one of the earliest homes built in the area (before 1800). The house, unoccupied for many years, was finally razed by the town. It has been said that the house was built here before the road was properly laid out. There was a huge central fireplace in the center of the home, with fireplace openings in each room. The outbuildings were unique because of an unusual fireplace in one of the buildings that could have been used as a community butchering place.

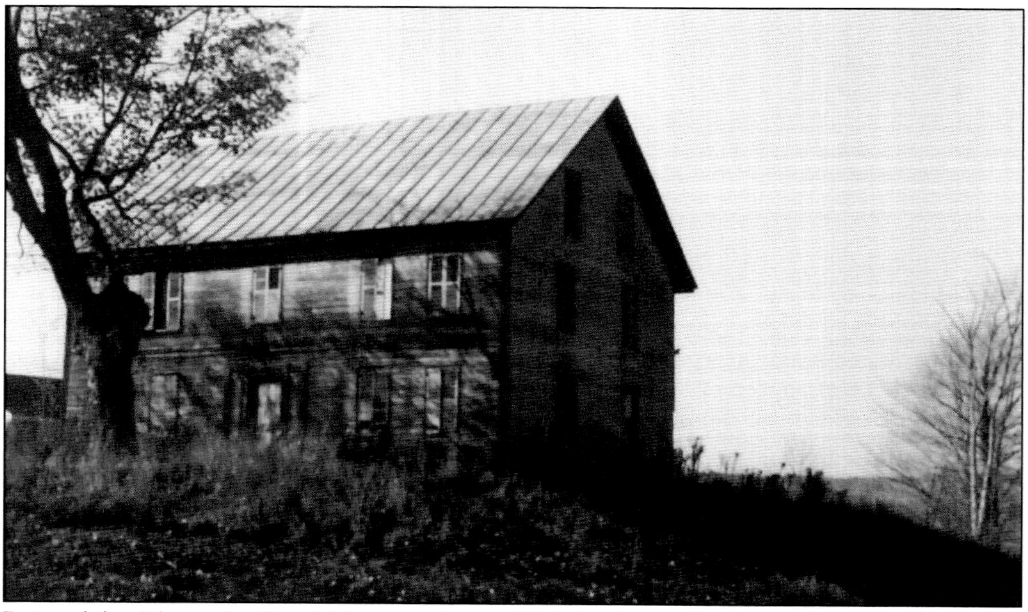

Ruin of the Alexander Weed Homestead, *c.* 1810. The Alexander Weed Homestead near the Malta Avenue and Old Post Road intersection stands as a silent sentinel to the past. It is said that the remains of a Dutch oven can still be seen in the cellar. Alexander was the son of John Weed and Hannah Mann of Milton. He married Esther Smith of Malta. Both families, Weed and Smith, were prosperous farmers in the early years of the town.

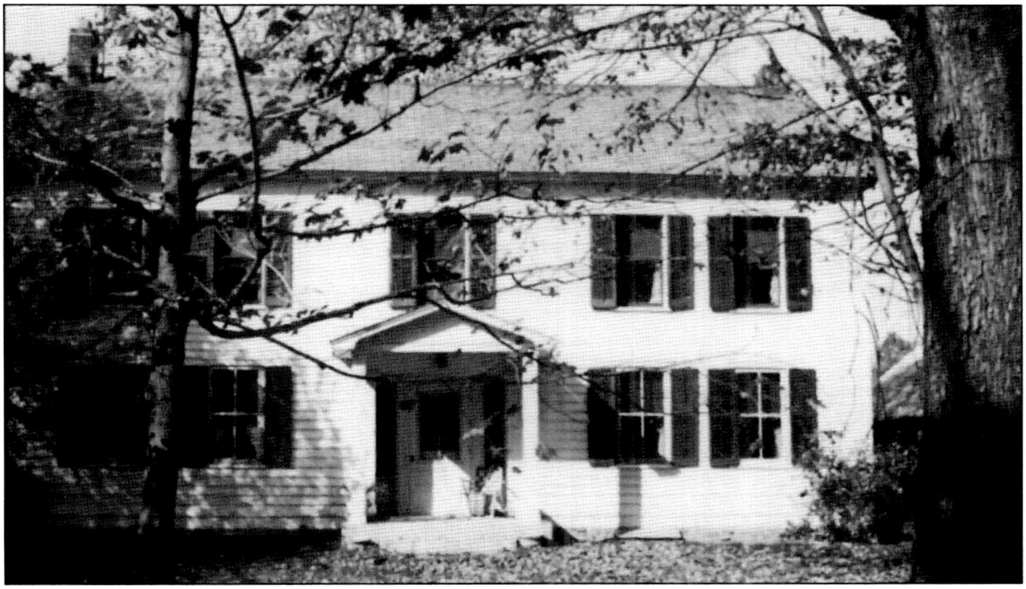

Millard/Emigh/Morehouse/Wolfe Homestead, Brownell Road, c. 1800. The Millard family lived here in the early 1800s, and the Emigh family followed in the latter half of the nineteenth century. The Morehouse family owned the property about the turn of the century. By the 1920s, the home belonged to the Wolfe family. The house is a fine example of late Federal period architecture; the many out buildings indicate the sufficiency of these pioneer families.

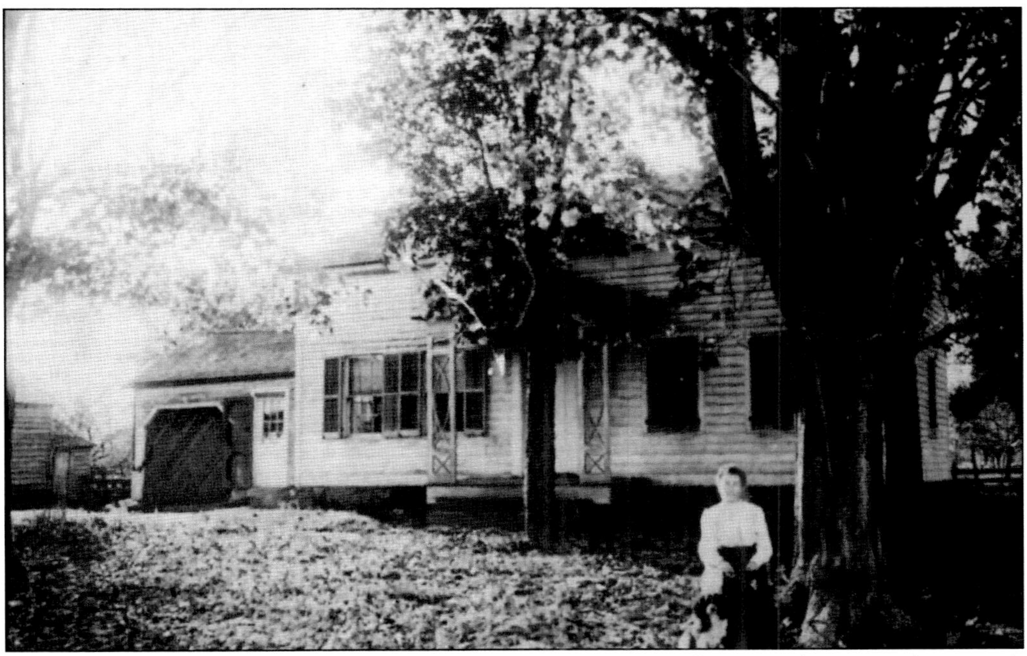

Cole/Fitzgerald Homestead. Mary Kerley Cole and her dog are shown in this 1901 photograph of the Cole/Fitzgerald Homestead at Halls Corners. Mary Kerley Cole was the grandmother of Robert, Walter, and Mary Fitzgerald. Today this is the home of Mr. and Mrs. Robert Fitzgerald at 304 Brownell Road. They are now the third generation living in this home.

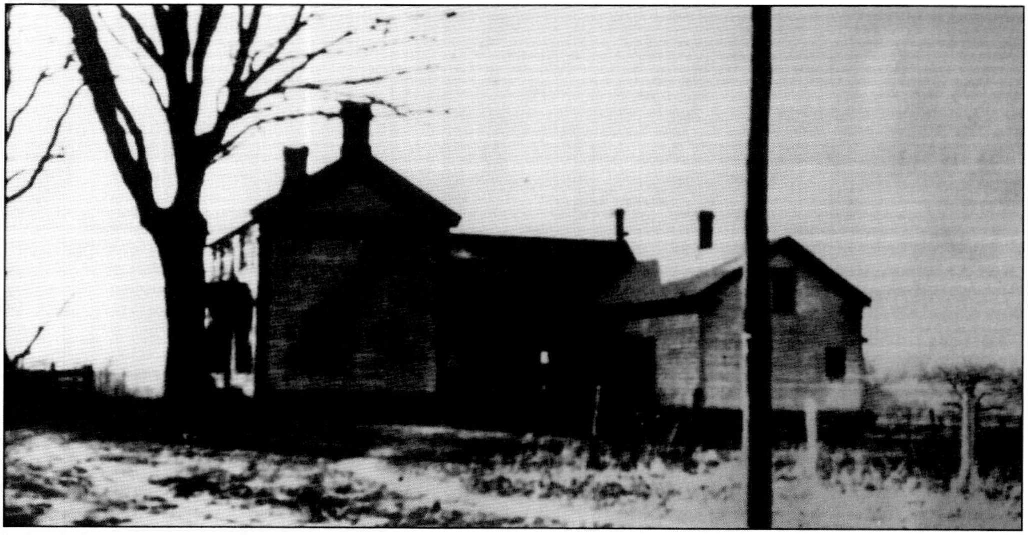

John Thompson Family Homestead, East High Street, *c.* 1840. This was the home of William A. Collamer Jr. in the 1860s. The house was taken down by the present owner and the barns burned many years ago. Once it was a large, productive dairy farm with a tenant house on the property. The house stood at the sharp bend in the road, where the road goes down a steep hill and then crosses the Adirondack Northway.

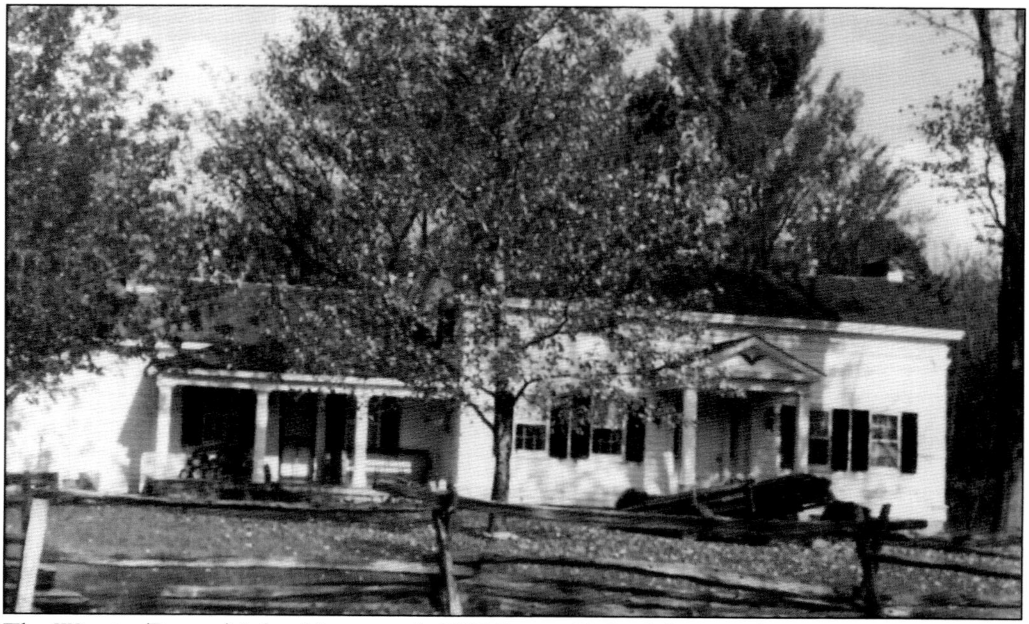

The Wiggins/Brown/Nolen Homestead, 2359 Route 9P. Built by David Wiggins in 1840, this is a fine example of a Vernacular Greek Revival house. After the 1874 death of Mary A. Wiggins, David's wife, the property was divided and sold. In 1900, Charles H. Brown bought two parcels of the former homestead, including the house. The Brown family remained in the home until 1965. In 1970, the home was purchased by Thomas V. and Sue Nolen and beautifully restored. It was designated as a historic landmark by the town of Malta in 1991. Mrs. Nolen presently serves on the town board of the town of Malta as a councilwoman.

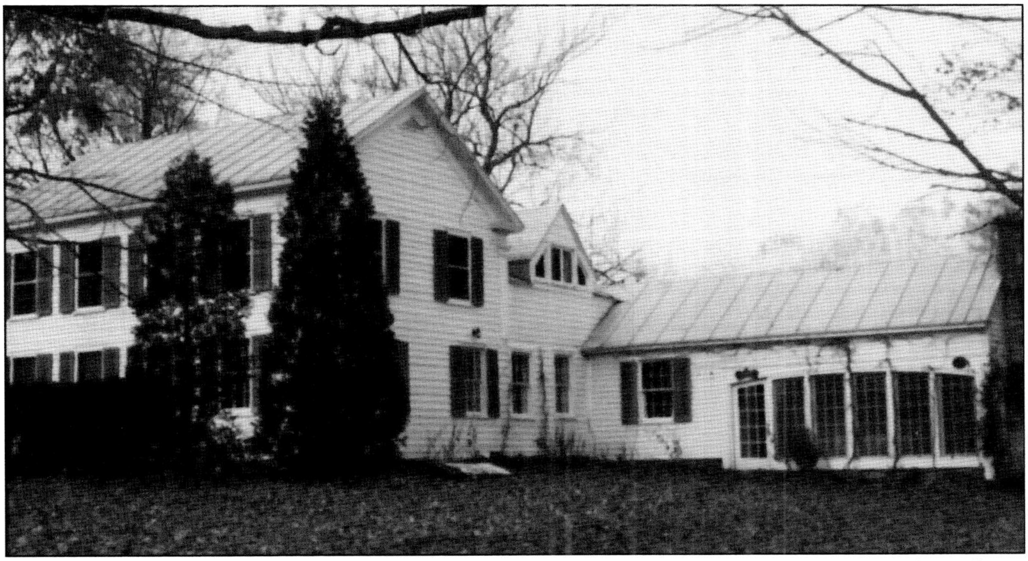

The Hill/Porter/Willison/Nolen house. This home at 165 Cramer Road is believed to have been built around 1830, and is a beautiful example of a nineteenth-century farmhouse. It was owned by the Hill family from 1857 until 1941, when it was purchased by Katherine Anne Porter. Miss Porter, a 1966 Pulitzer Prize-winning author known for her collection of short stories, also wrote the novel *Ship of Fools*. In 1946, George and Florence Willison purchased the home. Mr. Willison was famous for his book, *Saints and Strangers*, a historical work about the pilgrims. Recently this home has been purchased by Thomas V. and Sue Nolen, who plan to restore it.

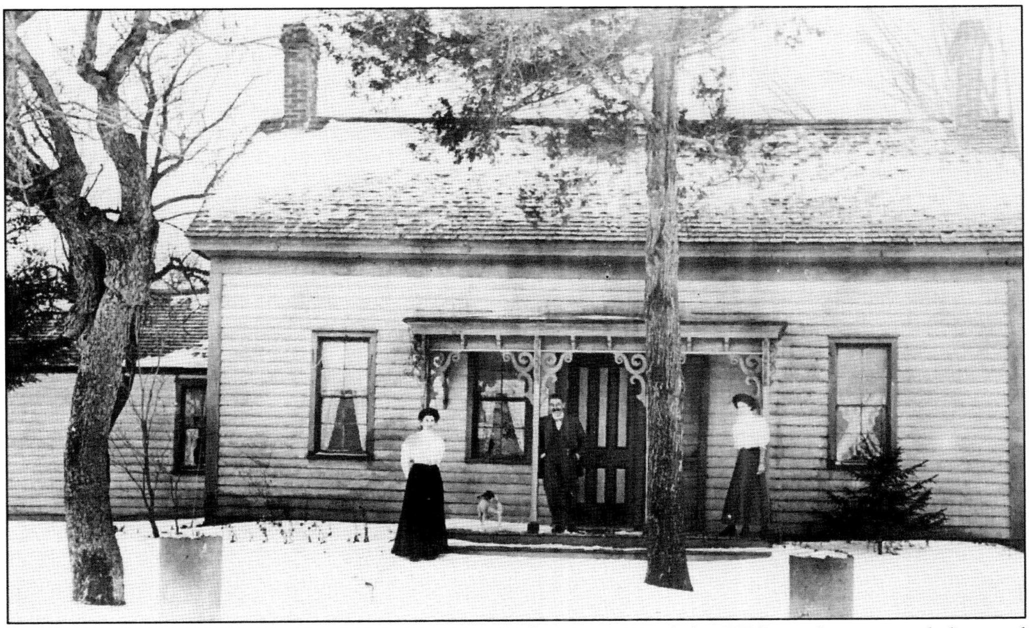

Homestead of Arthur G. and Bertha Wilmot. This picture of the Wilmot homestead, located on Round Lake Road, shows Bertha and Arthur Wilmot and their daughter, Mable Wilmot Vincent. Today this is the home of Emil M. and Marie Habesch.

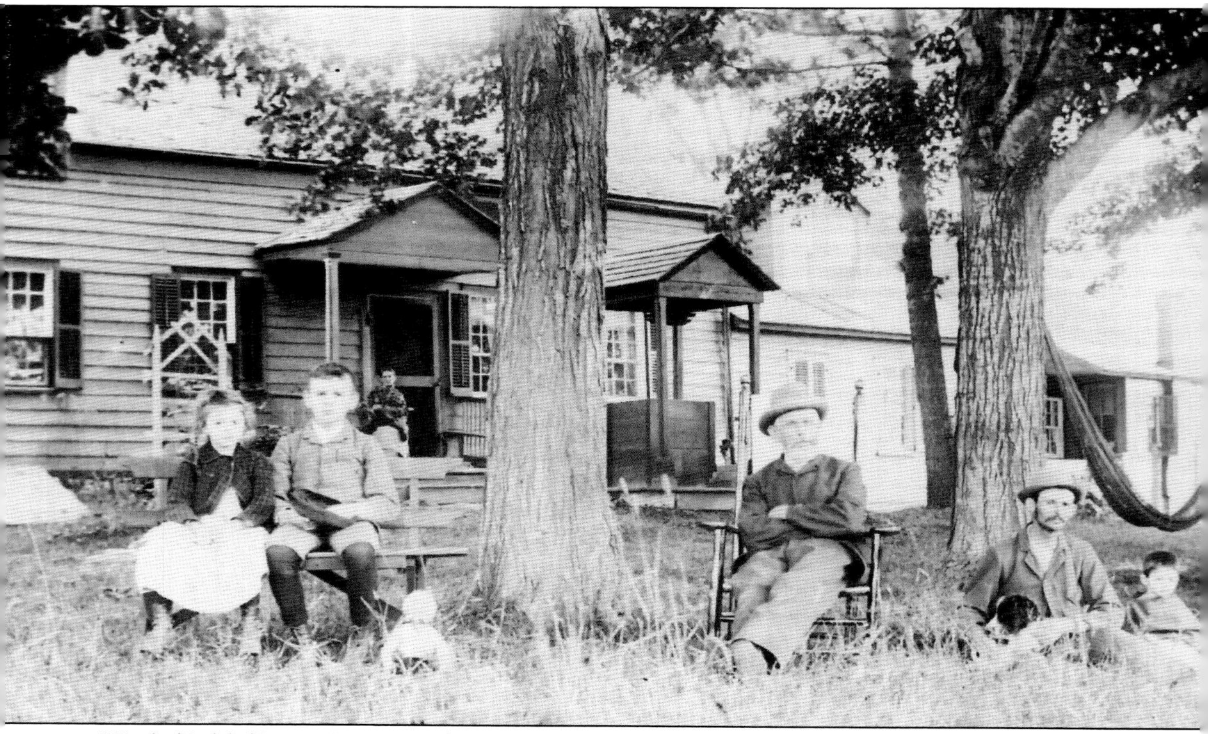

Weeks/Ruhle/Roerig Homestead, *c.* 1890. This home is situated on Ruhle Road. James Weeks came to Malta from Westchester County about 1787 with his wife, Freelove Brundage, and their children. He served in the Revolutionary War and was a prisoner of the British for four months in New York harbor. Pictured are Uncle Levi (grandson of James), Aunt Jane (his wife, seated on the porch), Elliott Weeks (their son, with his dog), and Elliott's children: Lelia, Harry, and Jessie. Today the homestead belongs to Paul and John Roerig, who are part of the eighth generation of the Weeks family.

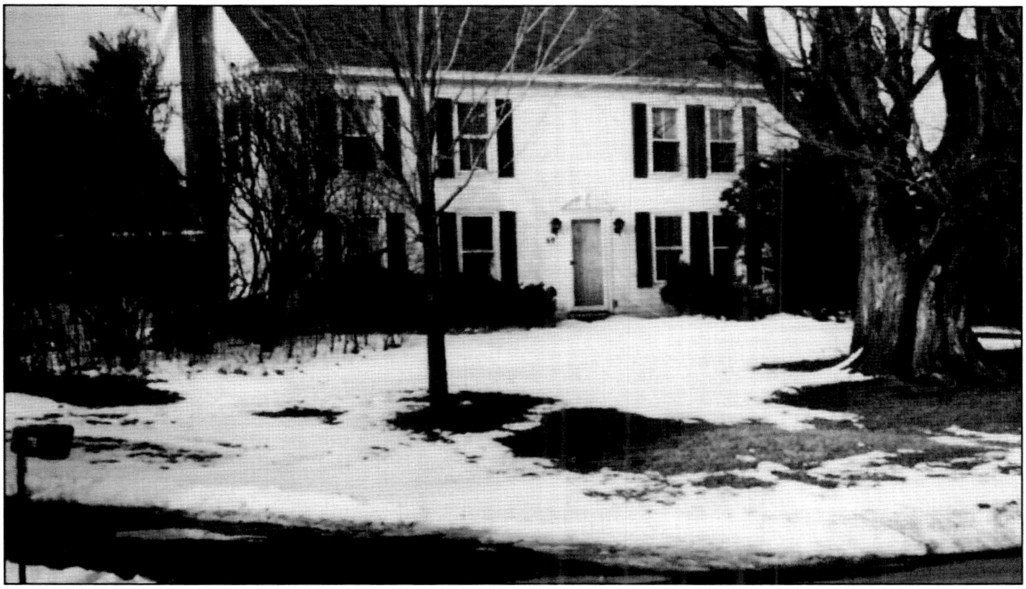

VanHyning/Roerig Homestead, County Highway 82 (Round Lake Road), *c*. 1830. Built by James and Amanda Cook VanHyning, the parents of seven sons and one daughter, this structure housed four generations of VanHynings. It later became the home of the Kaiser family, and in 1938 was purchased by August and Isabel Roerig. The homestead is still in the possession of the Roerig family. It was designated as a historic landmark by the Town of Malta in 1994.

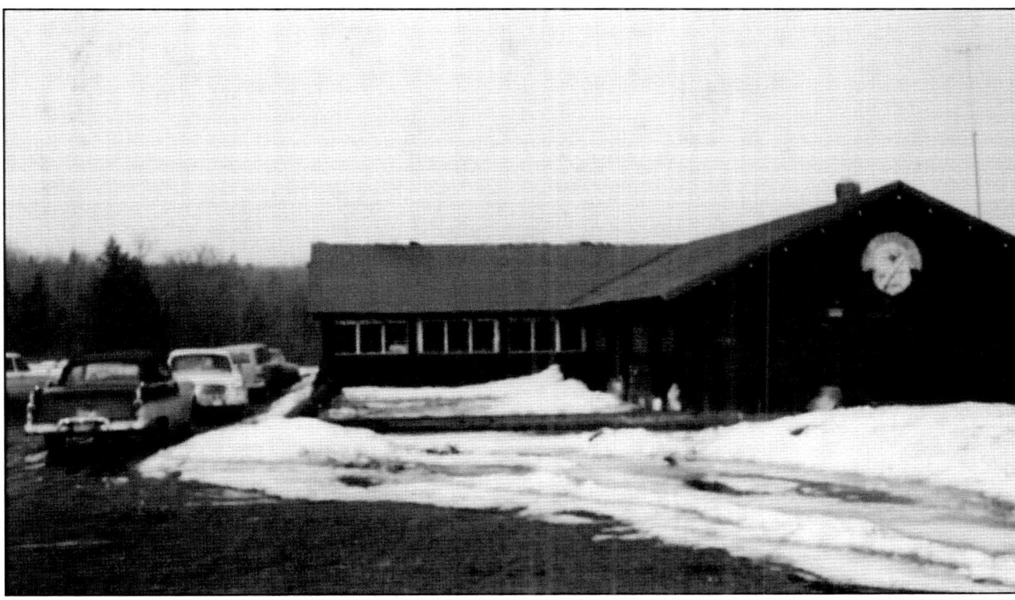

Round Lake Rod and Gun Club. Fifty-one men held an organizational meeting to form the club in 1954, and at a later meeting a land search committee was formed. In late 1956, the land committee selected a site that included 86 acres of land. The land was purchased from Harry Ruhle and construction of the clubhouse started in 1957. For over twenty-five years this organization served the sportsmen in the area; at present it is inactive.

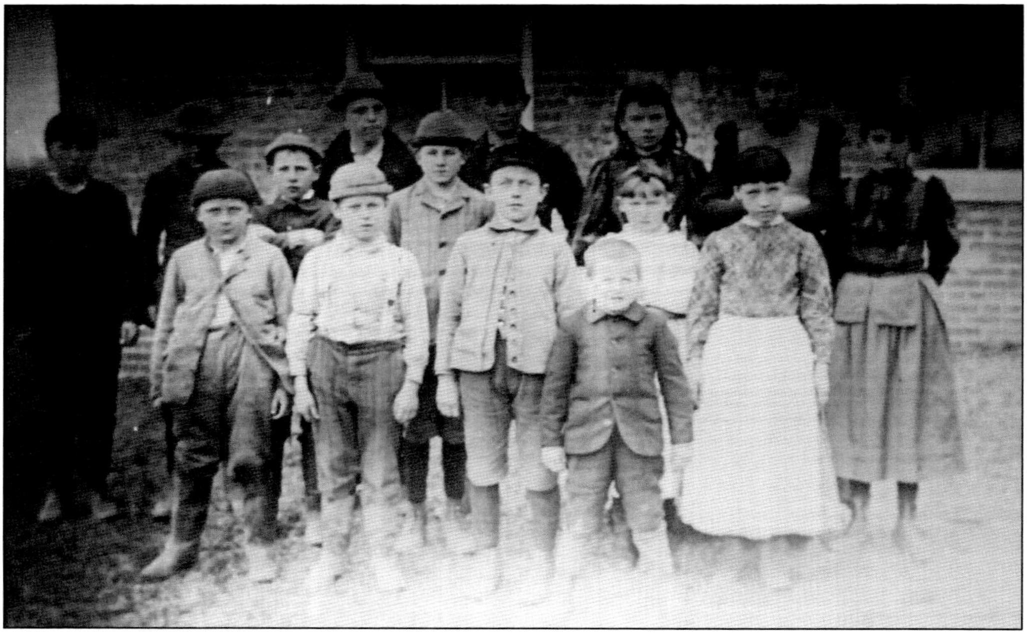

Students of Armstrong's Corner's Common School No. 5. The names of these 1892–93 students are unknown to us after the passing of nearly 105 years. However, we can still appreciate these sturdy and serious young citizens.

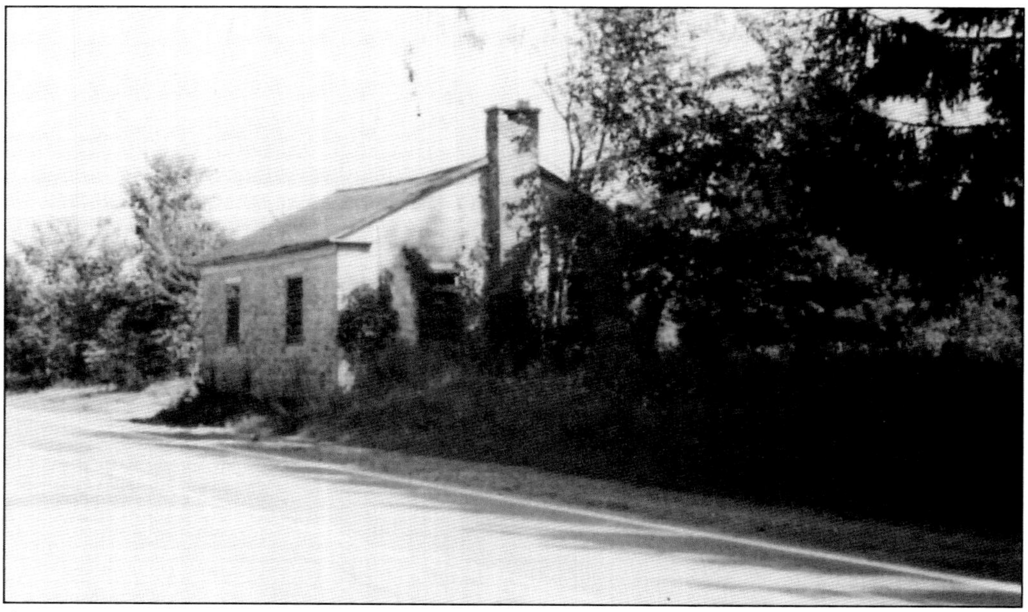

Armstrongs Corners Common School No. 5. This school site is believed to be nearly two hundred years old. The original schoolhouse was built of logs and has long since burned down. This second schoolhouse, built in 1825, was constructed of homemade bricks made in a brickyard somewhere near Round Lake. At one time there was an addition to the east or entrance side of the building that served as the woodshed and "privy." The school was demolished in 1976.

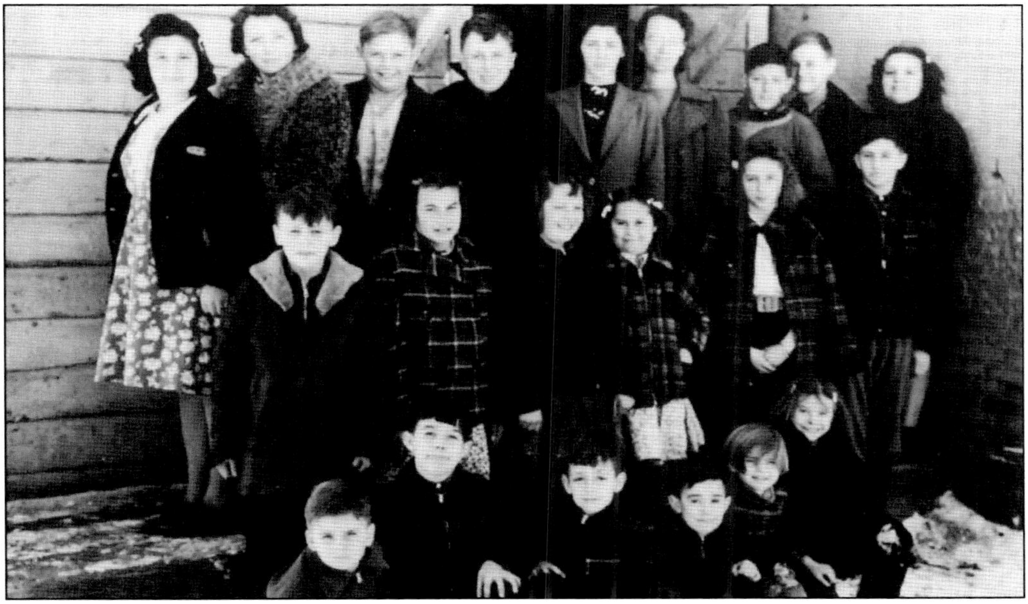

Students of Armstrong's Corner's Common School No. 5, *c*. 1938–39. From left to right are as follows: (front row) George Voelker, Billy Abeel, Donnie Abeel, Jimmy Abeel, Lorraine Voelker, and Delvina O'Keefe; (middle row) Loren Reed, Ruth Downing, Catherine O'Keefe, Agnes Johnson, Hazel Miller, and Robert Miller; (back row) Marjorie Johnson, Iona O'Keefe, Lester O'Keefe, Bob Downing, Jean Kelley, teacher Nevelyn Bruce, Stanley Kelley, Fred Simmons, and Marilyn Abeel. It is said that Ms. Nevelyn Bruce had a new car, a Willys, which constantly gave her problems. The truth was that the boys were tampering with the automobile.

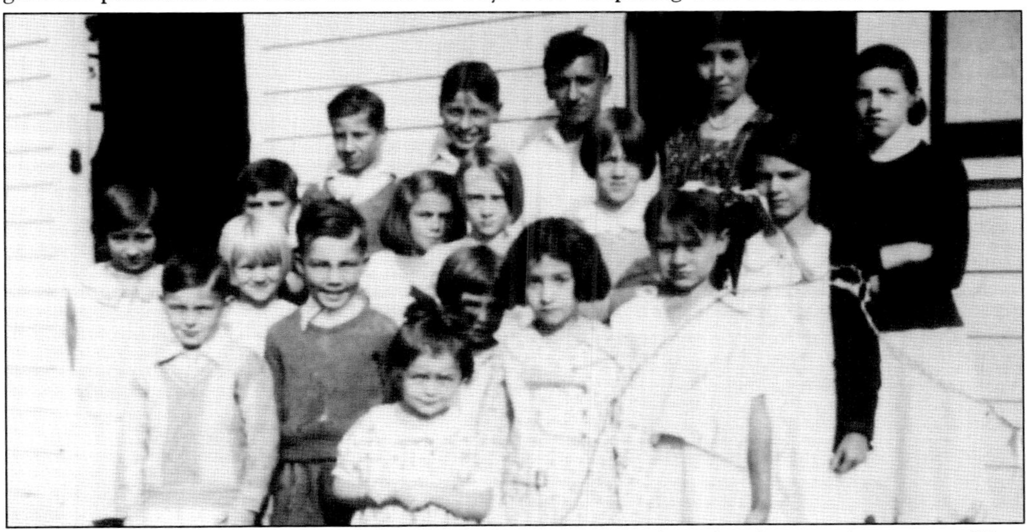

Students of Hall's Corners Common School No. 6, *c*. 1932. This school was at the corner of East High Street and Brownell Road. From left to right are as follows: (front row) Mary Fitzgerald; (second row) Bob Fitzgerald, Raymond Melander, Doris Melander, Marion Atkins, and Truman Grandy; (third row) Dorothy Brown, Shirley Read, Pat VanAernum, Mary Read, Norma Read, and Ruth Mosher; (fourth row) Bob VanAernum, Milton Atkins, Al Brown, Ed Swartz, Irene Atkins, and Ruth Atkins. The teacher is Ada Pierce.

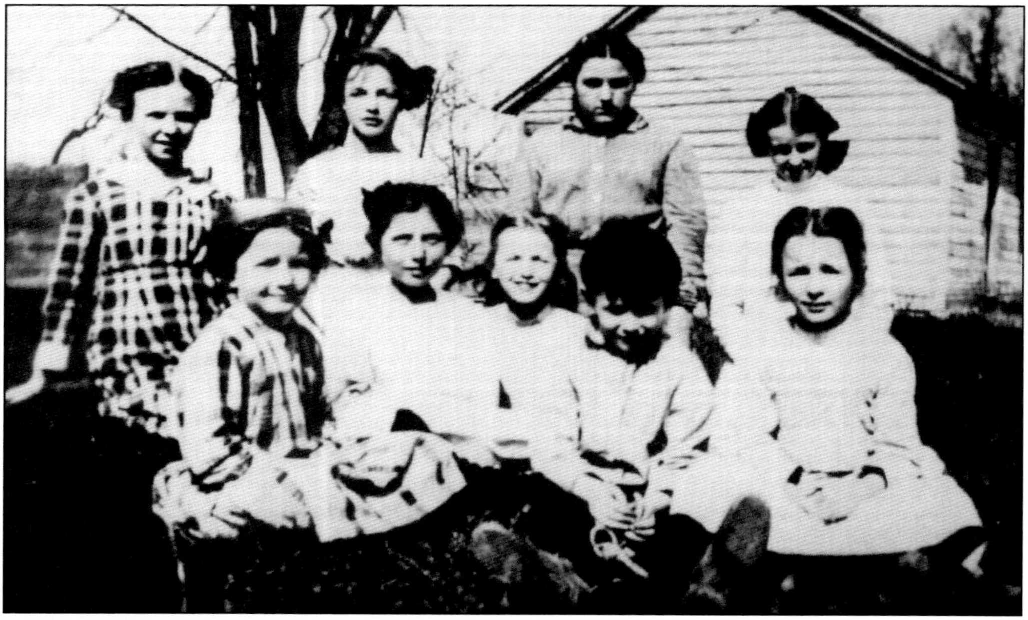

Students of Hall's Corners Common School No. 6, *c.* 1915. We notice one lone male surrounded by girls. Only two students have been identified from this class. In the back row, the third young lady from the left is Jane Glen Uline, and beside her in the fourth position is Anne Cole (Fitzgerald). This school was merged with the Ballston Spa School District in 1937.

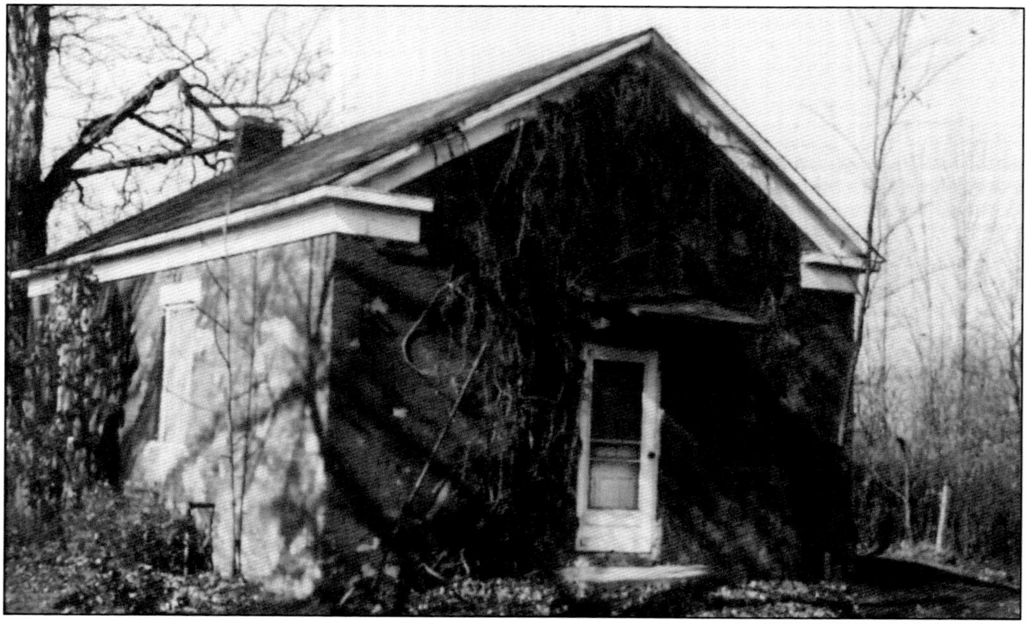

Green Corners Common School No. 7. This little brick schoolhouse was also known as the Greens Corners School. It was located on Cherry Choke Road, east of Route 9. This same road continues west of Route 9 and is named Old Post Road. In early times, this building was the home of David Rowley. Today it is home to Mr. and Mrs. Martin G. McCarthy, and is known as 15 Cherry Choke Road.

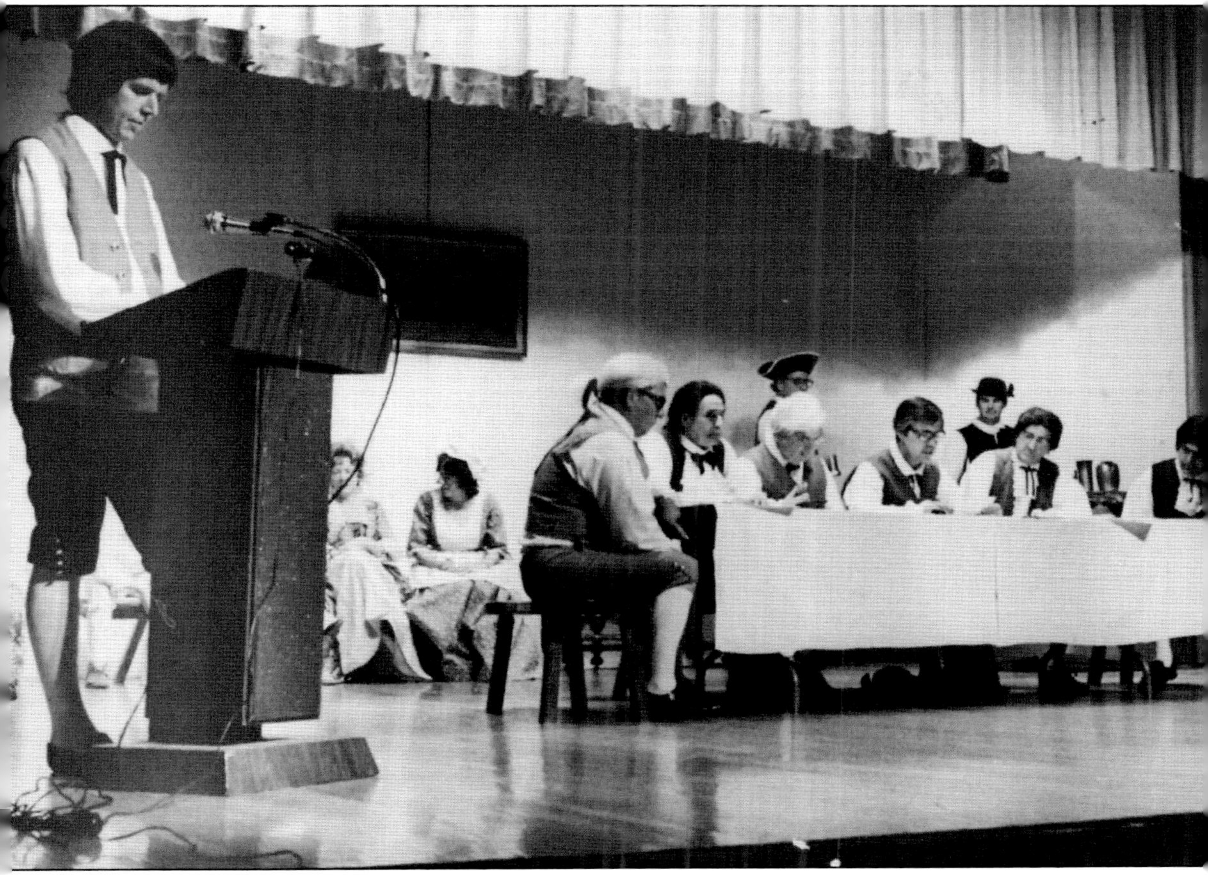

Reenactment of supervisors meeting. A reenactment of the 1791 first meeting of the supervisors of the newly formed Saratoga County was staged at the Stillwater High School on May 27, 1975; the scene of the first actual meeting was the tavern of William Mead. The narrator at the podium, David R. Meager, is addressing the supervisors and others gathered. For twenty-five years David R. Meager has served as supervisor of the town of Malta.

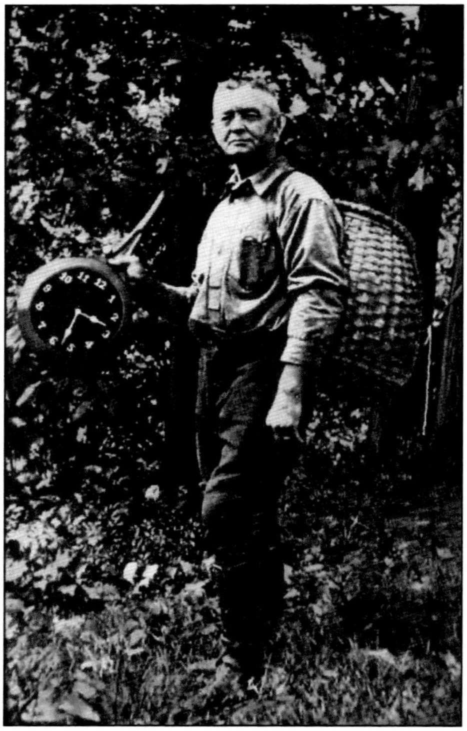

Mr. Noah La Casse, fire observer. Towers were built to observe the acres of reclaimed and reforested lands of Thomas Luther. Mr. Noah La Casse was a fire observer in Luther Forest for a number of years. La Casse acted as a guide to the party including Vice President Roosevelt on its notable trip up Mount Marcy on September 13, 1901. While they were lunching, the party received word that President McKinley's physical condition was grave and they rushed back. McKinley died on September 14 while Roosevelt was making his historic ride to a special train at North Creek.

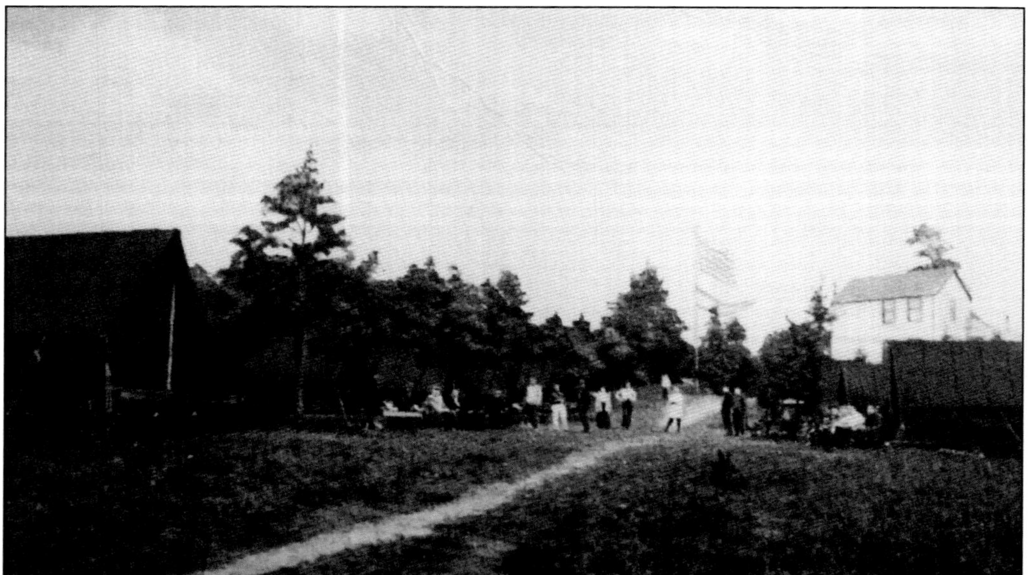

Cornell University Forestry School Camp on Luther's Preserve. In 1901, Thomas C. Luther, a lifelong resident of the area and proprietor of the White Sulphur Springs Hotel, became interested in reforestation. In that year, he bought up 65 acres of depleted, barren land in Malta and Stillwater and planted the land with young trees. By 1937, it is estimated that he had reforested approximately 15,000 acres. It was not unusual for Luther to plant a million trees in one season.

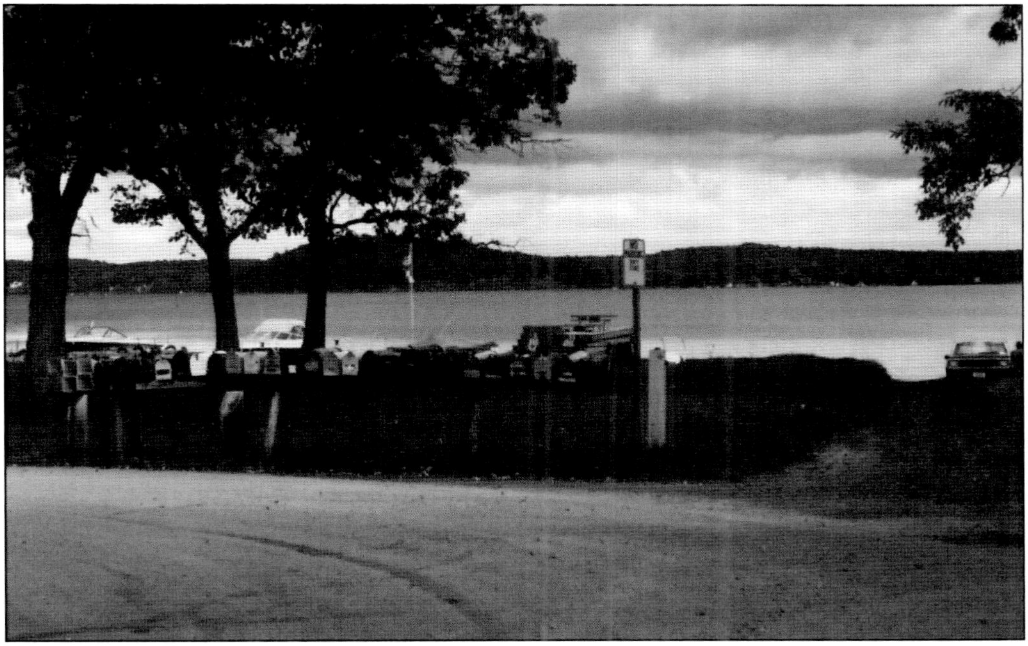

View of Saratoga Lake. This picture was taken from the Silver Beach area on Saratoga Lake. Snake Hill is on the opposite shore.

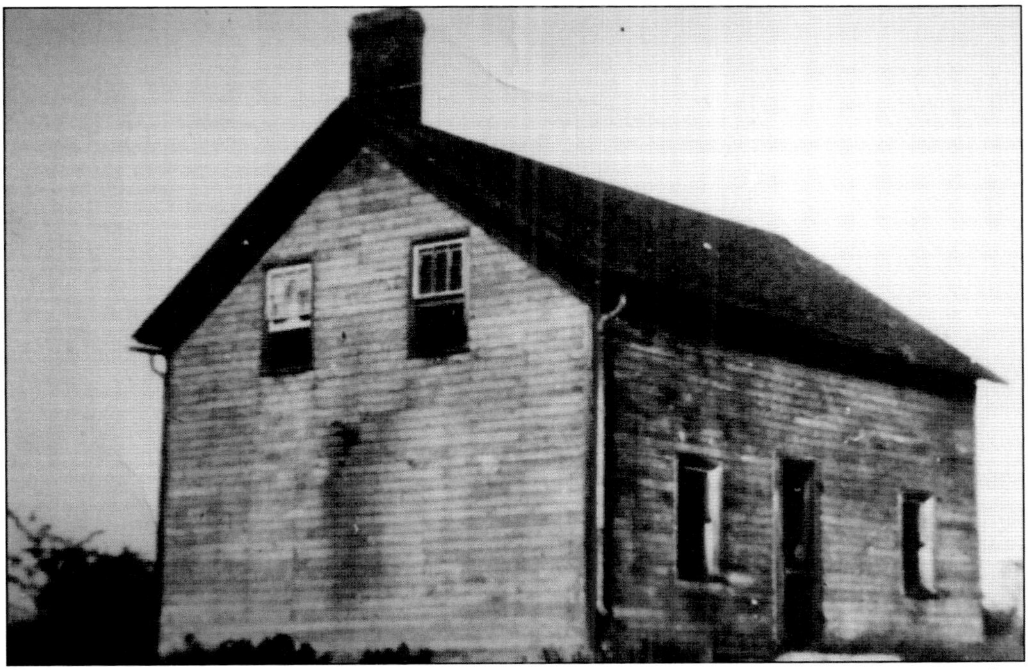

Collamer/Cain/Melander Homestead, built c. 1800. The homestead is pictured as it appeared in 1923 when it was purchased by Clarence Melander.

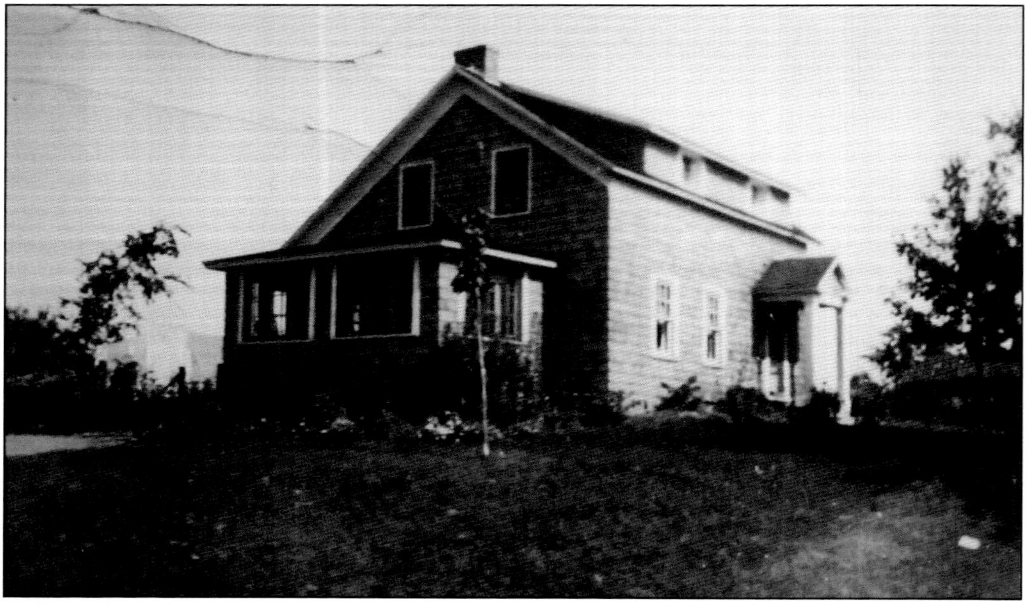

Collamer/Cain/Melander Homestead. The homestead is shown as it appeared years after undergoing remodeling and renovation work by the Melander family.

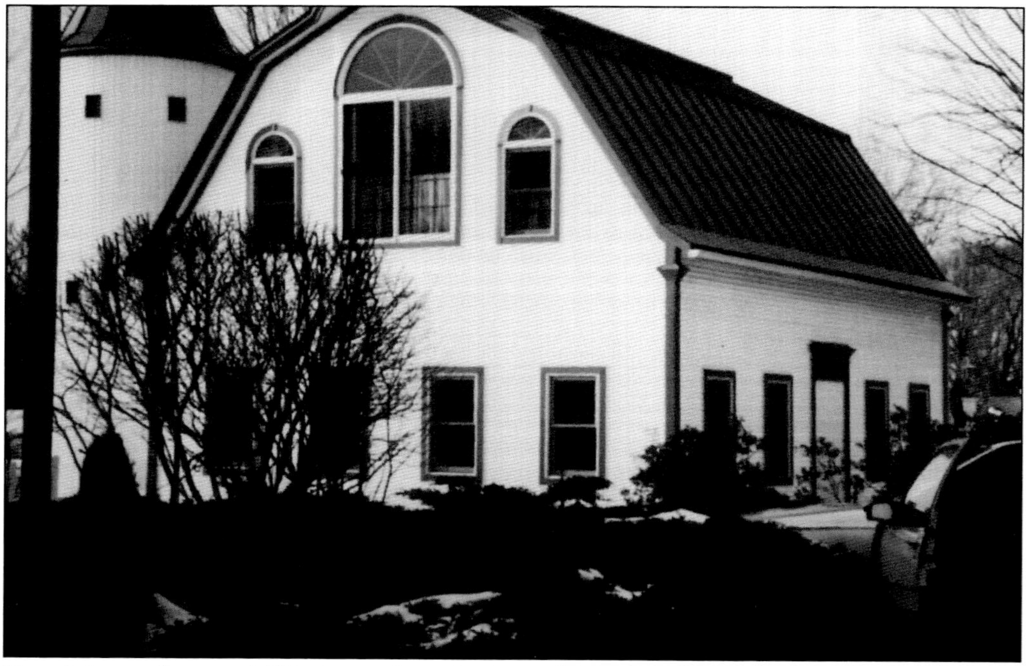

Kopp/Meager Barn, *c.* 1933. Located on the Round Lake Road intersection with Ruhle Road, this barn was built by Robert Kopp for his farm, which had in earlier times been the farm and homestead of the Rice/Dunning families. This unique building was adapted for office use in 1989 by James Robbins of Malta. At present the building is owned by David R. Meager, supervisor of the town of Malta. It was designated as a historic landmark by the Town of Malta in 1994.

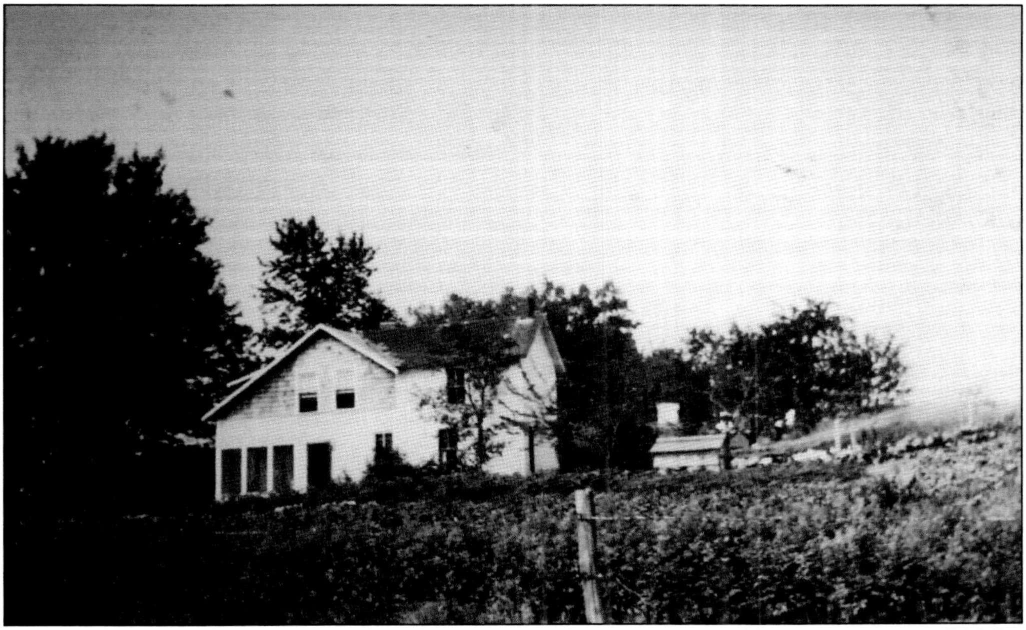

The Old Melander Homestead, situated on the northwest corner of the intersection of Malta Avenue Extension and Rowley Road. It is pictured here as it appeared on July 11, 1921. Carl and Jennie Melander, who came from Brooklyn in 1919, purchased the home in 1920. The Melanders lived there the rest of their lives, from 1920 through 1977. Unfortunately, today the house is vacant.

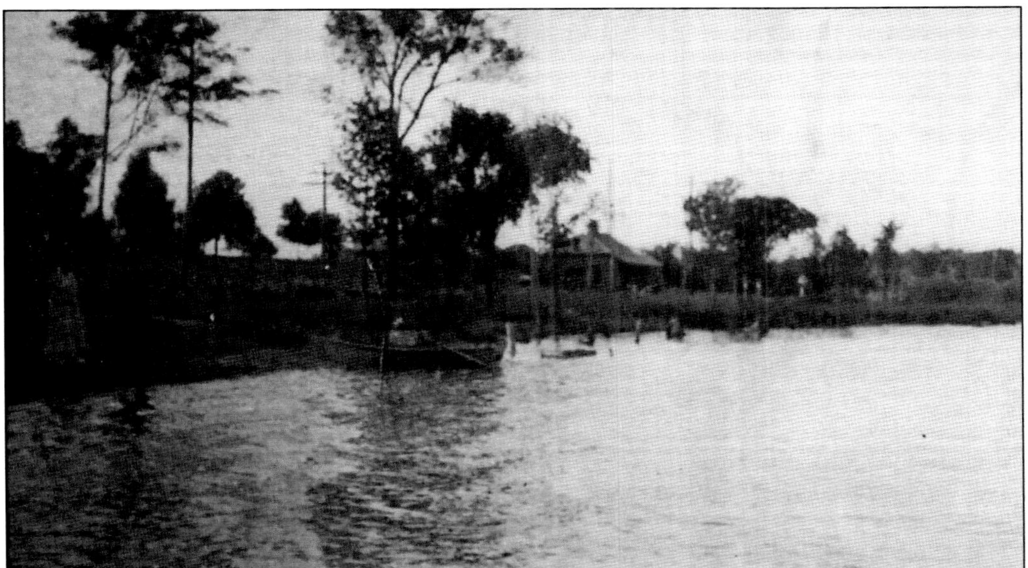

Round Lake trolley station, with a view of Round Lake.

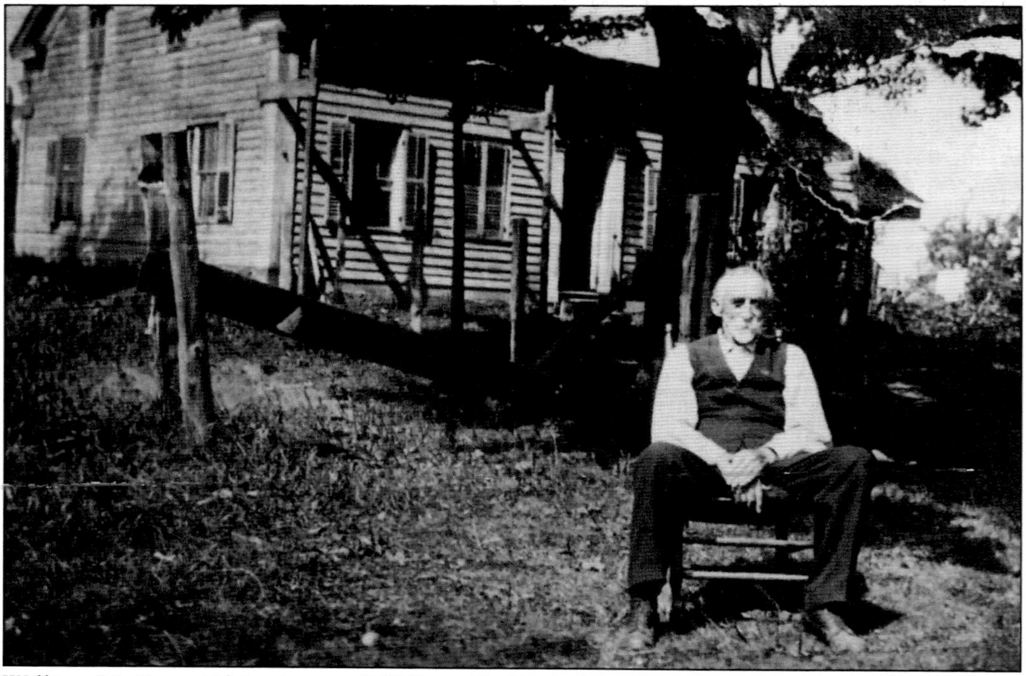

William H. Coon. This picture of William H. Coon shows him seated in front of his home on Raymond Road at East Line. Further information on this old homestead appears on p. 40.

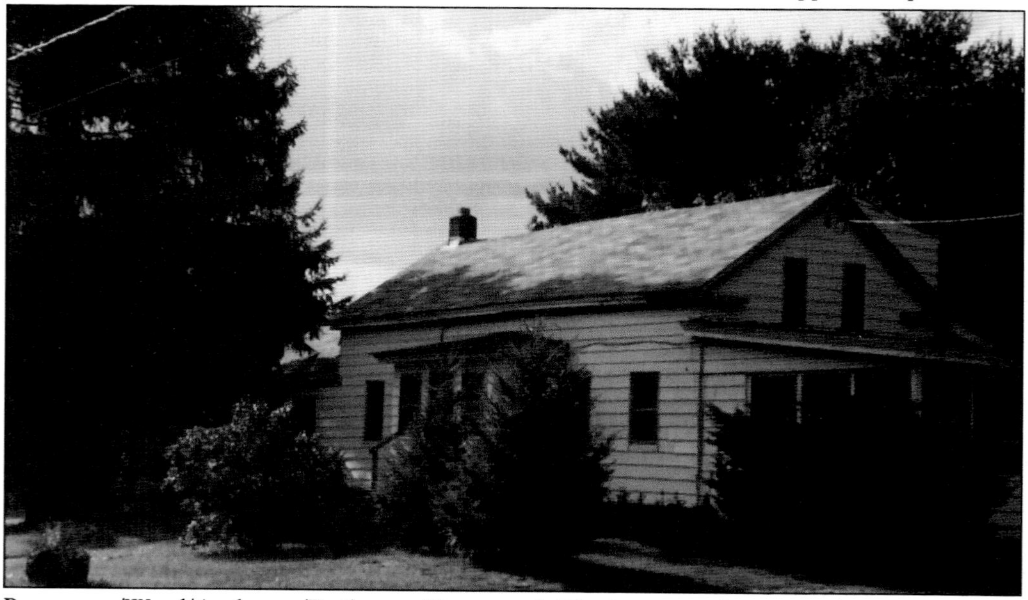

Bousmann/Weed/Anderson/Freiberger Homestead. The homestead is situated on Plains Road. William and Sarah Bousmann were early pioneer settlers who came to Malta. In 1827, the property was sold to David S. and Louisa Weed and family from Washington County. After the death of his wife and his son Leonard, David Weed moved on to Oswego County. The property was sold to George Anderson, whose descendants lived in the house for many years. Today the property is owned by Henry D. and Debra Freiberger.